THE ENCYCLOPEDIA OF
INFANTRY WEAPONS
OF WORLD WAR II

THE ENCYCLOPEDIA OF

INFANTRY WEAPONS

OF WORLD WAR II

IAN V. HOGG

Thomas Y. Crowell

A BISON BOOK

First published in the United States of America
1977 by
Thomas Y. Crowell Company Inc.
New York, New York

Copyright © 1977 Bison Books, London, England

Library of Congress Catalog Card Number: 76-51525
ISBN 0-690-01447-3

Printed in Japan

CONTENTS

Half title: The Vickers Gun Mark 1, with dial sight
Title page: A German infantry section takes a rest. Mauser rifles and stick grenades are prominent, while one man carries the mortar bipod
This page: The PPD sub-machine gun is brandished as Soviet infantry follow the flag, breaking out from Leningrad

INTRODUCTION

'All battles and all wars are won in the end by infantrymen.' *Field Marshal Viscount Wavell*

A legacy of the First World War, which persisted well into the Second, was the belief that the infantryman was a phlegmatic and somewhat simple individual, capable, after long instruction, of mastering the intricacies of the bolt-action rifle and the shovel and capable of executing simple orders if pointed in the right direction; the expression 'cannon-fodder' was quick to spring to the lips. This generalization might have been barely true in 1800, but it was a gross misrepresentation by 1918 and downright libel by 1939. The years 1914–18 had seen considerable expansion in the armory of the infantry soldier; more machine guns, the introduction of the mortar, the light machine gun, even in some cases the automatic rifle and the sub-machine gun. The grenade had been rediscovered, the mortar given a new appearance and lease of life. All these weapons were given to the infantryman and he had to master them.

When World War I ended these weapons were thinned out but not entirely cast aside, and were retained in small numbers and improved in subsequent years, so that in 1939 they were all in service. Every infantryman—and many soldiers of other corps—was expected to be capable of operating them should he be called upon to do so, irrespective of what his authorized position and weapon might be. Numerous young men, brought up on their fathers' reminiscences of rifle, bayonet and mud in the Ypres Salient, were given a sharp surprise when they found themselves wearing the new battledress in 1939 and saw the range of weapons they had to learn.

As the war progressed, more and more new weapons appeared; either because the old ones could not be produced in the quantities needed for global war, or because their performance was no longer adequate. Or because new tactical problems had arisen which demanded new solutions; or because new technical developments pointed the way to a more effective weapon to replace the old. As each appeared the infantryman had to learn afresh; and not merely learn, but learn so thoroughly that the new weapon became a part of him, used instinctively by day or night to the best effect. A British infantryman serving from 1939 to 1945 might well have been called upon during those years to learn three or four rifles, two sub-machine guns, three light machine guns, ten or a dozen types of grenade, two heavy machine guns, two mortars, an anti-tank rifle and an anti-tank projector, and possibly two or three anti-tank guns. If

he were in any sort of raiding force, such as the Commandos or the Airborne Forces, then he would also have been expected to know the rudiments of a similar number of enemy weapons, so that in an emergency he could pick up a weapon from the battlefield and use it. If he found himself attached to an Allied army, then he might have to learn the weapons of his new companions; if he were seconded away to instruct, he would have had to learn a collection of obsolescent weapons still used for instruction or issued to the Home Guard for local defence. Remember too that proficiency in weapons was (and still is) but one facet of the infantryman's expertise; he was also expected to be proficient in minor tactics so that he could use the weapons to best effect; he had to be able to look after himself, read maps, cook and do a thousand and one other things which all go to the making of a rounded professional soldier.

The collection of weapons shown in these pages covers those which were, at some time or another between the years 1939 and 1945, part of the authorized armament of infantry formations. However it must be admitted that there were a lot more weapons than those shown here which actually found their way into the hands of the infantry during the period in review; there were obsolescent, even obsolete weapons hurriedly resurrected from stores and handed out for training —the first rifle I ever had during the war was an Italian Vetterli-Vitali Model 1887 of 10.4mm caliber; thousands had, apparently, been captured in Eritrea and shipped back to England for use by Home Guards and others as training weapons. There was, of course, no ammunition for them. There were, from time to time, experimental weapons issued in small numbers on a troop trial basis to see if either the weapon or the theory behind it were of any use; the Sterling sub-machine gun, for example, never became an official British service weapon until the 1950s, but about a hundred of the prototype Patchett were made in 1944 and some were even used at Arnhem. Space restrictions have prevented the inclusion of such weapons as these; this is particularly the case with rifles, since every country had huge stocks of almost indestructible models of older pattern, and it would serve no useful purpose to catalogue all these museum pieces even if it were possible to produce an accurate list of them. The weapons shown here are those which were the standard issue models, and where variations have appeared they have been explained.

It might also be pointed out that one or two weapons which might be expected are missing, simply because, contrary to popular opinion, they were not infantry weapons at all. A notable example of this is the flame-thrower; only in the British and Japanese armies was it an infantry weapon. Every other army gave it to their engineers. Mines too were engineer stores, though it often fell to the lot of the infantryman to lift them and sometimes lay them as well. On the other hand, there are a number of weapons here which will probably come as a surprise to many readers, particularly in the section on Infantry Guns.

Organization

When contemplating the organization of infantry, it is as well to recall at the outset the famous remark quoted by Field-Marshal Sir William Robertson, which he said was made to him by a very senior General about the turn of the century:

'Never forget, Robertson, that we have two armies—the War Office army and the Aldershot Army. The first is always up to strength and is organized, re-organized and disorganized almost daily. The second is never up to strength, knows nothing whatever about the first, and remains unaffected by any of these organizing activities. It just cleans its rifle and falls in on parade.'

If for 'War Office' we substitute the word 'paper', and for 'Aldershot' the word 'field', then the amended quotation sums up the situation in every army in the world at any time in its history. The 'family trees' so beloved of lecturers rarely saw fulfilment in real life; partly because there were never enough soldiers to flesh them out, partly because what is an ideal combination on paper might well not be so ideal for some particular operation and the mixture was therefore modified.

As an example; the British infantry division of World War II was basically three brigades, each having three infantry battalions, with three artillery regiments and three engineer companies; it will be appreciated that this arrangement in threes made it easy to split off one brigade with one artillery regiment and one engineer company to form a smaller independent unit, should such be required. But in actual practice, additions were made from time to time; take, for example, the composition of 51st (Highland) Division in the Western Desert in 1942. In addition to the theoretical composition outlined above, there was an anti-tank artillery regiment, an anti-aircraft artillery regiment, an additional infantry battalion armed entirely with medium machine guns, and an armored reconnaissance regiment. On the other side, the Italian 'Brescia' division, which should have been composed on roughly the same lines as the British division, actually contained no more than three infantry regiments, one artillery and one engineer regiment.

As a good example of the theoretically perfect composition, the German Infantry Division as it stood in 1939 is as good as any and probably better than most. Due to limitations of space it is clearly not possible to illustrate adequately or completely the composition of every sub-unit, but without this it is still apparent that the ramifications of a full-strength division were far-reaching. The total strength of this formation was 518 officers, 15,752 NCOs and men, with 493 motorcycles, 1187 motor vehicles, 819 horse-drawn vehicles and 3804 horses—a set of figures which should dispose of the idea that the German division was a highly mechanized force. The firepower was tremendous; 432 machine pistols, 430 light machine guns, 116 medium machine guns, 81 anti-tank rifles, 84 anti-aircraft cannon, 75 anti-tank guns, 84 5cm mortars, 57 81mm mortars, twenty 75mm infantry guns, six 150mm infantry guns, 36 105mm field howitzers, four 105mm field guns, and eight 150mm field howitzers. The number of rifles and bayonets held has never been accurately calculated, but is estimated at about 10,000.

But this was the 'ideal' and rarely assembled in real life. To take but one sub-unit; the mounted infantry platoon was rarely seen after 1939. Moreover, many internal changes went on, some with and some without official blessing; thus, it was the practice to provide a pioneer platoon within the infantry battalion; this is not shown in the example as it was put together as and when needed by milking pioneer-trained men from the rifle companies.

However, using this example as a guide it can be seen how an infantry division was organized so as to be a self-sufficient entity. The nucleus is, of course, the infantry component, comprising three regiments, each of which contained three rifle battalions, a gun company having three platoons of two 75mm guns and one of two 150mm guns; an anti-tank company, four platoons of three guns plus a machine-gun section for their protection; the mounted platoon of three sections; and pioneer and signal platoons. The 'rule of three' once more obtains, so that each battalion can be split off with its share of ancillaries. The rule continues farther down the line; the battalion had three companies, each of three platoons; but the platoon splits into four sections so as to provide a balanced force for fire and movement tactics—two sections firing while the other two moved—if we exclude the mortar section. The basic section was made up of an NCO, three light machine gunners and six riflemen, their arms being nine rifles, a light machine gun and a machine pistol in the hands of the NCO.

The rest of the division was put together with the sole aim of supporting the infantry. The prime support came, of course, from the divisional artillery, three field batteries of 105mm howitzers each with twelve guns, split into three sections, and a medium battery of four 105mm long-range guns and eight 150mm howitzers. For aerial protection there was the Motorized Anti-Aircraft Machine Gun Battalion, armed with 20mm automatic cannon, three companies each with twelve guns, while anti-tank defense was in the hands of the

Italian Alpine trooper takes aim with a Beretta Model 1934 pistol

divisional anti-tank battalion, also three companies with twelve guns each. To deal with obstacles there was the divisional engineer battalion; the divisional signals unit took care of communications; the divisional reconnaissance unit, a peculiar mixture of armored cars and bicycles, acted as the eyes and ears of the division, the medical and veterinary companies took care of the division's health, and the 'Services' looked after such things as the field bakery, the butchery, fuel supplies, workshop facilities, and all the manifold housekeeping tasks which the assembly of 16,000 men and their attendant machinery and horses were likely to need.

It must be reiterated that this was the organization as it stood at the outbreak of war in 1939; and that as the war moved on and the situation changed, the make-up of the division changed with it. Obviously as new weapons appeared there were alterations in the establishment—the anti-tank rifle gave way, in due course, to the Panzerschreck launcher, and then the anti-tank capability was extended beyond the confines of the specialist section by the profuse issue of Panzerfaust one-man projectors to all and sundry. As more mechanical transport became available the workshops and supply services expanded and the veterinary section contracted, and when warfare was more or less static the reconnaissance regiment was removed and put to work somewhere else. Additional artillery was almost always attached from corps level or Army reserve, and self-propelled assault guns became an integral part of the division.

It must also be borne in mind that while infantry formed (obviously) part of the infantry division, they also formed part of the armored division; the old idea of an all-tank force swooping across the battlefield like a fleet at sea soon died and infantry, transported in trucks or armored cars to keep up with the armor, were needed to exploit the armor's gains, consolidate the ground won, and, on occasion, dismount and fight off other infantry who were giving the tanks a hard time of it. This concept reached its ultimate in the Red Army's 'Tank Rider Battalions'; armed with nothing except sub-machine guns, these men actually rode into battle on the engine decks of their tanks, dismounting to deal with opposition, remounting to proceed, leaping off and clambering on to another tank if their first choice was stopped by a mine or anti-tank gun.

By and large the planned strength of infantry divisions dwindled as the war progressed and the optimum mixture changed. As the war became faster and faster moving, more and more armor found its way into the infantry division, while in many cases the strength was reduced to make them more manageable and also to provide men for other types of formation. Thus the Red Army infantry division in 1939 was an unwieldy 19,000 strong; this was reduced after the Russo-Finnish War to 14,500 and by 1944 it was down to 9000. At the same time, the proportion of transport was increased so as to make the division capable of faster movement.

It follows from all this that sweeping generalizations on the lines of 'an infantry division contained 12,000 men' are liable to lead to serious misapprehensions. It all depends on what sort of division it was, at what period of the war, and where it was fighting. By and large though the division was the basic currency of war; as a fighting machine, irrespective of paper strength or theoretical configuration, one division was much the equal of another.

The Mauser rifle was the basic weapon of the German Army from 1898 to 1945

German infantry advance through a Russian corn field. The machine gunner in the foreground, carrying the MG34, is protected by his assistant gunner carrying a machine pistol 38

Two German soldiers with their MG34 man a defensive post on the Channel coast. The much vaunted Atlantic Wall was rather thin in places

German mountain troops engage a distant target with their MG42 machine gun

The MG34 mounted on its tripod with long range sights for the sustained fire role, as used by the Wehrmacht, still dressed in 'colonial' garb from the campaign in the Western Desert, in their defense of southern Italy

The German 5cm mortar in action. The mortar gunner has one hand on the traverse control and the other on the firing lever, while he watches the elevation scale. The loader is about to drop the bomb

A German infantry squad gather round their 37mm PAK36 anti-tank gun

Although the flame thrower was an engineer weapon, it was invaluable in assisting the advance of infantry against fortified positions. Here a combat engineer flames a Russian pillbox and removes another obstacle from the path of the Wehrmacht

THE WEAPONS

PISTOLS

A British General once said that he had seen thirty men wounded by pistol fire during the course of World War II, of which 29 were his own troops who had inadvertently shot themselves while cleaning or otherwise mishandling their pistols. Undoubtedly the pistol is a hazardous weapon, largely due to its size; it can be pointed in any direction quite inadvertently and far too easily discharged. As it happens it is less used by infantry than by other arms of the service; it is probably most used by armored formations, since it is more convenient to carry in and out of tanks than rifles or sub-machine guns. In the infantry its use is generally restricted to officers and specialists who have other things to do with their hands during battle than carry rifles. In real life it was rarely carried by officers, since it became appreciated that the man with nothing in his hands and a pistol at his waist was probably somebody important and thus a likely candidate for attention from a sniper.

The other thing militating against the widespread use of the pistol is that it is not, contrary to common belief (fostered by incredible feats on the silver screen) an easy weapon to use effectively. Most men (and women too), if given a rifle and some simple instruction, will put their first-ever shot into the bull. (This is unfortunate, since it immediately gives them the impression that they are born shots and need no further training; it takes another three or four hours of hard work to get their second shot into the bull.) But give the same person a pistol and the same amount of basic instruction and they are highly unlikely to get their first shot into the target at all, let alone into the bull. To become even a passable pistol shot takes a good deal of training and constant practice, and these are not generally available in wartime—or in peacetime for that matter.

As a result, the only infantry who used pistols at all extensively or effectively were Commando and similar units who specialized in close-quarter fighting and for whom the handiness of the pistol was a considerable asset; they were also able to devote the necessary time to practice so that when they were called upon to use them they got results. However, these gentry were individualists and in many cases found themselves pistols other than the regulation issue; thus, while the official British Army pistol was the .38 inch revolver, few Commandos ever used it; they preferred to acquire a .45 automatic pistol from the US Army, or 'liberate' a 9mm Walther P'38 if they could do so, or perhaps go into action brandishing father's .455 Webley which had last seen the light of battle on the Somme. It is in the nature of soldiers to want to use something other than that which the quartermaster issues, even if, in some cases, it isn't as good as the regulation weapon, but the Commandos had a good case; they generally selected weapons which had a better knock-down power than the issue revolver. The British Army had long been believers in heavy caliber revolvers, .455 inch being the preferred standard, but the problem of training recruits to handle these powerful weapons during the course of World War I led to a postwar study of smaller calibers, resulting in the adoption of a .38 inch revolver firing a 200 grain bullet. This meant a reduction in striking energy, from

248ft/pounds for the .455 to 187ft/pounds for the .38, but since it was generally accepted that 50ft/pounds was sufficient to knock somebody over, it seemed that there was enough energy available. Moreover, and this was the important feature, the lighter cartridge led to lighter recoil and easier shooting.

In fact, this question of 'stopping power' is far more involved than simply comparing striking energies. What really counts is the 'shocking power' of the bullet, the speed and violence with which it dissipates its latent energy into the human target, and this is something very hard to define in a purely mathematical way. The difference in effect between the impact of a .455 bullet and that of a .38 bullet is a lot greater than the simple 3:4 proportion of the relative striking velocities, and as a result, people whose lives depended on their pistols tended to hunt for weapons firing heavier bullets.

In the German Army the official weapon was the Walther Pistole '38, but vast numbers of the Parabellum (Luger) Pistole '08 were still in service and remained in use throughout the war. The Walther was undoubtedly the better pistol of the two when considered as a combat weapon; it was less fussy about ammunition, less prone to stoppage from dirt and dust, more robust, and easier to mass-produce in the first place. But for all that there was still a certain mystique about the Parabellum,

and those who had them were generally reluctant to part with them. The German forces in general used many more pistols, of course; notably the other Walther designs, the PP and PPK automatics, the Mauser Model 1934 and HSc and the Sauer Model 38, but these were never infantry weapons.

The United States Army had adopted their .45 automatic in 1911 and, except for some minor changes in the light of World War I experience, they had stuck to it ever since—and still do. Without any shadow of doubt, it qualifies as the finest fighting pistol in the world; simple, robust, reliable, and throwing a heavy bullet to deliver 375ft/pounds of impact force, it cannot be faulted for military use. Due to the rapid expansion of the Army a number of revolvers, made by Colt or Smith & Wesson, were also in use, but these were not first line infantry weapons.

The Russian service pistol was either the elderly Nagant revolver or the more up-to-date Tokarev automatic pistol, but in fact few of either of them were ever seen in infantry hands. In the first place, production of the Tokarev is believed to have been much smaller than is generally supposed, so that large numbers were never available for issue; and secondly the Russians appreciated the training problem. The rapid-firing sub-machine gun was much easier to teach and use effectively with little training, and to all intents and purposes the

sub-machine gun replaced the pistol in the hands of fighting troops.

With the Japanese Army the pistol retained its secondary role as a social symbol; let the war become as modern as it liked, the Japanese officer still went forth girded about with sword and pistol, and from all accounts he was not averse to using either if the need arose. But the quality of the pistols provided was not of the best, and more than one Japanese officer was sacrificed on the altar of second-rate design.

There were no wartime developments in the pistol field which actually saw service. All the pistols in use had been perfected and put into production before the war broke out, and the development of new designs was shelved in favor of work on more vital weapons. I only know of two designs developed during the war years; one was the British 'Tarn' 9mm blow-back pistol, tested and rejected as being unsafe, and the other the German 'Volkspistole', a mass-production design of delayed blow-back weapon intended for the rapid armament of the Volkssturm and which was not completed before the end of the war. There were a number of Walther designs put together during the war, but there is no evidence that they were ever offered for service acceptance. On the whole, there was no reason why they should have been. The pistols which started the war were the same ones which finished it.

F.B RADOM
1939r
VIS-wz.35
pat. Nr. 15567

The Enfield .38 Mark I at Arnhem

UK

Pistol, revolver, Webley, .38in, Mk 4

Caliber .352in (Nominally .38)
Length 10.5in
Weight 1lb 11oz
Barrel 5in long, 7 grooves, right hand twist
Feed system 6-chambered cylinder
System of operation Revolver, single or double action, top-break
Manufacturer Webley & Scott Ltd., Birmingham

The .455 revolver of World War I (also a Webley design) was admittedly an effective man-stopper, but it was a heavy and violent weapon which was generally only put to good use in the hands of a highly skilled revolver shot, and such men are not to be developed under the pressure of wartime training. As a result, after the war, the British Army did some research into revolver ballistics and decided that it would be possible to produce a sufficiently lethal result by using a 200 grain .38in bullet. The

Webley .38 Mark IV revolver

Webley & Scott company were, at that time, developing a .38 revolver for possible military and police use and this they submitted for trial.

The Army elected to develop its own design, however, and the Webley model was turned down; it was subsequently perfected by the company and became a commercial pattern, widely adopted by police forces throughout the world.

In 1941, with the expansion of the British Army under way, the manufacturing capacity of the Royal Small Arms Factory at Enfield to produce revolvers was strained to the limit, and in order to equip the forces it was necessary to go to commercial companies. Webley & Scott were asked to produce numbers of their .38 revolver, and it was officially introduced for service in 1942. Since the Enfield revolver had been largely based on the Webley design, the differences were very minor; the trigger was fitted through a slot in the underside of the body, instead of a separate side-plate being incorporated; the trigger guard was detachable and secured by two screws; the cylinder stop formed part of the trigger; and the contour of the grips was slightly different and had the name 'Webley' incorporated in the molding.

had the distressing habit of catching on various parts of the tanks as the crews scrambled in and out, a potentially dangerous situation when the pistol was loaded. As a result, the Mark 1* was approved on 22nd June 1938, a pattern which had the offending comb removed. This prevented the hammer from being thumb-cocked and thus converted the pistol to use in the double-action mode only. The mainspring was lightened to reduce the trigger pull from 13–15lbs to 11–13lbs, the grip sidepieces were slightly changed so as to give a better grip, and a brass disc for stamping regimental identification numbers, was secured in the right-hand grip.

This, of course, led to the problem of having to make sure that the Tank Corps always got Mk 1* pistols, so in order to simplify matters the Mark 1 was forthwith declared obsolescent and, as they were periodically withdrawn for overhaul or repair, were all converted to Mark 1* pattern. Due to this, unmodified Mark 1 pistols are now exceedingly rare.

The final change in design came with the introduction of the Mark 1** on 29 July 1942. This was a Mark 1* with the hammer safety stop omitted and one or two of the minor lock components modified, a step intended to simplify and thus speed up manufacture. It did this, but it also made the pistol liable to go off if dropped so as to land on the hammer; this was an unlikely event though, and the design was accepted as a wartime concession. As soon as

UK

Pistol, revolver, No. 2 Mk 1, 1* and 1** (Enfield)

Caliber .352in (Nominally .38)
Length 10.25in
Weight 1lb 11½oz
Barrel 5in long, 7 grooves, right hand twist
Feed system 6-chambered cylinder
System of operation Revolver, single or double action, top-break
Manufacturers Royal Small Arms Factory, Enfield Lock, Middlesex
Singer Sewing Machine Company, Clydebank, Scotland
Albion Motor Company, Glasgow, Scotland

As outlined in the remarks on the Webley revolver, the British Army began studying the adoption of a .38 model in the 1920s. The Webley & Scott pattern was generally acceptable, but for reasons which doubtless seemed good at the time, the lock mechanism was objected to. Using the basic outline of the Webley as their starting point, the Royal Small Arms Factory

designers developed their own model using a slightly different lock and trigger mechanism, and this was eventually approved for service on 2 June 1932.

This, the Mark 1, was capable of operation as a single or double-action revolver. However, among the principal users was the Royal Tank Regiment, and they objected to the hammer spur or 'comb', which

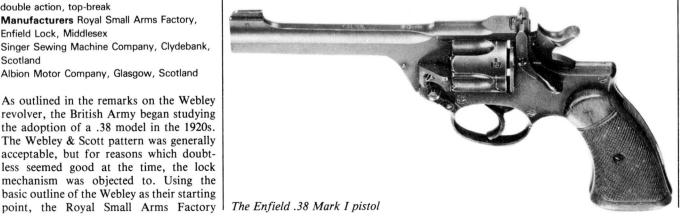

The Enfield .38 Mark I pistol

the war was over these models were all recalled and modified back to Mark 1* standards of safety.

The Webley and Enfield pistols were not often used in action, largely due to the unwelcome attention they drew from enemy marksmen. The Enfield, moreover, was unpopular, since the double-action-only feature made accurate and deliberate shooting almost impossible. The trigger pull for a single-action revolver is generally from three to five pounds; that of the Enfield was never less than 11lbs, and delivering that amount of effort with the forefinger invariably ruined the aim. As a hip-shooting emergency weapon it was serviceable enough, but I have been unable to find any reliable record of it being used to good effect.

Pistol, revolver, Smith & Wesson .38in

Caliber .357in (Nominally .38)
Length 10.125in (with 6 inch barrel)
Weight 1lb 8oz (with 6 inch barrel)
Barrel 4, 5 or 6in long, 5 grooves, right hand twist
Feed system 6-chambered cylinder
System of operation Revolver, single or double action, solid frame, side-opening, hand ejector
Manufacturer Smith & Wesson Arms Co., Springfield, Mass., USA

In 1940, after the losses at Dunkirk and with a rapidly expanding army to equip, the British Government went to the USA for the purchase of a variety of weapons. Among the items on the shopping list was a revolver, and a contract was placed with the Smith & Wesson Company to produce a model suited to the standard British Army .38in cartridge. The resulting weapon was the 'British Military' or '38/200' Model.

Basically it was no more than Smith & Wesson's standard 'Military and Police .38' which had been commercially available for several years, but the chambers were dimensioned to suit the British cartridge. As with most Smith & Wesson designs the chambers had a slight step at the point where the mouth of the cartridge case lay,

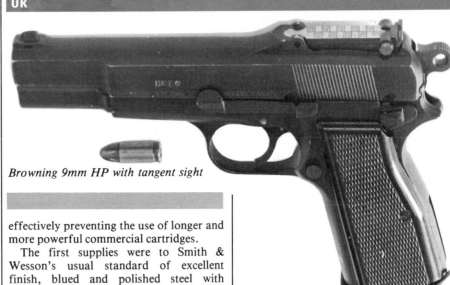

Browning 9mm HP with tangent sight

effectively preventing the use of longer and more powerful commercial cartridges.

The first supplies were to Smith & Wesson's usual standard of excellent finish, blued and polished steel with chequered walnut grips bearing the 'S & W' medallion in silver. These early models were supplied in three barrel lengths as tabulated above, though the four- and five-inch lengths were not common. After April 1942, under the pressure of war production, the finish was changed to sandblasting and the grips were of smooth walnut without the medallion. From that time too, only the six-inch barrel model was produced.

The remarks made previously about the carriage of revolvers by infantry apply equally well here. However it might be said that this was undoubtedly the most popular revolver ever issued. Light, well-balanced, accurate and reliable, it was a better fighting weapon than either the Enfield or the Webley and it was frequently carried by Commando and Airborne troops. It suffered from one slight mechanical defect in that after some years of use the mainspring tended to take on a permanent 'set' which weakened the hammer blow. This was never remarked upon in its previous existence as a police revolver in the USA, but became obvious some years after the war in British Service, due to the fact that military ammunition demands a somewhat harder striker blow to function the cap than does civil ammunition. However, repair was a simple task and the possibility of this defect never affected the popularity of the weapon.

Pistol, Browning (FN), 9mm, HP, No. 2 Mk 1*

Caliber 9mm
Length 7.75in
Weight 2lb 3oz
Barrel 4.65in long, 4 grooves, right hand twist
Feed system 13-round detachable box magazine
System of operation Recoil; Browning link
Manufacturer John Inglis & Co., Toronto, Canada

This pistol was designed by John Moses Browning in the late 1920s, developed by Fabrique National d'Armes de Guerre of Herstal, Belgium, and introduced by them in 1935 as the 'Browning High Power' or 'Model 35'. It was adopted by the Belgian Army and also taken into use by the Lithuanian and various other armies in small numbers prior to the outbreak of war.

Upon the outbreak of war the drawings were brought to Britain, but there was no particular need for the weapon at that time, nor indeed was there any manufacturing capacity available. In Belgium the FN factory was taken over by the Germans and the pistols were continued in production, known now as the Pistole Modell 35(b) and most of them were supplied to German SS and Paratroop units.

The records are not entirely clear on this point, but it appears that a very small number were made in Britain for evaluation in 1941. They were given the nomenclature 'Pistol Browning 9mm (FN) Automatic (Mk 1, UK)' but they were never formally introduced into service, and the design approval was subsequently cancelled in April 1945. In the interim, however, the drawings had been sent to Canada and the pistol was put into production there, the first output being supplied to the Chinese Nationalist Army. Once their demands had been met, the pistol was supplied to the Canadian Army, and numbers were sent to Britain and issued to Commando and Airborne forces.

As originally designed, the pistol was

Smith and Wesson revolver with .38 cartridge

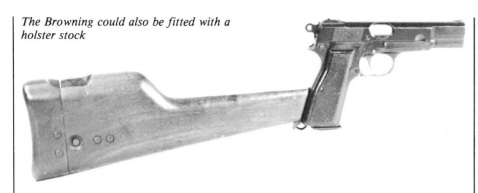

The Browning could also be fitted with a holster stock

supplied with an optimistic tangent backsight graduated to 500 yards and a wooden holster-stock which could be clipped to the butt to form a species of carbine. The weapons supplied to China were of this pattern, such exotic fittings being considered *de rigueur* in Chinese military circles. The models supplied to Canada and Britain substituted a simple fixed backsight and dispensed with the stock-butt.

The Browning was a highly popular weapon; firing the standard 9mm Parabellum cartridge as used in the Sten gun and freely obtainable on the continent, it was unusual in its magazine capacity of 13 rounds, far more than any other hand gun. This advantage was frequently exploited against those enemies who astutely counted shots and showed themselves after a count of eight, expecting to find the owner of the pistol occupied in changing magazines. They were in for a surprise.

USA

Pistol, automatic, .45 M1911A1

Caliber .45in
Length 8.5in
Weight 2lb 7½oz
Barrel 5in long, 6 grooves, left hand twist
Feed system 7-round detachable box
System of operation Recoil; Browning link
Manufacturers Colts Patent Firearms Mfg. Co., Hartford, Conn., USA
Remington Arms -UMC, Bridgeport, Conn., USA
Springfield Armory, Springfield, Mass., USA
Union Switch & Signal Co., Swissvale, Pa., USA
Ithaca Gun Co., Ithaca, NY., USA
Remington-Rand Inc., Syracuse, NY., USA

This is a modification of a design originated in 1911, designed by John Browning as early as 1908 for trials by the US Army to determine their future service pistol. Of the several models submitted, the Colt, Savage and Parabellum (Luger) were the most promising. The Colt was slightly redesigned to suit the Army's demands for simplicity, robustness and safety, and eventually was selected to become the issue pistol as the Model 1911.

This served well, but user experience during World War I indicated the need for some small changes. The contour of the butt was altered to fit the hand better; the trigger was shortened; the front edge of

Colt M1911 (left) and M1911A1 (right)

the butt was cut away to allow the trigger finger a better grip; and the hammer spur was shortened. With these changes it became the M1911A1, and this version dates from 1922. During World War II it was manufactured by a number of companies in order to provide the numbers required. As a point of interest it might be noted that a quantity of M1911 pistols were made in 1915–16 for the Royal Navy and Royal Flying Corps, chambered for the .455 Webley & Scott automatic pistol cartridge.

Firing a 230 grain bullet at 860 feet per second, the M1911A1 is the most powerful military pistol in service, and has been since the demise of the .455 Webley revolver in the 1920s. As a man-stopper it is without parallel; the impact of over 300 foot-pounds on any part of the body guarantees disablement. On the other hand, it must be said that such a powerful weapon is not easy to shoot accurately without a fair amount of practice.

The Colt .45 was, and still is, widely issued in the United States Army. As well as being an officer's weapon, it was carried by NCOs and was the personal arm for many operators of crew-served weapons such as heavy machine guns and mortars. Due to complaints of its uselessness as a long-range weapon, it was largely replaced by the M1 Carbine or M3 sub-machine gun after 1942, particularly among weapon crews. There is no doubt that it was the most widely used of all combat pistols (perhaps because the Americans are rather more 'hand-gun oriented') and there are innumerable stories of its effectiveness in combat. But for the Colt story to end all Colt stories, it is necessary to go back to 8 October 1918, when Corporal Alvin York, after shooting a machine-gun team with a rifle, rounded up 132 German prisoners and marched them into captivity at the point of an M1911.

USSR

Pistol, revolver, Nagant, Model 1895

Caliber 7.62mm
Length 9.06in
Weight 1lb 12oz
Barrel 4.3in long, 4 grooves, right hand twist
Feed system 7-chambered cylinder
System of operation Revolver, single or double-action, solid-frame, gas-seal, with swing-out cylinder and hand ejector
Manufacturers Nagant Frères, Liège, Belgium
State Arsenal, Tula, USSR

The Nagant revolver was an elderly weapon of unusual design which originated in Belgium. The inventor and patentee, Leon Nagant, took an idea attributed to another Belgian gunsmith, Pieper, and developed it into a workable pistol. The singular feature of this weapon is the mechanical arrangement which thrusts the cylinder forward on cocking, so that the coned breech end of the barrel enters the mouth of the aligned chamber to effect a

The Nagant with its cartridge

more-or-less gastight seal. The common or garden revolver merely aligns cylinder and barrel with as close a fit as possible and accepts the resulting gas leak as inevitable. To add a final touch, the cartridge case completely encloses the bullet, the mouth of the case extending in front of the bullet

nose, so that as the bullet left the case on firing, the case mouth was opened out into the barrel breech to perfect the seal.

In spite of all this complexity, it is arguable whether the results justified it; the sealing of the gas probably resulted in an increase in velocity of some 50 feet per

second. Nevertheless the Imperial Russian Government appeared to be convinced of its virtues and adopted the weapon in 1895. First supplies were made by Nagant, but in about 1901 the Russians purchased the patent rights and subsequently manufactured the weapon at Tula Arsenal. The vast majority of pistols were made before 1917, but manufacture continued after the Revolution, the later models being recognizable by the Red Star engraved upon them. According to some authorities, manufacture did not finally cease until well after World War II. It is interesting to note that a fairly modern Soviet target pistol uses the same gas-seal system and cartridge for international competition shooting.

The Nagant revolver was standard issue to officers in the Tsarist and Red Armies and was also carried to some extent by specialist personnel such as NCOs, telegraphists, messengers and machine gunners. Its use decreased during World War II since with the vast expansion of the Red Army it was quicker and easier to provide the members with sub-machine guns.

USSR

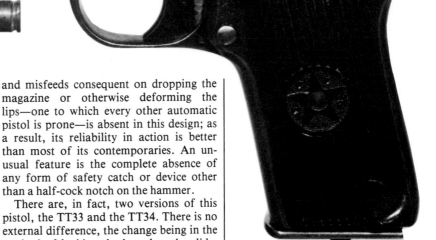

Pistol, automatic, Tokarev, Model TT33

Caliber 7.62mm
Length 7.68in
Weight 1lb 13oz
Barrel 4.57in long, 4 grooves, right hand twist
Feed system 8-round detachable box
System of operation Recoil, Browning link
Manufacturer State Arsenal, Tula, USSR

The nomenclature TT33 indicates design by Tokarev, manufacture by Tula and adoption in 1933; and that, due to the old Russian custom of encouraging other people to mind their own business, is about as much as we are ever likely to know about its design and development. However, a certain amount can be pieced together. In the first place, the Tokarev pistol is based on the John Browning design as exemplified by the US Colt M1911 pistol; it uses the same swinging link system of locking barrel and slide together. The only major change is the absence of a grip safety and the manufacture of the firing pin, hammer and lock mechanism in a removable sub-unit. A second notable feature is the machining of the feed lips, normally part of the magazine, into the frame of the pistol. As a result the magazine itself is a relatively simple box, and the danger of malfunctions

and misfeeds consequent on dropping the magazine or otherwise deforming the lips—one to which every other automatic pistol is prone—is absent in this design; as a result, its reliability in action is better than most of its contemporaries. An unusual feature is the complete absence of any form of safety catch or device other than a half-cock notch on the hammer.

There are, in fact, two versions of this pistol, the TT33 and the TT34. There is no external difference, the change being in the method of locking the barrel to the slide. The TT33 has two ribs formed on the upper surface of the barrel, which engage in two grooves on the underside of the slide top, in the usual Browning fashion. The TT34, on the other hand, has the ribs running completely around the barrel; this simplified and speeded up production, since the ribs could now be turned on a lathe while the rest of the barrel was being finished to correct dimensions, instead of having to be milled out in a separate operation.

Tokarev TT33 with its cartridge attached to it

The exact distribution of these pistols is not known, but it can be assumed it was a general issue to infantry officers, although there is some doubt as to whether it was ever turned out in sufficient quantities to make its use widespread. Small numbers were first seen during the Russo-Finnish War, but as already pointed out, the sub-machine gun tended to become the individual weapon of the Red Army during the latter stages of the war against Germany, the pistol being less prominent.

The Tokarev is a powerful weapon, despite its small caliber; the cartridge is derived from the 7.63mm Mauser, and propels an 86 grain bullet at almost 1400 feet per second, to give a striking energy of 365 foot-pounds, quite sufficient to cause considerable damage. As a corollary of this power, due to the pistol's lightness, it is a rather violent weapon to shoot.

Pistole, Parabellum, Modell 1908 (P'08)

Caliber 9mm
Length 8.75in
Weight 1lb 14oz
Barrel 4in long, 8 grooves, right hand twist
Feed system 8-round detachable box magazine
System of operation Recoil; toggle joint
Manufacturers Deutsche Waffen und Munitionsfabrik, Berlin
Royal Arsenal, Erfurt
Simson & Cie, Suhl
Mauserwerke AG, Oberndorf
Heinrich Krieghoff Waffenwerke, Suhl

The Parabellum Pistole '08, familiarly known as the Luger, was perfected at the turn of the century by Georg Luger, using the earlier Borchardt Pistol as his starting point. The Borchardt introduced the toggle joint system of locking and other mechanical features in a pistol which, while a workable proposition, was at best a cumbersome device. Luger refined the mechanics, his principal change being in the arrangement of the mainspring, which had been a coiled clock-type spring and which now became a flat leafspring in the rear edge of the butt. This changed the whole outline of the weapon and made it much better balanced. Further improvement followed, the mainspring being changed to a coil and the original 7.65mm caliber being improved to 9mm caliber in order to make the bullet rather more combat-effective. In 1908 it became the standard pistol of the German Army, having already been accepted by the Swiss Army in 7.65mm caliber and the German Navy in 9mm.

It was widely tested in the years 1906–14 by almost every army in the world, and A .45 caliber came very close to being adopted by the US Army in 1908. Numbers remain in service today, and it was in military use recently by the Portuguese Army in Angola and Mozambique.

Although of distinctive appearance it is not among the most reliable of weapons; the toggle lock is too dependent upon consistent ammunition quality and the multiplicity of exposed moving parts are prone to suffer from mud and sand. Nevertheless it served the German Army well enough in 1914–18 to be retained after the war. By the middle 1930s, however, it was clear that a large and expanding army needed a pistol which could be mass-produced faster than the Parabellum, and in 1938 manufacture of a replacement, the Walther P'38, began. In spite of this the P'08 was continued in production until about 1942 for the German Army, and later than that for export, the last batch, in 7.65mm caliber, sold to Portugal in 1944.

The Pistole '08 was issued throughout the German Army, and its infantry role was as an officer's sidearm and also by weapon crews, despatch riders, signallers and NCOs. It saw wide combat use, though tales of individual feats of arms with the weapon are rare. It was, of course, highly prized as a souvenir by Allied troops, and many thousands must still be in private hands today.

Pistole, Modell 38 (Walther)

Caliber 9mm
Length 8.38in
Weight 1lb 13½oz
Barrel 5.0in long, 6 grooves, right hand twist
Feed system 8-round detachable box magazine
System of operation Recoil; wedge lock; double action firing lock
Manufacturers Carl Walther Waffenfabrik, Zella-Mehlis
Spreewerke GmbH, Berlin
Mauserwerke AG, Oberndorf

During the early 1930s the company of Carl Walther of Zella-Mehlis, who had been making a series of pocket pistols of excellent quality for many years, began work on a military pistol in 9mm Parabellum caliber. Completely forsaking their earlier designs, they produced a locked-breech pistol using an internal hammer which had the ability to function at double-action. When the

Pistole '08: note the raised extractor, indicating the loaded condition

Pistol '38, standard German sidearm

gun was loaded and cocked, applying the safety catch lowered the hammer. To fire, after moving the safety catch to 'fire', the firer pulled the trigger to raise and then release the hammer. After this initial shot the hammer remained cocked and was fired in the usual automatic pistol single-action mode.

This weapon was known as the Modell AP (Armee-Pistole) and a very small number were made. Offered to the Army it was refused on the grounds that the hammer was invisible; the soldiers liked to see the hammer as an outward and visible sign of the state of readiness of the weapon. Walther promptly redesigned it with an external hammer, and while it was being considered by the Army, offered it commercially as the Modell HP (Heeres-Pistole). In 1938 it was adopted as the standard sidearm of the Wehrmacht and changed its name once more to Pistole '38, although as the HP it was still commercially available until the summer of 1939.

The P'38 was also taken into use by the Swedish Army in 1939 as the Model 39, though it is doubtful if they received many. During the war its mass-production virtues were tested to the full, three factories being devoted to its production, as well as numerous sub-contractors who were making components for assembly at the major plants. It was this characteristic which had led to its adoption, since the design of the Walther demanded less of the traditional pistolsmith's art than did the Parabellum '08. Production stopped after the war, of course, but it was later revived by the new Carl Walther company at Ulm in 1957 and has since been re-adopted by the Bundeswehr as the Pistole 1.

As with the P'08, the P'38 was widely distributed to all and sundry of the German Army. Although described by one American critic as a 'sheet metal and wire spring wonder' it is a remarkably robust weapon and showed up particularly well on the Russian Front, where extreme cold conditions put numerous otherwise sound weapons out of action. It was also accurate and easy to shoot well, attributes which accounted for its combat popularity and effectiveness.

Maschinenpistole, Mauser, Modell 1932 (Schnellfeuerpistole)

Caliber 7.63mm
Length 12.25in (without butt)
Weight 2lb 14½oz (without butt)
Barrel 5.5in long, 6 grooves, right hand twist
Feed system 10 or 20-round detachable box magazine
System of operation Recoil; rising block lock
Rate of fire (cyclic) 850rpm
Manufacturer Waffenwerke Mauser AG, Oberndorf-a-N

The well-known Mauser 1912 Military Pistol was widely imitated in Spain and China, particularly after World War I, when economic conditions gave these cheap and cheerful versions a considerable price advantage. One modification which appeared in Spain was a version with a selector mechanism which allowed the weapon to be fired at full automatic; with the familiar wooden butt-stock and a 20-round box magazine, it became a species of machine pistol or sub-machine gun; utterly impractical but attractive to the less technically sound Chinese warlords and banana republic generals.

Unwilling to be outmaneuvered by these competitors, Mauser proceeded to make their own version, using their 1926 Model pistol as a basis. As might be expected, the result was rather better engineered than the Spanish versions; two types appeared, differing only in the selector mechanism. The first model, produced in 1932, was designed by Josef Nickl and is identifiable by the fire selector, on the left side of the frame, being in a diamond shape. In 1936 a second model with a selector mechanism due to one Karl Westinger appeared, in which the fire selector was rectangular.

Like all such weapons the Schnellfeuer-pistole is a poor substitute for a sub-machine gun. The rate of fire is impossible to control in such a light weapon, with the result that the second and subsequent shots of a burst rarely land on the target; moreover, due to its automatic pistol origin it fires from a closed breech. When the trigger is released after firing a burst, the bolt closes, loading a fresh round, but the hammer does not fall. This means that the cartridge is sitting in a warm chamber, and if the gun has been heated up by firing several bursts, a cook-off—the spontaneous ignition of the cartridge in the chamber due to heat absorption—is inevitable. Experiments have shown that three ten-round bursts are sufficient to make the chamber hot enough to guarantee the next round cooking-off within seconds.

So far as can be ascertained, the few Schnellfeuerpistolen acquired by the German Army appear to have been issued to Waffen SS units on the Eastern Front. Photographs showing them in use have been seen, but no details of their employment or effectiveness are known. They were also supplied to the Chinese and Yugoslavian Armies in prewar days. The German government, both prior to and after Hitler's accession to power, supported Chiang Kai-shek's Chinese government, but ceased to do so after the Anti-Comintern Pact with Japan was signed. Hitler also supported Yugoslavia after 1934. A few of the latter seem to have turned up in the hands of Marshal Tito's men during the war. As a guerrilla weapon it was doubtless useful, being readily broken down and concealed, and if restricted to use as a self-loading single-shot carbine it would be a highly effective weapon.

Mauser Model 1932 as produced for the Chinese Army of Chiang Kai-shek

Austria/Germany

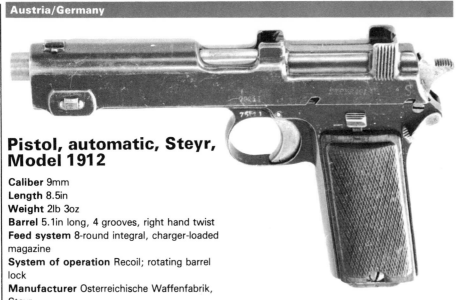

Pistol, automatic, Steyr, Model 1912

Caliber 9mm
Length 8.5in
Weight 2lb 3oz
Barrel 5.1in long, 4 grooves, right hand twist
Feed system 8-round integral, charger-loaded magazine
System of operation Recoil; rotating barrel lock
Manufacturer Osterreichische Waffenfabrik, Steyr

As with early European revolvers, so with early European automatic pistols; there was considerable cross-fertilization during the early development of these weapons, and it becomes difficult to state with any certainty who might have been the 'onlie begetter' of any particular design. The Steyr Model 1912 is one of these confused weapons, and it seems to have been developed by the Steyr factory along lines originating in earlier designs by Georg Roth, together with features attributable to

Steyr M1912 of the Austrian Army

those ubiquitous Bohemians, Rudolf Frommer and Karel Krnka. In any event, it was adopted in 1911 by the Austro-Hungarian Army.

Originally it was chambered for the 9mm Steyr cartridge, the round and pistol being developed together, and the cartridge being used with no other weapon. The 9mm Steyr is longer than the 9mm Parabellum round and was usually provided with a rather pointed, steel-jacketed bullet; fired

at 1250ft/second it delivered 400 foot-pounds and was a most powerful and long-ranging round.

In consequence, when the Austrian Army was merged with the German Army in 1938, the majority of their Steyr pistols were fitted with new barrels chambering the 9mm Parabellum cartridge. The only other alteration, except for chamber size, was the design of a new feed ramp on the barrel to deal with the shorter and more blunt Parabellum bullet. Converted weapons were stamped ''08' or 'P'08', referring to the standard German pistol cartridge the 'Patrone '08'. These weapons remained in service throughout World War II in the hands of German troops, where they were known as the 'Pistole Modell 12(ö)'.

Like other pistols, precise information on employment in specific actions is not available, but it appears to have been moderately well distributed. It was an excellent pistol, and one is inclined to respect the Austrians for electing to modify it rather than to accept a substitute. Its only drawback was that the system of loading was archaic and cumbersome; the slide was drawn back and locked by the safety catch, a charger holding eight rounds inserted into guides in the slide, and the rounds then forced into the integral magazine by the thumb. To unload quickly the slide was pulled back and a catch on the frame depressed; this pulled a restraining clip to one side and allowed the magazine spring to eject the contents.

Poland/Germany

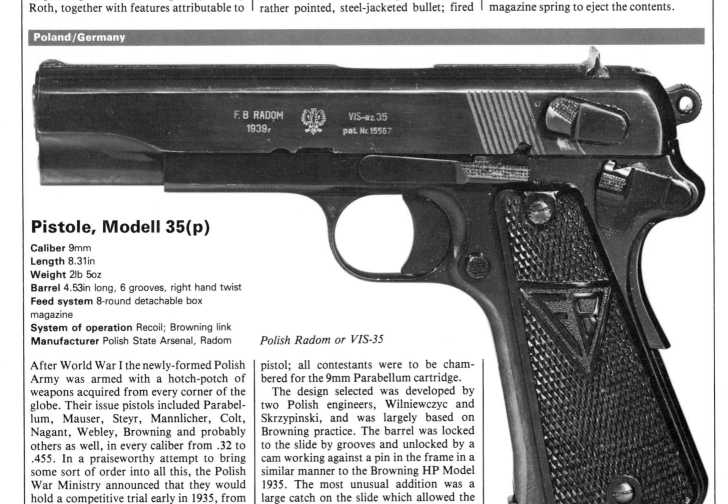

Pistole, Modell 35(p)

Caliber 9mm
Length 8.31in
Weight 2lb 5oz
Barrel 4.53in long, 6 grooves, right hand twist
Feed system 8-round detachable box magazine
System of operation Recoil; Browning link
Manufacturer Polish State Arsenal, Radom

After World War I the newly-formed Polish Army was armed with a hotch-potch of weapons acquired from every corner of the globe. Their issue pistols included Parabellum, Mauser, Steyr, Mannlicher, Colt, Nagant, Webley, Browning and probably others as well, in every caliber from .32 to .455. In a praiseworthy attempt to bring some sort of order into all this, the Polish War Ministry announced that they would hold a competitive trial early in 1935, from which they would select one standard

Polish Radom or VIS-35

pistol; all contestants were to be chambered for the 9mm Parabellum cartridge.

The design selected was developed by two Polish engineers, Wilniewczyc and Skrzypinski, and was largely based on Browning practice. The barrel was locked to the slide by grooves and unlocked by a cam working against a pin in the frame in a similar manner to the Browning HP Model 1935. The most unusual addition was a large catch on the slide which allowed the hammer to be lowered safely on to a loaded chamber, so that the pistol could be carried fully loaded and brought to a state of readiness by simply cocking the hammer. The hammer had a grooved top surface, which some authorities aver was to permit a cavalryman to cock it quickly by rubbing the rear end of the pistol down the side of his breeches; what virtue there is in this movement is hard to see; it seems no less simple to thumb the hammer back, and ribbed tops are commonly found on pistols with no pretensions to being cavalry weapons. But bearing in mind that the cavalry was still the *corps d'élite* of the Polish Army, perhaps the designers felt that such a gesture would get their support in the trials.

The pistol went into production in 1936 and is known variously as the 'VIS' (derived from the initials of the designers) or the 'Radom', from its place of manufacture. After the German occupation in 1939 production continued for the German Army, these being recognizable by the marking 'P Mod 35(p)' on the slide in place of the Polish Eagle engraved on prewar models.

Due to the relatively small number manufactured and issued in Poland prior to 1939, Polish use appears to have been limited to cavalry, with a few issued to infantry officers. It received wider use in the German Army, where it was particularly favored by parachute troops and Waffen SS units.

As a combat pistol, the Radom was among the best in the world. Immensely strong and reliable, excellently made from first-class material (except some made under occupation in 1943–44) it was on the heavy side for its caliber, which made it an accurate and pleasant pistol to shoot.

Italy

Pistola de Rotazione, M1889, System Bodeo

Caliber 10.35mm
Length 9.25in
Weight 2lb 1oz
Barrel 4.375in long, 4 grooves, right hand twist
Feed system 6-chambered cylinder
System of operation Revolver; double action; solid frame; rod ejection
Manufacturers Castelli, Brescia
Fabricca d'Armi, Brescia
Metallurgica Bresciana, Brescia
Siderurgica Glisenti, Turin
Royal Fabrica d'Armi Glisenti, Brescia

During the 1880s and 1890s new revolver designs appeared almost daily, and there was a good deal of copying and adapting of other people's ideas, so that it is generally difficult to pin down a specific model of revolver as one man's effort. This applies to the Model 1889 'Bodeo' pistol; although called 'System Bodeo', Signor Bodeo appears to have done little more than run up a serviceable design using features already in use and of proven worth. The lock mechanism is more or less the same as that used on the French

Italian Bodeo revolver

M1892 revolver and seems to have been derived from some Belgian designs of about 1875. The loading system used a gate to allow single rounds to be loaded, and as this gate was opened the hammer mechanism was disconnected, both as a safety measure and to allow the cylinder to be rotated for loading the chambers; this feature seems to have been borrowed from an earlier Portuguese design. The only unique feature seems to be the adoption of a hammer-block, which moved in front of the hammer and only allowed a cartridge to be struck when the trigger was properly pressed. Dropping the gun, or accidentally allowing the hammer to slip while thumb-cocking, would not fire the weapon. This may well have been Bodeo's contribution, though it has not been possible to trace a relevant patent specification for this weapon to date.

The original model used an octagonal barrel and was without a trigger guard, the trigger folding forward under the frame, dropping into the action position when the hammer was thumb-cocked. The design was later improved by the adoption of a rounded barrel and the provision of a conventional trigger and guard; this model is frequently referred to as the 'Glisenti M1894'. Glisenti may indeed have inaugurated the modifications, but the weapons were still manufactured by the other companies as well.

Although largely superseded by the Glisenti and Beretta automatic pistols, numbers of Bodeo revolvers remained in use during World War II; indeed manufacture had continued well into the 1930s. The cartridge fired was among the last of the 19th-century low-velocity large-caliber types to see military service; originally using a plain lead bullet, final issues generally had a brass-jacketed bullet of unusual skirted shape—to the casual glance, it looks as if the whole round is made from one piece of brass. But due to the low muzzle velocity (827 feet/second) the energy is only 258 foot-pounds, a poor performance for a weapon of this size and caliber.

Italy

Pistola automatica, M1910 (Glisenti)

Caliber 9mm
Length 8.25in
Weight 1lb 14½oz
Barrel 3.5in long, 6 grooves, right hand twist
Feed system 7-round detachable box magazine
System of operation Recoil; hinged block lock
Manufacturers Metallurgica Bresciana, Brescia
Siderurgica Glisenti, Turin

The history of the Glisenti pistol is somewhat obscure, but it appears to have first seen the light of day as the Hansler-Roch pistol in 1905, which was issued originally to Carabinieri officers. With some modification it was later put into production by Glisenti of Turin and taken into Italian Army service as the Model 1910. The matter is not made any more clear by contemporary records referring to it as the 'Brixia' pistol. It was, apparently, offered to numerous armies under one or the other name, but only the Italians adopted it.

The Glisenti cannot be claimed to be among the world's better pistols; the breech lock is not particularly strong and the construction of the weapon is mechanically and structurally weak. Moreover the ammunition situation is hazardous; it is chambered for the 9mm Glisenti cartridge, which is dimensionally the same as the 9mm Parabellum, but loaded less powerfully to give 1050 ft/second instead of the Parabellum's 1300 ft/second. Provided the Glisenti pistol is used with Glisenti ammunition, there is a margin of safety, but if it is inadvertently loaded with Parabellum cartridges, this margin is exceeded and an accident could easily result.

It has not been possible to discover much about the use of the Glisenti in combat. It was officially an officer's weapon, but in fact most officers appear to

Glisenti automatic pistol of 1910

have preferred to use the Beretta Model 1934. Few Glisenti pistols were found in the Western Desert fighting in 1941–42, and it seems that the principal issue was to non-combatant elements such as quarter-masters and clerks.

Italy

Pistola automatica, M1934 (Beretta)

Caliber 9mm Short (.380 Auto)
Length 6.0in
Weight 1lb 7½oz
Barrel 3.75in long, 4 grooves, right hand twist
Feed system 7-round detachable box magazine
System of operation Blowback
Manufacturer P. Beretta, Gardone

The firm of Pietro Beretta was founded as far back as 1680 to produce sporting guns, and made its first essay into the modern military pistol field with the production of a simple and reliable blowback pistol in 1915. This was immediately accepted into service by the Italian Army and thereafter was gradually improved through a number of models, culminating in the M1934. The simplicity and robustness of this model, as well as its small size, made it highly suc-

cessful, and to a large degree it replaced the earlier Glisenti throughout the combat units.

The 9mm cartridge fired by this weapon is not the universally accepted Parabellum, but the 9mm Short, known also as the .380 Automatic cartridge. This has a light bullet travelling at low velocity and it delivers only about 160 foot-pounds of energy at the muzzle; while this is, of course, lethal, it lacks the shock value and knock-down ability of heavier or faster bullets. During the years between the wars it had become extremely popular as a police and military cartridge in southern and eastern Europe, but since 1945 it has been completely abandoned as a military loading.

Another odd feature of the Beretta is the absence of a slide stop; when the last round has been fired, the action stays open by virtue of the slide being held against the magazine platform. This often leads to difficulty in removing the magazine due to the pressure of the slide.

Since the end of the war the Italian Army has fallen into line with the rest of Europe and adopted the 9mm Parabellum round as standard, with a new model of Beretta pistol to suit. However the Model 1934 is still commercially available under the name 'Cougar'.

The M1934 first saw action in the Italian-Abyssinian War in 1935–36, and after that it was supplied in considerable numbers to Franco's forces in the Spanish Civil War. Both these affairs showed its reliability, and World War II saw it widely

Beretta Model 34 with short 9mm cartridge

distributed throughout the Italian Army. While serviceable enough, it can only be considered as a purely close-range self-defense weapon; the low power and poor accuracy—due to a short barrel which soon lost its alignment—prevented more aggressive use.

Pistol, revolver, Meiji 26

Caliber 9mm
Length 8.5in
Weight 2lb 4oz
Barrel 4.7in long, 6 grooves, left hand twist
Feed system 6-chambered cylinder
System of operation Revolver; hinged-frame, double-action only, self-ejecting
Manufacturer State Arsenal, Nagoya

The Meiji 26 revolver was adopted in 1893, the 26th year of the Meiji Era. Although a Japanese design it was put together from a combination of features derived from various Western weapons. The Japanese Navy had purchased a number of Smith & Wesson revolvers in 1879, and the barrel latch and cylinder lock were copied from this; the basic construction came from Belgian Nagant designs, and the lock mechanism leaned heavily on the contemporary Dutch service revolver. It also featured a hinged side-plate which could be opened for cleaning or repair of the lockwork, which seems likely to have been inspired by the French M1892 revolver.

On the face of it, such a combination ought to have resulted in a reasonable weapon, but in fact something went wrong in the assembly, and the result was muzzle-heavy, hard to fire (due to its double-action lock) and poorly made of inferior material. Its accuracy was equally poor, and the round of ammunition, a peculiar 9mm rimmed cartridge unknown outside Japan, developed no more than 136 foot-pounds at the muzzle—one of the least effective rounds ever taken into military service.

Initial issues of the Model 26 revolver were apparently to cavalry, but after the general adoption of the Nambu automatic pistol, the revolver then found its way into the hands of other corps. During World War II it was principally issued to reserve and home defense units, but numbers of NCOs of infantry units in the South Pacific were found to be carrying one. There are no definite reports regarding its effectiveness or otherwise in combat.

Pistol, automatic, Taisho 04 (Nambu)

Caliber 8mm
Length 9.0in
Weight 1lb 15½oz
Barrel 4.7in long, 6 grooves, right hand twist
Feed system 8-round detachable box magazine
System of operation Recoil; hinged block lock
Manufacturers Japan Special Steel Company State Arsenal, Nagoya

The remarkable thing about the Nambu pistol is that, so far as can be ascertained, it was never officially accepted into Japanese military service, although thousands were carried by Japanese officers.

The Taisho 04 takes its nomenclature from the fact that it was perfected and offered for sale in the fourth year of the Taisho reign, or 1915 in the Christian calendar. The name 'Nambu' comes from Colonel Kirijo Nambu, the designer. According to contemporary Japanese newspaper reports, Colonel Nambu first demonstrated this pistol before the Emperor at the graduation ceremonies of the Toyama Military Academy in September 1909.

Although resembling the Parabellum to some degree, and sometimes referred to as a 'Japanese copy of the Luger', there is no mechanical similarity between the two guns; there is, however, a good deal of internal resemblance to the Italian Glisenti pistol, and the indications are that Nambu took the Glisenti as his starting point. The breech-locking mechanism, a drop-down block beneath the bolt, is almost identical to that of the Glisenti, but an oddity of the Nambu design is that it is quite possible to assemble the pistol without the breech lock in place, which makes it extremely dangerous to fire. Another small peculiarity is the small-diameter single recoil spring lying in a recess on one side of the receiver, which gives the weapon an oddly lop-sided appearance.

The cartridge is an uncommon bottle-necked round carrying a 100-grain jacketed bullet of poor stopping power. Apart from its use in Japanese sub-machine guns, the cartridge has never been used in any other weapon.

Widely used by Japanese officers, the Taisho 04 made frequent appearances in

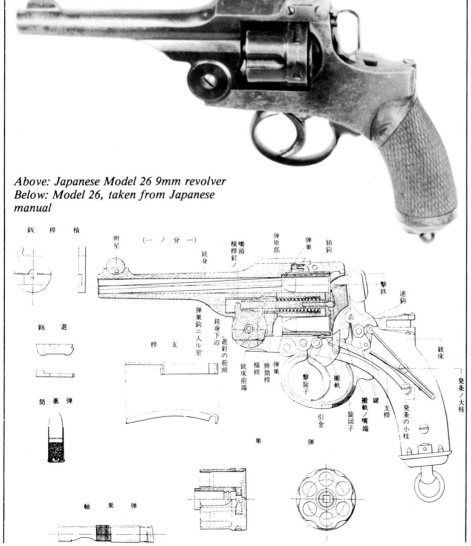

Above: Japanese Model 26 9mm revolver
Below: Model 26, taken from Japanese manual

Taisho '04 Nambu pistol, which was still in use throughout World War II

combat. Its principal defect seems to have been a weak striker spring, which soon lost its resilience and gave light striker blows and misfires. This was sufficiently well appreciated for the standard holster to be provided with a special pocket for carrying a spare spring, and it was significant that when these weapons were captured by Allied troops, the holster pocket rarely contained a spare spring.

Japan

Pistol, automatic, Taisho 14 (Nambu)

Caliber 8mm
Length 8.95in
Weight 1lb 15¾oz
Barrel 4.75in long, 6 grooves, right hand twist
Feed system 8-round detachable box magazine
System of operation Recoil; hinged block lock
Manufacturer State Arsenals

Although still called the Nambu and easily confused with the 04 model, this version was not, so far as can be ascertained, actually designed by Colonel Nambu. Its development appears to be the work of a government arsenal design office, probably that of Nagoya Arsenal, in order to supplant the 04 by a more easily manufactured pistol, and this model was actually approved as a service issue. The model number indicates its adoption in the 14th year of the Taisho reign, or 1925.

The changes from the 04 design consisted of adding a safety catch in such a position that it could only be operated by the firer's free hand; replacing the single offset recoil spring by two springs, one at each side of the frame; and some minor internal changes to simplify manufacture. Nothing was done by way of improving the striker spring, so that this was still the weak point of the design. Another disadvantage was that the bolt was held open after the last shot had been fired by abutting against the magazine platform. The pressure of the two recoil springs, plus that of a strong magazine retaining spring, made the empty magazine difficult to

remove. When the fingers are slippery with oil or perspiration and the gun at all dirty, it is almost impossible to change magazines quickly.

There are one or two minor variants of this weapon; the 'Baby Nambu' is a smaller model taking a special 7mm cartridge. Developed as a commercial pistol, the entire production appears to have been taken over by the Japanese Air Force. The 'Kiska Model' is a Taisho 14 with an extra-large trigger guard to allow using it with gloved hands. This was developed for use in Manchuria in the early 1930s, but takes its (unofficial) name from the fact that it was first found by Allied troops in the Aleutian Islands campaign.

As with the 04, this model was widely used and found in combat throughout the Greater East Asian Co-Prosperity Sphere. The only specific reference I have come across to its use in combat was in a manuscript by the late Lt-Col R. K. Wilson, RA, in which he related an encounter in Burma with an unfortunate Japanese officer who, having emptied his pistol at the approaching British, was shot while vainly attempting to remove the empty magazine; a victim of the defective design feature noted above.

Japan

Pistol, automatic, Type 94

Caliber 8mm
Length 7.125in
Weight 1lb 12oz
Barrel 3.125in long, 6 grooves, right hand twist
Feed system 6-round detachable box magazine
System of operation Recoil; vertical sliding lock
Manufacturer State Arsenals

Like most totalitarian states, Imperial Japan was reluctant to announce any information about its weapons, so that the history of the Type 94 pistol is not known.

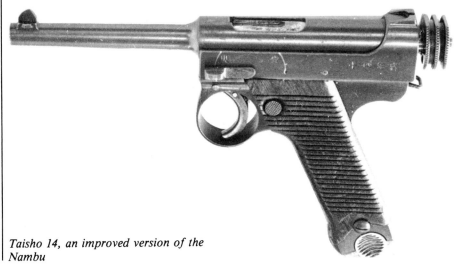

Taisho 14, an improved version of the Nambu

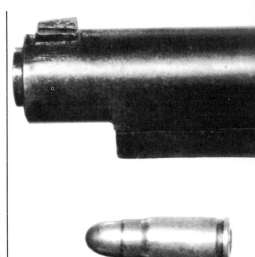

Japanese Type 94 automatic pistol

It appears to have been developed in the early 1930s in a further attempt to develop a weapon simple to mass-produce. Some authorities speak of it having been offered for sale commercially in prewar days, notably in South America, but the evidence for this is very slender and it was unknown to the outside world until specimens were captured during the war. It was introduced for military service in 1934, the nomenclature 'Type 94' coming from the equation of 1934 with the year 2594 in the Japanese calendar.

The Type 94 is, in my estimation, a prominent contender for the title of worst military pistol ever issued. The ammunition is that of the Nambu pistols and, fired from such a short barrel as this, it develops no more than 180 foot-pounds at the muzzle. The pistol itself is an odd-looking weapon which sits awkwardly in the hand, and although generally of sound material is usually poorly finished. It exhibits two startling mechanical defects: the disconnector and lock mechanism are so constructed that it is possible to release the striker and fire the pistol before the barrel and breech are locked together; and the sear which releases the striker is an exposed metal strip on the left-hand side of the frame, capable of being depressed and thus firing the weapon by simply grasping it carelessly. Minor defects of design include the exposure of the recoil spring, and the general accessibility of the mechanism to any dirt and dust which happen to be flying about. Taken all round, it is an astonishing weapon; in the 1930s the Japanese were not averse to copying any design they thought might be useful in other fields of activity, and it is thus all the more surprising that they went to the trouble of producing this monstrosity instead of copying a more workmanlike pistol.

So far as employment goes there is little information; it was a general issue to officers, but appears to have been most favored by the Air Force and is not often found in the hands of infantry. There are no reliable reports of its use in action.

Pistol, revolver, M1892 (Modèle d'ordonnance or Lebel)

Caliber 8mm
Length 9.25in
Weight 1lb 10½oz
Barrel 4.5in long, 6 grooves, right hand twist
Feed system 6-chambered cylinder
System of operation Revolver; double action; solid frame, side-opening, hand ejector
Manufacturer Manufacture d'Armes de St. Etienne

Sometimes called the 'Lebel' revolver, it appears doubtful if Nicholas Lebel, a foremost weapon authority of the French Army in the 19th Century, had anything to do with the design of this pistol. Its design is attributed instead to a M. Richard, Inspector-General of the Manufacture d'Armes de St. Etienne. Production began in 1892 and is said to have continued, off and on, until 1945.

The design is not outstanding, being more or less the same sort of thing as most of its contemporaries, the most interesting innovation being the use of such a small caliber at a time when heavy caliber revolvers were the general rule for military use. Two unusual design features are firstly that the cylinder swings out to the right, in opposition to the design of every other side-opening revolver, and secondly the making of the left-hand side of the frame into a hinged cover which can be freed by loosening a screw and opened forward to reveal all the lockwork.

The cartridge used with this pistol was rarely seen outside France, though one or two gunmakers produced commercial revolvers for it in the 1890s. It fired a 120 grain bullet at 715 feet per second to give about 135 foot-pounds at the muzzle, which was a poor performance by the standards of the day.

The Model 1892 was widely distributed throughout the French Army and remained in use until World War II; indeed, it is said that Army depots still carry several thousands as reserve stocks. It was exten- sively used in combat throughout its life, in the French Foreign Legion's desert activi- ties as well as in the two World Wars, and numbers were left behind in Indo-China. Doubtless as ammunition supplies dwindle it will fade away, but it qualifies as one of the longest-serving weapons of any army.

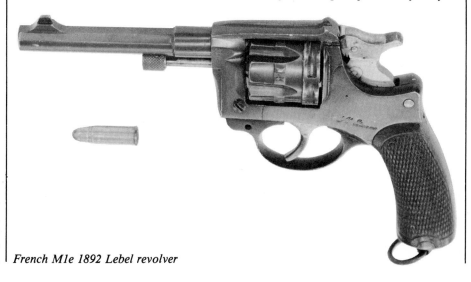

French M1e 1892 Lebel revolver

Japanese military terms and characters

Important military characters

歩兵	騎兵	砲兵	師團	旅團	聯隊	大隊	中隊	小隊
Infantry Hohei	Cavalry Kihei	Artillery Hohei	Division Shidan	Brigade Ryodan	Regiment Rentai	Battalion Daitai	Company Chutai	Platoon Shotai

Characters used in the nomenclature of army stores

Date

年號 = Nengo

年 = Year

明治 = Meiji

年內 = Within the year

大正 = Taisho

月 = Month

昭和 = Shōwa

日 = Day

紀元節 = Anniversary of Jimmu

式 = Pattern

Numbers

〇 = 0

一 = 1

二 = 2

三 = 3

四 = 4

五 = 5

六 = 6

七 = 7

八 = 8

九 = 9

十 = 10

十一 = 11

十二 = 12

二〇 = 20

二一 = 21

二二 = 22

三〇 = 30

三一 = 31

三二 = 32

Examples

九 = 9
八 = 8
式 = Pattern
一 = 1
〇 = 0
〇 = 0
式 = Pattern
三 = 3
年 = Year
式 = Pattern

Date

昭和 = Shōwa
十六 = 16
年 = Year
四 = 4
月 = Month
十五 = 15
日 = Day

or

昭和16·4·15

Pistol, automatic, MAS M1935A, M1935S

Caliber 7.65mm
Length 7.45in
Weight 1lb 10oz
Barrel 4.3in long, 4 grooves, right hand twist
Feed system 8-round detachable box magazine
System of operation Recoil; Browning swinging link
Manufacturers Sociètè Alsace de Constructions Mechanique (SACM)
Manufacture d'Armes de St. Etienne (MAS)
Manufacture d'Armes de Tulle (MAT)
Manufacture d'Armes de Chatellerault (MAC)

French MAS 1935A pistol

The Model 1935 pistol was designed by a Swiss, Charles G. Petter. What little is known of him indicates a colorful background, including a tour of duty with the French Foreign Legion, from which he was invalided out after being severely wounded. In the 1920s he worked for SACM, eventually taking charge of their firearms department. During this period he worked on a pistol design which he patented in 1934; the principal feature of this was the construction of the lock mechanism as a separate unit. This is the same as the system used on the Russian Tokarev pistol, but since at that time precious few Tokarevs had been made, and the pistol was entirely unknown outside Soviet military circles, there seems no doubt that this coincidence is the result of two good designers thinking about the same problem and coming up with the same answer completely independently of each other.

In other respects Petter's design is basically Browning, using the usual system of locking the breech by a rib on the barrel mating with a recess on the undersurface of the slide top, and unlocked by a cam beneath the breech. The prototype was submitted to the French Army for trials and adopted for issue as the Model 1935. In about 1937 the design was reworked by the St. Etienne design staff with a view to making it easier to manufacture; after this the original model was known as the M1935A, while the new simplified model became the 1935S. The differences are immediately apparent; the 1935A is a much smoother product, with the butt shaped to fit the hand and with an excellent finish. The 1935S, on the other hand, has a straight butt, an angular and slab-sided appearance, and the finish is to a much lower standard.

There is little available evidence of the use of the M1935 pistols by the French Army; what is even more remarkable is that there is no record of this weapon having been taken over by the German Army, and they were generally quick to adopt a good design. Two reasons can be advanced for this; in all probability very few weapons had been made and issued

before the outbreak of war; and secondly the M1935 was chambered for a very odd cartridge, the 7.65mm Longue, or French Service Auto. This round, which fired an 85 grain bullet at 1120 feet per second to give 240lbs/ft of muzzle energy, was marginally effective as a combat round, and had been developed specifically for this pistol; it was only used in one other weapon, a prewar French sub-machine gun.

In later years the Petter patents were taken over by the Schweizer Industrial Gesellschaft, and the current SIG 210 pistol, generally conceded to be the finest automatic pistol in the world —and certainly the most expensive—is the present-day descendant of the M1935A.

The 'utility' MAS 1935S pistol

RIFLES

Traditionally, the weapon of the infantryman is the rifle—together with its bayonet—and that remains true even today, though as World War II progressed, fewer and fewer infantrymen carried rifles and more and more carried some other form of weapon. Nevertheless, the rifle was still the basic military arm, the one which every soldier learned as the foundation of his military competence and which every soldier was expected to be able to handle if the need arose. The bayonet was less vital; again, every soldier seems to have been taught the rudiments of bayonet fighting, but there is room for considering that the time might have been better spent. As far back as 1914, Fortescue, in his lectures on Military History at Cambridge, was pointing out a few truths about the bayonet:

'English and French both talk much of the bayonet; but in Egypt in 1801 they threw stones at each other when their ammunition was exhausted, and one English sergeant was killed by a stone. At Inkerman, again the British threw stones at the Russians, not without effect; and I am told on good authority that the Russians and Japanese, both of whom profess to love the bayonet, threw stones at each other rather than close, even in this twentieth century.'

Within a few months of this statement, the bayonet was in greater evidence than ever before, but postwar analysis showed that the number of injuries attributable to it were miniscule in comparison to those caused by other agencies. World War II was little different, and in the writer's own experience, British troops in Korea resorted to stone-throwing much as their ancestors had done at Inkerman. The American cartoonist Bill Mauldin, in the *Stars and Stripes* had the last word on bayonets when he drew a cartoon showing an astounded GI holding a rifle and bayonet.

'I'll be damned,' he says. 'Did you guys know this can-opener fits on the end of a rifle?'

World War II sounded the Last Post for the bolt-action magazine rifle which had armed most of the world since the 1880s, while it ushered in the automatic rifle. The automatic, or more properly, self-loading, rifle had been knocking at the doors of the world's war offices since the turn of the century, but apart from one or two experimental examples produced in small numbers, little interest had been aroused. There were two stumbling blocks; firstly it had to be absolutely and unquestionably reliable under the most unlikely conditions and in the hands of the most cretinous soldier imaginable; and secondly there was always the fear that given such a weapon, the soldiers—particularly hastily-trained conscripts—would blast off every round they possessed in the general direction of the enemy during the first two minutes of the battle and thereafter sit waiting to be overrun. There were some grounds for this second argument, for that very thing had happened once or twice even with magazine rifles; moreover the load on the supply services to deliver the vast amount of ammunition which would be needed to feed these voracious weapons would be insupportable. In fact, the same sort of arguments had been advanced against the quick-firing field gun in days gone by, and eventually seen to be groundless, but that didn't stop them being offered all over again.

But in order not to appear too reactionary, from time to time the war departments would issue notices to the effect that they would be interested in seeing and testing some automatic rifles if any inventors would care to compete. Usually the specifications and conditions which appeared with the notice were enough to deter all but the most eccentric or the most dedicated. The following announcement was published by the British War Office on 1 August 1909 and is a good example of the type:

'Any rifle submitted for consideration must be addressed to the Director of Artillery not later than 1 May 1910. Only rifles in a complete state can be accepted, and 300 rounds for a preliminary trial should accompany the rifle.

1. *The rifle should be simple, strong and compact* as possible, and *the mechanism should be well protected from the entrance of sand, rain and dirt and free from risk of derangement due to accident, long wear and tear, rough usage on active service, exposure to wet or sand, or fouling from long continued firing.* It should be easily cleaned and inspected, and, if after long use any part breaks down, it should be easily and cheaply repaired. *Such parts of the mechanism as require to be cleaned and oiled by the soldier should be capable of being stripped without the aid of tools.*

2. *Filling the magazine and loading the cartridges into the chamber should be done with ease and certainty.*

3. Cartridges may be rimless.

4. As regards the ballistics of the rifle, the range for the maximum height of trajectory of $5\frac{1}{4}$ feet must be not less than 800 yards.

5. The weight of the bullet, which should be pointed, must not be less than 150 nor more than 180 grains.

6. The caliber must not be less than .27 inch nor greater than .28 inch.

7. The working pressure must not exceed 21 tons to the square inch at 80 degrees Fahrenheit.

8. The rifle must be as light as possible and, in any case, must not exceed $9\frac{1}{2}$lbs with magazine empty and without bayonet.

9. The rifle must be capable of being used either as an automatic-loading rifle or as a magazine rifle, the change from one to the other being simply and rapidly effected. The rifle must work correctly as an automatic rifle both with and without the

bayonet fixed; the bayonet being attached to the fore-end and not to the barrel.

When used as a magazine rifle *the bolt or block must work freely by hand, without excessive force having to be used.*

The magazine must contain not less than five cartridges and is to be filled either by means of a 'charger' or a 'clip'.

The rifle is to fire only one shot for each pressure of the trigger.

After the last round in the magazine has been fired, the fact should be indicated by the bolt remaining open or by some other conspicuous arrangement.

10. *The direction in which the fired cases are ejected should be such as not to incommode the firer or men at his side.*

11. *The bolt or block supporting the base of the cartridge must, at the moment of firing, be locked positively to the barrel or to some part securely attached to the barrel, and must not depend merely on its inertia, or friction, or on the pressure of springs to resist separation of the breech bolt or block from the barrel on discharge; it must be impossible to fire the cartridge by pressing the trigger until the locking is complete.*

12. An efficient safety device must be provided to prevent the rifle being fired when the safety device is used, and, on putting the safety device out of action, the rifle must remain cocked and ready for firing.

It is instructive to read through that carefully and then contemplate how many present-day self-loaders could meet all the demands.

As if the specification were not enough, it was followed by a *Memorandum for Inventors* which was no less daunting:

1. Persons who desire to submit any invention . . . should do so by letter.
2. The letter should state the nature of the invention and give sufficient particulars to enable its merits to be fully considered, and adduce any evidence there is of the usefulness of the invention obtained by actual previous experiment. All designs, plans, drawings, models, samples or papers submitted are at the owner's risk. . . .
6. Expenses. Expenses or loss of time incurred before or after the submission of an invention will give no claim unless authority for such expenses has been previously given by letter signed by the Secretary or the Assistant Secretary of the War Office or by the Director of Artillery, and the liability will be strictly confined to the limits . . . authorized in such letter.
7. Should the Army Council consider it desirable to try an invention, the inventor will, as a general rule, be required to bear the expense of the provision of the article, its carriage, fitting up and removal. . . .
8. The Army Council reserve the right to retain for future reference any designs, plans, drawings, models, samples or papers forming an essential part of the description of the invention. . . .
9. Should the invention be adopted . . . terms for its use will be fixed by subsequent agreement, and such terms will include the supply of two copies of all designs, drawings, patents, patterns, and particulars relating to the invention which may be considered necessary . . . ; and it is to be understood that all such designs, etc., will be absolutely at the disposal of His Majesty's Government for all purposes whatever, and that for them reasonable prices only will be paid . . . to cover the cost of draughtsmanship and manufacture.
10. No claim for remuneration for an invention will be held to be established unless the invention has been adopted into the Service.
11. All claims for remuneration will be carefully considered; but any award which may be made will only be payable to the claimant when approved by the Treasury and money is available from funds voted by Parliament for such purposes.'

One is not very surprised to hear that the pavement outside the War Office was not thronged with inventors of automatic rifles in 1910. What is more surprising is that in 1940 another announcement was published for the guidance of firms desirous of submitting automatic rifle designs, and in the specification all the phrases in italics above were repeated word-for-word; there had been very little change of heart in thirty years.

As a result, although numerous designs were tested in Britain, none came up to the stringent demands, and World War II was fought entirely with the bolt action Lee-Enfield; and it says much for the Lee-Enfield that it acquitted itself well, so well that it was exceptionally rare for a British soldier to acquire a rifle of enemy or Allied origin in preference to his issue weapon, something which cannot be said in the pistol or sub-machine gun categories.

The Americans had been experimenting with automatic rifles since 1918 and in 1936 began issuing the well-known Garand. This made a reputation for reliability which was second-to-none, and was, more than anything else, the factor which led to the acceptance of the automatic rifle in other armies. If it worked for the Americans, then it must work for us, was the attitude, and as a result, once the American adoption of the Garand was seen to be crowned with success, everybody began to look again at the automatic rifle question. The Russians had been toying with a design for some time and forthwith went into production; they regretted their haste shortly afterwards, and withdrew the rifle, replacing it with an improved model in due course. But they never armed their entire army with them as did the Americans, and the production figures of Soviet automatic rifles prior to 1945 are relatively minute.

The Germans had also been playing with automatic rifles for many years, numerous private companies offering designs for consideration, which makes it all the more remarkable that when they finally did decide to adopt one they chose an abominable design which they later had to get rid of. But after this false start they managed, in spite of enormous production and political obstacles, to produce two of the best automatic rifles ever seen, and in the bargain began the rise of a new class of weapon, the 'Assault Rifle'.

In Japan and Italy the automatic rifle hardly got started. So far as we are aware no wartime work was done on an automatic rifle design in Italy, in spite of the fact that an Italian design, the Cei-Rigotti was one of the first ever to appear, back in 1905. But this failed to live up to its promise and probably colored Italian opinion thereafter. The Japanese experimented with one or two designs taken from foreign sources, one of them a copy of the Garand, but none of their designs was ever perfected to a state of reliability where it could have gone into production on any large scale.

Rifle No. 4 Mark 1

Experimental British No. 4 rifle with plastic stock

Caliber .303in
Length 44.43in
Weight 9lb 1oz
Barrel 25.19in long, 5 grooves, right hand twist
Feed system 10-round detachable box magazine
System of operation Lee turn-bolt
Manufacturers Royal Ordnance Factory, Fazakerley
Royal Ordnance Factory, Maltby
Birmingham Small Arms Co., Tyseley
Savage Arms Corporation, Chicopee Falls, Mass., USA
Long Branch Arsenal, Ontario, Canada

The well-known Lee-Enfield rifle began its service with the British Army in 1895 and ran into some 27 different models before being replaced by a self-loader in 1957. The most famous model was probably the Mark 3, the 'Short' Lee-Enfield, so-called because it introduced a new idea into military rifles. Prior to its introduction (in 1903) it was customary to produce two rifle-type weapons, one a long rifle for infantry use and one a short carbine for cavalry and other mounted troops such as engineers and artillery. The 'Short' Lee-Enfield was shorter than a normal 'long' rifle, and longer than a carbine, and thus it was possible to standardize on one weapon for all branches of the Army.

Below: British rifle No. 4 in action protecting a Bren gunner. This revised specimen was the best of its type and is still in use today by NATO forces, though now chambered for the 7.62 NATO round

Excellent as the Mark 3 was, it had some drawbacks, and the major one was that its manufacture was time-consuming, demanding much machining and hand-fitting. The other principal complaint was that the nature and location of the back-sight (an open-topped U in front of the chamber) made it difficult to master quickly. Because of these points, work began immediately after the Armistice in 1918 to try and develop a rifle which retained the Lee-Enfield's many virtues—robustness, speed of operation, reliability—but which had better sights and was easier to make. The first attempt was the 'No. 1 Mark 5' (a new system of nomenclature had been adopted after the war) which was little more than a Mark 3 with an aperture sight at the rear of the receiver. It was never adopted as a service weapon. The design was then simplified into the 'No. 1 Mark 6' which used a heavier barrel, a new design of bolt, less woodwork, and a projecting muzzle on to which a spike bayonet could be fixed. This too was never adopted, but with a little more improvement it became the 'No. 4 Mark 1', the standard World War II rifle.

The No. 4 rifle was much like the earlier Mark 6, but there were numerous small changes which simplified production. It was first issued late in 1939, though not officially adopted until 13 February 1941. Well over a million were made during the war, both in Britain and across the Atlantic in the USA and Canada, and after some misgivings by old soldiers who missed the immaculate finish of the Mark 3, the No. 4 became liked and trusted in its turn. It remains in service today as a sniping rifle, using 7.62mm NATO ammunition.

Variants
Mark 1* This model was made almost entirely in the USA and Canada, and differed from the Mark 1 in the method of removing the bolt. Numbers of these rifles also had rifling which differed from the standard five grooved pattern, using only two grooves in order to speed up production.
Mark 1(T) This was the sniper's version, differing from the standard pattern by having a rather better backsight, having the necessary fittings for mounting a telescope No. 32, and with a wooden cheek rest on the butt.
No. 5 Mark 1 A shortened version of the No. 4, designed for use in the jungle. The weapon is some 5 inches shorter and has a prominent flash hider on the muzzle. The woodwork is shortened, leaving a considerable amount of exposed barrel, and a rubber shoulder pad is fitted to the butt. Although light to carry it was violent to shoot, and was never notable for its accuracy. Neither was it very popular.

US rifle, cal .30 M1903

Caliber .30in
Length 43.25in
Weight 8lb 11oz
Barrel 24.0in long, 4 grooves, left hand twist
Feed system 5-round integral box magazine
System of operation Mauser turn-bolt
Manufacturers Remington Arms Co.
L. C. Smith Corona Typewriter Corp.
Springfield Arsenal
Rock Island Arsenal

Although the M1 Garand was the standard rifle of the US Army during World War II, many thousands of the older bolt-action M1903 remained in use. In the earlier part they were still carried by first-line troops before production of the M1 reached sufficient quantities to supply them, and later it was relegated to reserve and guard use as well as for initial training of recruits.

The M1903 is commonly known as the 'Springfield' since it was designed and developed, and largely manufactured, at Springfield Arsenal. The first magazine rifle of the US Army was the Krag-Jorgensen, but after a very few years of this weapon, work began on developing a replacement. After considering all the designs then available, it was decided to adopt the Mauser system of bolt-action and magazine, and for $200,000 the United States Government purchased a licence from the Mauser company. The original

design was a long rifle with a 30-inch barrel, but while work was in progress, the British Army introduced its 'Short' Lee-Enfield and the US Army decided that they too would adopt this idea of one rifle for all troops. The design was modified to use a 24-inch barrel and the first models were issued in 1905.

The original bullet for which the rifle was designed was a 220 grain round-nosed pattern, but in 1905 the German Army introduced their 'Spitzer' or pointed bullet, which promised improved performance, and the rest of the world hurried to follow suit. The US Army adopted a 150 grain pointed bullet, and the rifle sights were modified to match its ballistics.

Although basically of Mauser pattern, there were one or two features which made the Springfield unique. The firing pin is in two pieces, the ejector is not spring-loaded, and an ingenious bolt stop allows bolt removal and acts as a cut-off, so that the rounds in the magazine can be held there while the rifle is used as a single-loader.

Variants

M1903A1 As for the M1903 but with a new stock of pistol-grip pattern, the forward finger grooves omitted, and the surface of the trigger milled to give surer grip.

M1903A2 A proposed barrel and action fitted into a special mounting for use as a sub-caliber training weapon for tank guns. The requirement was subsequently cancelled.

M1903A3 The rear sight was moved back to the rear of the receiver. Various small changes were made in construction to simplify and speed up manufacture. This model may have a straight or pistol-grip stock, and may have a barrel with only two rifling grooves. The design was standardized on 21 May 1942.

M1903A4 As for A3 but with a Weaver 330C sighting telescope and the iron sights removed. The bolt handle was also modified by cutting and bending so that it did not foul the telescope when operated. Like many bolt-action rifles with telescopes mounted centrally, this could only be used as a single-loader, since the location of the telescope prevented the magazine from being charged by the usual charger system.

US Springfield 1903 rifle with bayonet

or 'Enfield' by the Americans. In all, 2,193,429 Pattern 17 rifles were produced before the contracts were terminated in 1918.

After the war they were placed in store and were brought out once more in 1940 when over a million were sent to Britain to arm the Home Guard (who also were given large numbers of Pattern 14 which had been stored in Britain). The remaining M1917 were issued to the US Army to fill their needs until sufficient Garand rifles were produced. It is, in fact, doubtful if any Pattern 17 (or Pattern 14) rifles were ever used in combat, but they were certainly widely used for training.

As a military rifle, the Pattern 14/17 is not among the world's best, which is probably why it was never revived after World War I; it is, certainly to British troops accustomed to the Lee-Enfield, a cumbersome and badly balanced weapon. But as a target rifle it is certainly worth some respect, which rather reflects the target-shooting bias of the people who originally clamored for the design to replace the Lee-Enfield. It was used as a sniping rifle during World War I, but when it came to fighting, the British troops were in no doubt about which rifle they preferred.

US rifle, cal .30 M1917

Caliber .30in
Length 46.25in
Weight 9lb 10oz
Barrel 26.0in long, 2, 4 or 5 grooves, left hand twist
Feed system 5-round integral magazine
System of operation Enfield (modified Mauser) bolt action
Manufacturers Remington Arms Co. Winchester Repeating Arms Co., New Haven, Conn., USA

After the introduction of the Short Lee-Enfield rifle in 1903, the British Army were somewhat taken aback by its reception outside military circles. At that time there was considerable national interest in the Army's weapons, and numerous experts assailed the Lee-Enfield as being inaccurate, poorly designed, and generally of a standard well below that set by the armies of the rest of the world. Time—and World War I—showed that the Army were right and the experts were wrong, but just in

case there was a grain of reason in the outcries, work began on a fresh design, using a longer barrel and a bolt action with frontal locking lugs based more or less on the Mauser system. The new rifle was in .276 caliber, and a small number were issued for trial in 1913 as the 'Pattern 1913'. They were not particularly successful, most of the troubles stemming from the exceptionally powerful cartridge, and when war broke out the development was shelved, never to be revived.

However, due to the shortage of rifles, and since the 'P13' had been designed with an eye to rapid production in wartime, the design was changed to accept the standard .303 cartridge and several thousand were made on contract in the USA as the 'Pattern 14'. When the United States entered the war, they too had a rifle problem, and solved it by re-designing the Pattern 14 to take the standard US .30 cartridge, and then getting the same manufacturers to continue with production, this version being called the 'Pattern 17' by the British and the 'M1917'

US rifle, cal .30 M1 (Garand)

Caliber .30in
Length 43.0in
Weight 9lb 8oz
Barrel 24.0in long, 4 grooves, right hand twist
Feed system 8-round integral magazine, clip-loaded
System of operation Gas piston, turning bolt
Manufacturers Springfield Arsenal Winchester Repeating Arms Co., New Haven, Conn., USA

John C. Garand first produced a repeating rifle for trial in 1920, but it used an unusual system of operation, relying on

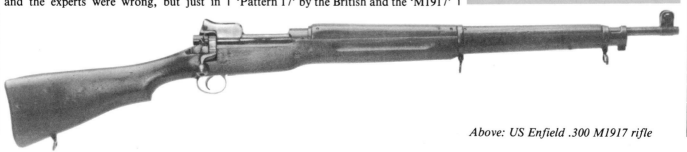

Above: US Enfield .300 M1917 rifle

US Garand rifle M1

Loading the Garand with an 8 round clip

the expansion and set-back of the primer cap in the cartridge to unlock the bolt action. While the system worked, it was not entirely practical, but Mr. Garand later joined the design staff of Springfield Arsenal and went on to develop the rifle which will always be associated with his name. In 1929 a series of tests of competing designs of rifle were held at Aberdeen Proving Ground, as a result of which a Garand design of gas-operated rifle was selected as the most promising. Further development took place, and in 1936 it was standardized as the US Rifle M1.

The operation is by gas tapped very close to the muzzle end of the barrel, driving a long-stroke piston backwards. This, by means of a cam, rotates and opens the bolt and cocks the firing hammer. The return spring is carried in the gas piston, an arrangement which keeps the action body short and compact. Feed is from a magazine loaded by an eight-round clip, and upon the last round being fired the clip is ejected and the action held open for re-loading. This is probably the least desirable feature of the Garand, since single rounds cannot be loaded to 'top up' the magazine; it has to be a full clip or noth-

A US Marine takes aim with his M1 rifle at Iwo Jima in 1945. The fighting on Iwo was fierce, as the Japanese put up some of the stiffest resistance in the war

ing. It also led to a tactical disadvantage in that the ejected clip made a most distinctive noise if it fell on hard ground, thus alerting the enemy to the fact that the rifleman was now holding an empty rifle. But in spite of this small defect, the Garand proved reliable and accurate in service all over the world. Indeed the postwar rifle, the M14, is largely based on Garand's design.

Variants

M1E1 An experimental model with slight changes in the cam angle of the bolt-opening section of the operating rod.

M1E2 An M1 fitted with an International Industries telescope sight for trials as a sniping rifle.

M1E3 The bolt was fitted with a roller cam and the operating rod altered accordingly. Experimental only.

M1E4 The gas system was altered so as to cut off the supply of gas and allow expansion in the gas cylinder to operate the action. Provided a less violent action. Experimental only.

M1E5 Shortened M1 with a folding stock and 18in barrel. Intended for airborne use, it gave excessive muzzle blast and was not adopted.

M1E6 An M1 fitted with an offset sighting telescope to allow use of either the standard sights or the telescope without adjustment. Not accepted.

M1E7 An M1 fitted with a Griffin and Howe telescope mount and a Lyman 'Alaskan' or Weaver 330 telescope, and a leather cheek pad on the butt. This was standardized in June 1944 as 'Rifle M1C (Sniper's)' and some models were fitted with a flash-hider in January 1945.

M1E8 As for the M1E7 but using a tele-

scope mount evolved by Springfield Arsenal and a Lyman telescope. Standardized as 'Rifle M1D (Sniper's) Substitute Standard' in September 1944.

M1E9 Similar to the M1E4 but had the piston-head separate from the rest of the piston so as to act as a tappet. Experimental only.

T26 The action and barrel of the M1E5 in a conventional wooden stock. This was demanded in July 1945 by the HQ Pacific Theater and an order for 15,000 was given but cancelled in August 1945. A small number were made and these later appeared on the surplus market described as the 'Tanker's Model'.

US carbine, cal .30 M1

Caliber .30in
Length 36.0in
Weight 5.0lb
Barrel 18.0in long, 4 grooves, right hand twist
Feed system 15-round detachable box magazine
System of operation Gas; rotating bolt
Manufacturers Inland Mfg. Division of General Motors, Dayton, Ohio
Winchester Repeating Arms Co., New Haven, Conn.
Saginaw Steering Gear Div. of General Motors, Grand Rapids, Michigan
Underwood-Elliot-Fisher, Hartford, Conn.
Rochester Defense Corp., Rochester, NY.
Quality Hardware Corp., Chicago, Ill.
Rock-Ola Corp., Chicago, Ill.
National Postal Meter Corp., Rochester, NY.
Standard Products Co., Port Clinton, Ohio
International Business Machines Corp., Poughkeepsie, NY.

The US Carbine M1 originated in 1938 with a request from the infantry for a light rifle, comparable with the carbine of older days, which could replace the standard rifle and the pistol in arming drivers, machine-gunners, mortar squads, cooks, clerks, and others whose primary function was not rifle-shooting but who, in emergency, might need a weapon with a better reach than the pistol. The request was turned down, doubtless on the usual financial grounds, but was revived in 1940 and this time met with a more favorable reception, since the Army was now expanding and the production of standard rifles was stretched to its utmost. By October 1940 a draft specification had been prepared and circulated to numerous gunmakers, and a specification was issued to the Win-

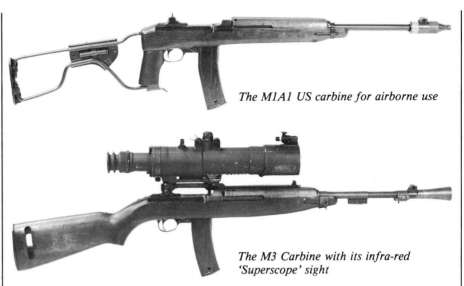

The M1A1 US carbine for airborne use

The M3 Carbine with its infra-red 'Superscope' sight

chester company to develop a special round of ammunition, using a 110-grain bullet and giving a velocity of 1860 feet per second. This was officially called the '.30 Short Rifle Cartridge' and was largely based on a much older commercial round, the Winchester .32 Automatic sporting rifle cartridge.

Eleven companies submitted weapons for test; some were rejected immediately, others sent back for further development where they looked promising, and finally seven models were subjected to trial. The

Winchester design, using a modification of the Garand bolt with a short-stroke gas piston originally developed for a potential military rifle, was selected for adoption and was standardized as the Carbine M1 late in 1941.

The gas action uses a captive piston with a travel of about one-third of an inch. This strikes an operating slide, delivering sufficient energy to drive the slide back to cam the bolt open against the power of the return spring. The rearward movement of the bolt also cocks a hammer before the

*Above: An M1 carbine in an unusual setting: a US PT boat pulls a Japanese survivor from the Surigao Strait in 1944
Left: US carbine M1 with spare magazines*

spring returns it, loading a fresh round and locking the bolt.

It has been estimated that something in the region of six and a quarter million carbines were made during the war, and they were widely distributed throughout the Army. Opinions as to their utility differ; they were without doubt a very handy weapon, light and easy to use, but the bullet was a pistol bullet rather than a rifle bullet and consequently their accuracy at anything other than short range was far from satisfactory; it was also somewhat deficient in stopping power in my experience.

Variants

M1A1 As for the M1, but with a pistol grip and folding skeleton stock; this pattern was intended primarily for airborne troops.

M2 Full automatic fire version. It resembles the M1 except for having a fire selector lever on the left of the receiver. Standardized in September 1944, a special 30-round magazine was developed for it. The cyclic rate of fire was approximately 750 rounds per minute.

M3 An M2 with the open sights removed and fitted with an infra-red 'Sniperscope' sight. Standardized August 1945.

T3 The development model number of the design standardized as M3.

T4 The development model number of the design standardized as M2.

USA

Browning automatic rifle, M1918A2

Caliber .30in
Length 47.75in
Weight 22lb
Barrel 24.0in long, 4 grooves, right hand twist
Feed system 20-round detachable box magazine
System of operation Gas; lifting bolt
Rate of fire (cyclic) 500rpm
Manufacturers Colt Patent Firearms Manufacturing Co.
Winchester Repeating Arms Co., New Haven, Conn.
Marlin-Rockwell Corporation

When the United States Army entered World War I in 1917 it was in no sense equipped with automatic weapons; it merely possessed an assortment, and one of its first tasks was to acquire a supply of

machine guns. John M. Browning stepped into the breach with two designs, one of which was this automatic rifle. Unfortunately, organizing production took time, and it was not until the summer of 1918 that issues began. From then until after World War II it remained the squad light automatic of the US Army.

While it was laudable to equip the army with an American weapon, it has to be said that the Browning was not one of the best of its kind. It was originally intended to be used during the assault, firing from the hip, a French theory for giving covering fire while crossing no-man's-land which, along with a lot of other peculiar French theories, was adopted by the US Army. But the action of the weapon is so violent that accurate fire under these conditions is almost impossible, and the gun was later provided with a bipod so that it could be used in the more conventional prone position.

The mechanism used a tipping bolt operated by a gas piston, a system more or less based on Browning's pump-action shotgun of 1904, but the lightness of the weapon (15½lbs without bipod in original form) led to light reciprocating parts, and in order to keep the rate of fire within reasonable bounds, it was necessary to include a shock absorber in the return spring assembly. In spite of this, the violence of the action led to rapid wear, and the rate of attrition in action was higher than for other light automatics.

Another drawback was the bottom-mounted 20-round magazine, inconvenient to change in action and with a limited capacity for automatic fire. In spite of all this, however, it had the advantage of being designed with mass-production in mind, and it was relatively easy to produce.

As well as being standard in the US Army it was widely adopted by other countries as a light machine gun, and large numbers were supplied to Britain during the war when it was used to arm Home Guard detachments.

Variants

M1918 The original model; no bipod, sights not adjustable for windage; selective full automatic or single shot fire.

M1918A1 Hinged butt plate; bipod attached just ahead of the fore-end stock.

M1922 Basically a 1918 with the barrel finned to improve cooling. Few of this pattern were issued.

USA

Johnson, cal .30 rifle, M1941

Caliber .30in
Length 45.5in
Weight 9lb 8oz
Barrel 22.0in long, 4 grooves, right hand twist
Feed system 10-round rotary integral magazine
System of operation Recoil; rotating bolt
Manufacturer Johnson Automatics Trust Inc., Providence, RI

This rifle was the last of a series of designs by Melvin M. Johnson. It is said that he developed 23 earlier versions before producing a serviceable design in 1936. This was improved still further, and in 1940 the Dutch Government contracted to purchase a number, which gave Johnson the opportunity to go into production.

The Johnson is one of the very few recoil-actuated rifles to reach any degree of success. Recoil operation demands movement of the barrel, which is not a desirable feature in a shoulder arm; nevertheless the Johnson worked well and at one time was strongly tipped as a potential service rifle for the US Army. The operation of the weapon is governed by the recoil of the barrel in the stock; on firing, it moves back for about three-eighths of an inch. The first portion of this movement occurs while the bullet is passing up the barrel, but after this the movement causes a cam in the bolt to engage an actuating face on the stationary receiver. This rotates the bolt 20 degrees to unlock it; the barrel completes the recoil stroke and, under spring pressure, returns to the forward position; the bolt continues to the rear, extracting and ejecting the spent case, and then returns under spring pressure to chamber the next round and lock into the breech.

The magazine is also unusual, being a spring-driven drum. The loading aperture is closed by a dust cover which is automatically pressed aside by inserting a standard 5-round charger or by inserting single rounds.

In 1940 the Dutch Government ordered 50,000 of these rifles for use in the Netherlands East Indies. Before delivery could be completed the Japanese overran the

The Browning automatic rifle Model 1918A1

Johnson automatic rifle Model 1941

Indies. The balance of the order was then taken over by the United States Marines who were finding it difficult to obtain sufficient M1 Garand rifles for their needs. The Johnson was primarily issued to parachute units, due to its lightness and due also to the fact that it could be rapidly stripped down into a small compass and stowed about the paratrooper's person.

We have been unable to find specific records of the use of the Johnson in combat, but the general concensus of user opinion seems to be that the weapon was not as reliable in action as was hoped. Numerous small modifications were made from time to time, but the design was never really finalized and the rifle was declared obsolete after the war ended.

Rifle, Model 1930G

Caliber 7.62mm
Length 48.5in
Weight 8lb 11oz
Barrel 28.7in long, 4 grooves, right hand twist
Feed system 5-round integral box magazine
System of operation Turn-bolt
Manufacturer State Arsenals

The Model 1930G (sometimes called the 1891/30) is one of a series of rifles based on the Mosin-Nagant Model 1891 and which formed the standard rifles of the Russian Army until 1945.

The title 'Mosin-Nagant' commemorates the original design, basically that of the Belgian Nagant brothers with modifications due to Colonel S. I. Mosin of the Imperial Russian Army. Its turnbolt action is much the same as any other, though the three-piece bolt is an unnecessary compli-

cation, probably adopted in order to avoid difficulties with the myriad rifle patents in force at that time. An unusual feature of the design is the provision of a cartridge control catch. One of the difficult problems of weapon design is the efficient feeding of rimmed cartridges from a magazine; the pressure of the magazine spring tends to jam the rims together and give rise to stoppages. The Mosin-Nagant used a spring-loaded latch, controlled by the operation of the bolt, to hold down the second round in the magazine and thus take pressure off the top round so that it could be easily loaded into the chamber by the closing bolt without the danger of the rim of the second round interfering due to the upward pressure of the spring.

The original 1891 model was a 'long' rifle, and was always used with its bayonet attached. It was partnered by a slightly shorter weapon, known as the 'Dragoon Rifle', but this was by no means as short and handy as the contemporary carbines in use by other armies. In 1931 the Soviet Army introduced the 1930G which was more or less the Dragoon Rifle with improved sights and with the design somewhat simplified so as to make production easier. It became the standard infantry rifle and remained so throughout the war, although it was widely supplemented by the later model of carbine (see below) and, of course, by the ubiquitous sub-machine guns which were a lot cheaper and quicker to make.

Numbers of the Model 1891/30 were fitted with sighting telescopes for use by snipers. In addition to the Mosin-Nagant rifles, Russian troops were issued with ex-Polish Mauser and ex-Lithuanian FN-

Mauser rifles, captured when those countries were overrun in 1939–40; the numbers were not significant, and some authorities claim that these weapons were principally issued to partisan groups, since they were chambered for the standard German Army 7.92mm cartridge.

Variants
Carbine 1938G Originally intended for mounted troops, this was the same basic pattern as the 1930G rifle but with the barrel shortened to 20.45in.
Carbine 1944G This was almost identical to the 1938G but with the addition of a folding cruciform bayonet attached to the muzzle. This, if it did nothing else, simplified the problem of what to do with it when it wasn't on the alert, a problem which often puzzled Russian recruits since bayonet scabbards were never a standard Russian issue item.

Tokarev automatic rifle, SVT–40

Caliber 7.62mm
Length 48.1in
Weight 8lb 8oz
Barrel 24.60in long, 4 grooves, right hand twist
Feed system 10-round detachable box magazine
System of operation Gas; tipping bolt
Manufacturer State Arsenals

The SVT-40 was derived from an earlier model, the SVT-38, the differences between them being largely a matter of simplifying production and improving reliability. The Model 40 was issued in relatively small numbers during the war and can be distinguished from the Model 38 by having more of the barrel exposed, by having a two- or three-baffle muzzle brake instead of the six-baffle pattern of the earlier one by using a shorter bayonet.

The action is by gas, this being tapped off close to the muzzle to drive a gas piston operating in a cylinder above the barrel. This in turn drives an operating rod to the rear, and this protrudes above the breech to strike the face of a bolt carrier and drive it to the rear against a return spring. Bolt movement is imparted by the bolt carrier by means of cam tracks which

Top: Soviet Model 1938G carbine
Above: Soviet Model 1944 carbine with bayonet in fixed position

The Tokarev SVT-40 in original form

lift and unlock the bolt and then hold it firmly to be withdrawn by the remaining rearward movement of the carrier.

The return spring is in the bolt carrier and receiver body, which accounts for the length of the action, and this returns carrier and bolt, loading a fresh round as it does so. A separate spring returns the operating rod and gas piston.

Mechanically speaking, this is a sound and commonplace design, but at this period of its development there seems to have been a lot of minor problems which

had not been cleared up. In any event, the Model 1938 proved to be fragile in service and was withdrawn in favor of the 1940; this, in turn, suffered from an inability to withstand the rigors of active service unless carefully nursed. It appears that these rifles were generally issued to NCOs of infantry regiments, but were later withdrawn and the majority of them converted to sniping rifles, an application where the self-loading action was advantageous and where the sniper could devote some time to careful maintenance of the weapon.

Variants
Although not graced with distinctive model numbers, there appear to have been some minor variations on the basic design. In 1941 the six-port muzzle brake was changed for a more simple two-port pattern. A carbine version is also known, although the specimen examined appears to have been modified from a standard rifle and not designed and built as a distinctive pattern. There was also a selective fire version, sometimes called the AVT-40, which had a change lever fitted to allow full automatic fire in the machine gun role, but few of these seem to have been made and it is believed that the mechanism proved to be unreliable under sustained fire conditions.

Germany

Karabiner 98K

Caliber 7.92mm
Length 43.6in
Weight 8lb 9oz
Barrel 23.6in long, 4 grooves, right hand twist
Feed system 5-round integral box magazine
System of operation Mauser turn-bolt
Manufacturers Basically Mauserwerke AG, but innumerable factories built either rifles or components on a sub-contract basis during the war.

The Karabiner 98K was the last of the long line of Mauser rifles used by the German Army and based on the original Mauser Gewehr 98. This 1898 model was an improved version of that designed in 1895 for the Chilean Government and featured a third locking lug at the rear of the bolt, and a rather unusual tangent backsight in front of the chamber.

With Britain's adoption of the Short Lee-Enfield in 1903, and the American introduction of their 'short' Springfield, the German Army, seeing the sense of the idea, developed a short version of the Gew 98, calling it the Karabiner 98; this was slightly confusing, because they had already produced a 'proper' carbine version and called it the Karabiner 98, but since the new short rifle rapidly replaced the carbine, the anomaly did not last for long. The principal change was, of course, the loss of six inches from the barrel, but the bolt handle was also turned down and the wood of the stock beneath cut away to allow the bolt to be grasped more easily. The rear sight was also simplified. This

became the standard infantry weapon during World War I and afterwards completely replaced the Gew 98 rifle; in its postwar version it was re-Christened the Kar 98a.

During the early 1930s one or two small changes were made in the design, largely, as usual, to facilitate mass-production, and the resulting weapon was adopted as the standard rifle for the new Wehrmacht in 1935 as the Kar 98K. It was produced by the million in a number of factories, and production continued until the end of the war in 1945, since the development of automatic rifles never reached the point at which production of bolt-action rifles could be terminated.

German infantry, armed with Karabiner 98K rifles as well as grenade throwers, take a position near Brest-Litovsk in the first stage of Operation Barbarossa

Variants
Kar 98K/42 This appears to be a production variation of the 98K and is rarely encountered. The principal differences are that the foresight is enclosed in a tunnel, and the butt-plate is of a cupped form which encloses the end of the butt for a depth of half an inch or so.

Kar 98B This bears no resemblance to the 98K. It is, in fact, no more than a Gewehr 98 rifle with its bolt handle turned down and with some improvements to the sights.

The German Gewehr 98 Mauser rifle

The Gewehr 41(W) automatic rifle

Gewehr 41(W)

Caliber 7.92mm
Length 44.5in
Weight 11.0lb
Barrel 21.5in long, 4 grooves, right hand twist
Feed system 10-round integral box magazine
System of operation Gas; locking flaps
Manufacturer Carl Walther Waffenfabrik,
Zella Mehlis, Thuringia

While numerous automatic rifle designs had been put forward in Germany since the turn of the century, and one or two of them actually tried in service, it was not until 1937 that the German Army really began to take an interest in the question of providing a self-loader to replace the bolt-action Mauser; probably the action of the United States in standardizing the Garand in 1936 had something to do with the timing of this decision. As a result of their demands the first self-loading rifle to be produced in any quantity was the Gewehr 41, two versions of which were developed, the 41(M) built by Mauserwerke, and the 41(W) built by Carl Walther.

Both these weapons used an unusual system of operation, a muzzle expansion chamber which turned some of the emerging gases backwards to actuate an annular piston surrounding the barrel. This in turn drove an operating rod to the rear to manipulate the bolt. The 41(M) had its operating rod beneath the barrel and used a rotating bolt opened and closed by cam surfaces. Although theoretically sound (as one might expect from Mauser) the design failed to stand up to trials and no more than a few were ever made.

The 41(W) had its operating rod above the barrel and used a totally different bolt locking system in which two flaps were pushed outwards to lock the bolt to the receiver as the firing pin moved forward; this method was derived from the Frijberg-Kjellman machine gun of the early 1900s and had achieved prominence in the Russian Degtyarev designs of 1928. The Walther version was easier to make and much better suited to the rough and tumble of service use, and it was adopted in preference to the Mauser design.

Several thousand rifles were made, the vast majority of which were sent to the Eastern Front and eventually lost there. While the 41(W) worked, it could not be called popular; its muzzle cone design carried the penalty of considerable fouling, and thus demanded constant and meticulous maintenance. Moreover the weapon was ill-balanced, with a pronounced muzzle preponderance, making it difficult to handle, and it was extremely heavy for an infantry rifle. As a result, when something better came along, the soldiers were not slow to discard the Gewehr 41, though it remained officially 'on the strength' throughout the war.

Gewehr 43

Caliber 7.92mm
Length 44.0in
Weight 9lb 9oz
Barrel 22.0in long, 4 grooves, right hand twist
Feed system 10-round detachable box magazine
System of operation Gas; locking flaps
Manufacturers Carl Walther Waffenfabrik, Zella-Mehlis
Berliner-Lubecker Maschinenfabrik AG, Lubeck
Gustloffwerke, Suhl

Experience with the Gewehr 41(W) soon showed the areas in which improvement was desirable. The bolt locking system was satisfactory, but the weight was excessive and the muzzle cone acted, in the words of one authority, as a 'built-in fouling generator'. As a result of these criticisms the gas operating system was changed to the more conventional piston type, the gas being tapped from the barrel about halfway between chamber and muzzle and directed into a gas channel above. Around this channel was a cup-like tubular piston, driving an operating rod which emerged above the chamber to drive a bolt carrier —a very similar layout to that of the Soviet Tokarev. This gives rise to the question of how many times the designer looked at the Tokarev during his designing.

The bolt locking system was the same as that used on the G41(W), pivoting flaps controlled by the movement of the firing pin assembly, which in turn was controlled by the bolt carrier. The whole weapon was much lighter and better balanced than its predecessor, and, moreover, had been designed with rapid production in mind so that it was an easier proposition to turn out in quantity. One unusual feature (for a military rifle) was the inclusion in the design of a machined-out dovetail section on the receiver to act as a seating for a sighting telescope, and a large number of these rifles were issued for sniping, fitted with the Zundblickfernrohr 4 telescope.

The G43 was extensively used on the Eastern Front, being first issued in 1943 and was found in much lesser numbers on other fronts. An interesting comment on the increasing difficulty of production in Germany is the gradual change in the appearance of the weapon as produced in 1944 and 1945; originally finished to a reasonably high standard and with solid wooden furniture, the external finish gradually deteriorated until final versions exhibited numerous tool-marks, and the furniture was of resin-bonded plywood laminations or phenolic plastic compounds. Nevertheless, the internal quality was always to a satisfactory standard, and the weapon had a good reputation for accuracy and reliability. It remained in production until the end of the war and was afterwards adopted by the Czech Army as their standard sniping rifle—which is something of a compliment when one considers the considerable firearms expertise of the Czechs. In addition, several thousand were disposed of commercially in postwar years.

Gewehr 43 with sniper's telescope

Maschinenpistole 43 or Sturmgeschütz 44

Caliber 7.92mm Short
Length 37.0in
Weight 11lb 5oz
Barrel 16.5in long, 4 grooves, right hand twist
Feed system 30-round detachable box magazine
System of operation Gas; tipping bolt
Manufacturers C. G. Haenel Waffen- und Fahrradfabrik, Suhl
B. Giepel GmbH, Waffenfabrik 'Erma', Erfurt
Mauserwerke AG, Oberndorf

During the 1930s the German Army spent some time assessing the basic requirements for an infantry rifle, and they came to the conclusion that the traditional rifle cartridge was unnecessarily large and powerful, since analysis revealed that the vast majority of infantry rifle fire was over short ranges. As a result work began by the Deutsche Waffen & Munitionsfabrik to develop a short 7mm caliber round; while this promised well, it was eventually stopped in favor of a 7.92mm design by Polte of Magdeburg, since this was of standard caliber and utilized a shortened version of the normal cartridge case, features which simplified production since much of the work could be done on existing machinery.

With the design of cartridge settled, contracts were placed with Carl Walther and Haenel for the production of suitable rifles. The resulting weapons were known as the Maschinenkarabiner 42—MkB42(H) and MkB42(W). The Walther design used an annular gas piston surrounding the

barrel to operate a tipping bolt, while the Haenel pattern used a more conventional gas cylinder and piston mounted below the barrel, also operating a tipping bolt. About 4000 of the Walther and 8000 of the Haenel model were produced in 1942–43 and issued to selected units on the Eastern Front for evaluation. As a result of their reports the Haenel pattern was selected for further development, particularly as far as simplification for mass-production was concerned, and the finalized design was issued as the Machine Pistol 43.

The nomenclature 'Machine Pistol' arose not from any attempt at security but was due to internal politics. Development began under the name 'Machine Carbine' as we have seen with the MkB42, but in spite of favorable reports from the trials,

The Stu .44 assault rifle with 'vampire' infra-red sight

Hitler rejected the weapon because he demanded longer range for infantry weapons, basing this decision on his alleged experiences in World War I and because he wanted, particularly for the battles in North Africa, a rifle capable of long-range fire. Moreover, according to a statement by Hauptdienstleiter Saur, then chief of the Technical Office of the German Ministry of Munitions, 'it was also rejected on the grounds that there were, at the time, 8 milliard (eight thousand million) rounds of standard 7.92mm ammunition in stock, and nobody would take the responsibility that these would become worthless.'

The German MP43 in standard form

The MP43 with 'Krummlauf' bent barrel attachment

The MKb42 (W), an unsuccessful design which led to the MP43

The Army Weapons Office therefore continued the development under the guise of 'Machine Pistol 43', development alleged before Hitler to be concerned with improvements to current machine pistol designs. Eventually experience with the first models of the MP43 on the Russian Front led to clamorous demands from the rest of the Army, and the Weapons Office, in a masterly political move, armed the personnel of the Guard Detachment of Hitler's Headquarters with the new weapon. This finally convinced Hitler of its utility, and following a demonstration in which its principal advantage—of firing full automatic during the assault phase of an attack—was demonstrated, it was officially christened the 'Sturmgewehr' or 'Assault rifle', originating the term which has since become associated with this class of weapon.

The MP43 was one of the first German weapons in which production was put before finish, no importance being attached to fine appearance or close tolerances except where they were vital. Indeed the original design (by Hugo Schmeisser) had to be considerably modified by the Merz Company of Frankfurt, who were specialists in metal pressing and stamping, to enable production to be done on simple presses. Nevertheless the design was exceptionally robust and reliable; one German report stated, 'Of all infantry weapons, the Sturmgewehr was the only one which always worked unobjectionably in Russia's dirt, cold and snow-dust, had no misfires and was resistant to stoppages.'

In spite of this, a contract was issued in 1944 to develop an even better weapon, tentatively known as the Sturmgewehr 45. Numerous designs were put forward, the most successful being that by Mauserwerke. But the war ended before development was very far advanced; the design was later taken to Spain and further developed into the CETME rifle, and then returned to Germany where, considerably improved, it is now produced as the Heckler & Koch Gewehr 3 and as well as being the standard rifle of the Bundeswehr is widely used throughout the world.

Germany

Fallschirmjägergewehr 42 (FG 42 or FjG42)

Caliber 7.92mm
Length 37.0in
Weight 9lb 15oz
Barrel 19.75in long, 4 grooves, right hand twist
Feed system 20-round detachable box magazine
System of operation Gas; turning bolt
Rate of fire (cyclic) 750rpm
Manufacturer Heinrich Krieghoff Waffenfabrik, Suhl

When the MP43 development began, the German Parachute Troops took an interest in it, since they felt that a selective-fire weapon would fill a void in their armory, since airborne operations always demand the maximum firepower in the smallest package. On further examination, however, they rejected the design on the grounds that the short cartridge, around which the new weapon was being developed, was insufficient for their particular needs, and they demanded a similar weapon taking the full-sized service round. This demand arose from experience in Crete, where they had been the targets for long-range rifle fire by British troops, and also from the fact that they considered that the standard 7.92mm round would be more easily available on any fighting front. The Army were not interested in such a weapon, so, since the Parachute troops were part of the Luftwaffe, they resubmitted their demand through Air Force channels and had it approved.

The weapon was designed by Rheinmetall-Borsig of Sommerda, who received the specification late in 1940 and had a prototype ready for testing in mid-1942. The specification had, in fact, been put out to eight companies, but only the Rheinmetall design was considered worth pursuing. Although it was eventually put into production there were numerous design changes and modifications, and the design was still not finalized when the war ended. A relatively small number were made—7000 is generally quoted—since during the development priorities had changed; the airborne assault on Crete, while providing the Paratroops with a useful case for having the weapon, had also shown that such operations were too expensive to be repeated, and the airborne forces spent the rest of the war fighting as conventional ground forces. Moreover the production facilities were controlled by the Army Weapons Bureau, who were reluctant to allot factory capacity to a weapon which they considered superfluous.

The FG42 was a sound design, based on well-tried principles. It was gas operated, and the bolt mechanism was so designed that when firing single shot the bolt closed on the cartridge, after which pressing the

The FG42 as made by Krieghoff

The FG42 Rheinmetall-Borsig Model, in early prototype form

trigger fired the weapon, which then automatically re-loaded. On automatic fire, however, the bolt remained open when the trigger was released so as to allow the chamber and barrel to cool down between bursts. Much of the weapon was fabricated from steel pressings, while the furniture was of laminated wood or plastic.

While it was an ingenious and effective weapon, it was difficult to shoot accurately due to the heavy recoil of the full-sized cartridge, and due to its lightness and flimsy bipod it was hard to control in the automatic mode.

It is said that the first use of the FG42 was in the raid to release Mussolini in September 1943; the majority of weapons were issued to units on the Western Front, large numbers being captured by Allied troops in 1944, which gave rise to the belief that the weapon was being produced in greater numbers than was the case.

Italy

Mannlicher-Parravicino-Carcano Modello 91

Caliber 6.5mm
Length 50.79in
Weight 8lb 6oz
Barrel 30.71in long, 4 grooves, right hand twist
Feed system 6-round integral box magazine, clip-loaded
System of operation Turnbolt
Manufacturer State Arsenals

This basic Italian army rifle was developed at the Turin Army Arsenal in 1890 and the names given to it tend to be a little misleading. In fact the only Mannlicher feature of the weapon is the magazine, using a 6-round clip; the only feature attributable to Carcano is the safety catch; while General Parravicino's name appears to have been attached from courtesy, he being the officer in charge of the commission charged with development of a new rifle design. As for the rest of it, it might just as well have been called 'Mauser-Carcano', since the general effect is that of a modified Mauser rifle.

The Mannlicher clip system perhaps warrants some explanation. Although almost everyone calls them 'clips', most rifles load from what are properly called 'chargers'; metal clips which grip the bases of the cartridges and from which the rounds are stripped by thumb-pressure into the magazine, after which the charger is discarded. All Lee-Enfield and Mauser rifles use this system. In the clip system, the clip remains attached to the rounds on loading and forms an essential part of the magazine system, a follower arm forcing the rounds out of the clip and presenting them in turn to the bolt for loading. When the last round has been loaded, in the Mannlicher system the clip drops through a hole in the bottom of the magazine. With the Garand, the only other clip-loader in use during World War II, it will be recalled that the clip is ejected after the last shot has been fired.

On the whole the M1891 was a serviceable enough weapon and on a par with its contemporaries, and it served as a basis for a host of variations over the years. Its principal drawback was the somewhat weak 6.5mm cartridge which it fired; the Italians became aware of this deficiency and in 1938 introduced a 7.35mm cartridge which they hoped would replace the 6.5mm. Unfortunately their financial masters thought otherwise, and the planned change of caliber never took place to the extent they had hoped for. A small number of rifles and carbines in 7.35mm were eventually issued, but the 6.5mm weapons were by far the most common throughout the whole of the war.

Variants
There were a large number of variant models, only two of which were of significance to the infantry:
Carbine M1891/24 After World War I the Italians decided to fall in line with the major powers and do away with the separate 'long' rifle and carbine models; the 1891 rifles were cut down to a barrel length of 17.7in, the bolt handle bent

A Mannlicher-Carcano 1891/24 with a 45mm grenade launcher attached

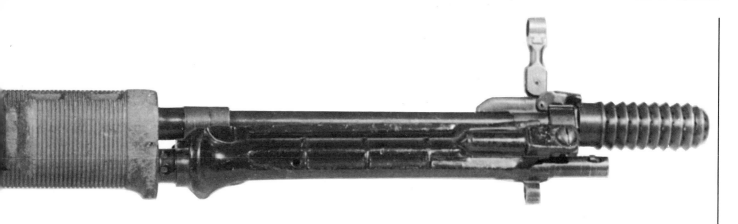

down and the sights improved. This then became the standard army rifle.

M1938 The introduction of the 7.35mm cartridge demanded a slight re-design since it was too powerful to be fired comfortably through a barrel as short as that of the 1891/24. A new rifle with a 21in barrel but otherwise much the same as the 1891/24 was developed. With the failure of the 7.35mm changeover, numbers of this pattern were made in 6.5mm caliber; they were probably the best Mannlicher-Carcano rifles ever built.

Japan

Arisaka rifle, Meiji 38

Caliber 6.5mm
Length 50.25in
Weight 9lb 8oz
Barrel 31.45in long, 6 grooves, right hand twist
Feed system 5-round integral box magazine
System of operation Mauser turnbolt
Manufacturer State Arsenals

When the Japanese Army decided to adopt a magazine rifle they, like many other nations, decided that the Mauser system had the most to offer. But, also like other countries, they preferred their own products and had their own ideas about what constituted a good rifle; so, taking

銃兵歩式八三

面断ルタキ開ヲ底遊

Mauser as a starting point, they developed their own variation. The design was the work of anonymous technicians, but the Commission appointed by the Emperor to develop the rifle was headed by Colonel Arisaka, and ever since the rifles have been known by his name.

The Meiji 38 model was introduced in 1905 (38th year of the Meiji reign), replacing the original 1897 model and displaying one or two improvements over it. The mechanism is basically Mauser but with a large mushroom-headed safety knob at the rear end of the bolt, which in turn led to a redesign of the striker mechanism. An unusual addition, though rarely found on specimens today, was a sheet-metal bolt cover which reciprocated with the bolt but served to keep rain and dust out of the mechanism. While it did all

Center: The mechanism of the Arisaka rifle, an illustration taken from a Japanese manual
Above: The Japanese Model 38 carbine with bolt cover in place

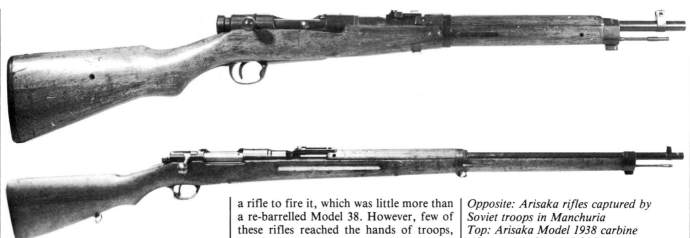

that was claimed, like most other devices of a similar nature it was flimsy and prone to rattle at inopportune moments, giving away the owner's location, and the vast majority were 'lost in action' at the earliest opportunity.

Like the Italians, the Japanese came to the conclusion that their elderly 6.5mm cartridge was no longer efficient, and in the 1930s they developed a 7.7mm round to replace it. As a corollary they developed

a rifle to fire it, which was little more than a re-barrelled Model 38. However, few of these rifles reached the hands of troops, for the Japanese were no more successful than the Italians in making their change-over though the reason lay in manufacturing problems. As a result the 6.5mm round and its associated rifle remained the standard throughout the war. It became Japan's most well-known infantry weapon.

Variants
Carbine M1938 Ostensibly for cavalry and artillery troops, this was also used by infantry and apparently preferred by them

Opposite: Arisaka rifles captured by Soviet troops in Manchuria
Top: Arisaka Model 1938 carbine
Above: Arisaka Model 1897 rifle

since it was about a foot shorter and a half a pound lighter. The mechanism was the same as that of the rifle.
Snipers Rifle M97 This was the original Arisaka rifle with the addition of a bipod and a low-power sighting telescope offset to the left to allow the rifle to be charger-loaded. The bolt handle was turned down to prevent the firer's hand fouling the sight when operating the bolt.

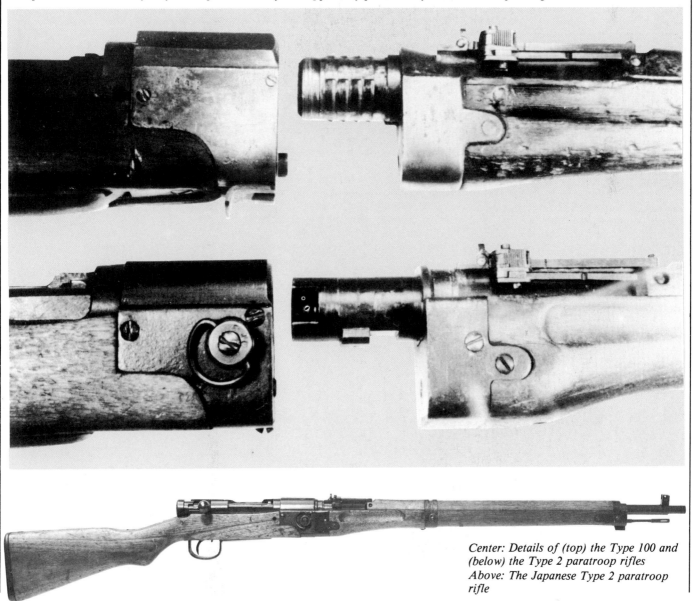

Center: Details of (top) the Type 100 and (below) the Type 2 paratroop rifles
Above: The Japanese Type 2 paratroop rifle

SUB-MACHINE GUNS

The sub-machine gun was born during the last year of World War I, and came into prominence during the intervening years when it appeared firstly in the hands of various anti-social elements in the United States and then, more martially, in the Gran Chaco War and the Spanish Civil War. It was regarded with some mistrust by most armies however; the British *Textbook of Small Arms 1929* dismissed the sub-machine gun in a single paragraph, making no comment on its possible worth or tactical use. But the Spanish Civil War opened a number of eyes and pointed to the advantage of a simple automatic weapon in the hands of partly-trained or even untrained irregular troops. The Soviets appear to have been the first to take heed, and began developing mass-production capacity for sub-machine guns in 1938, while the Germans were a little behind them, taking some time over deciding which model to adopt. The British Army became aware of the weapon at about the same time, and conducted tests of as many different models as they could obtain—and that was a surprising number even as early as 1938. But even if the Army thought the sub-machine gun was a desirable property, the Treasury didn't, and what money was available had to go on more vital types of armament. Thus, when the war broke out it was necessary to purchase weapons from abroad; when asked for an opinion the Ordnance Board observed that unquestionably the best they had seen was the Suomi, a Finnish design. But by then the Finns were battling with the Russians and the Ordnance Board, 'assumed that the Suomi, which in their opinion is the best of all the machine carbines, would be unobtainable, and the Thompson, the least desirable of all on technical grounds, was likely to be available.' So the Thompson was purchased in some numbers from the United States. But the hunt for a good sub-machine gun went on, particularly after Dunkirk when it seemed likely that England would be the German Army's next objective, and eventually it was decided to build a copy of the German Bergmann MP28, calling it the 'Lanchester' after the engineer who did the re-design to suit it to British production methods. But just before the Lanchester was due to go into production, came the '9mm Machine Carbine N.O.T. 40/1' which, after successfully passing the usual tests, entered service as the Sten Gun. The Lanchester, it may be said, did go into production, being issued solely to the Royal Navy. While all this was going on, more designs appeared and were tested; they can best be summed up by this extract from a report on an American weapon submitted for trial: 'The whole behavior of this carbine was so eccentric and erratic that it was difficult to assess the actual causes of the malfunctioning . . . '

In Germany there had been a small number of sub-machine guns in use more or less continuously since 1918, though during the years when the Versailles Treaty had relevance they were largely in the hands of police forces. As a result there had been constant, if slow, development of this class of weapon by one or two German manufacturers, and when the High Command decided that a sub-machine gun was needed in quantity, a design was waiting. This became the MP38, later the MP40, the familiar 'Schmeisser' (a misnomer) without which no film portrayal of the German soldier is complete. Undoubtedly it is one of the classic weapon designs of all time; absolutely functional, without an ounce of ornamentation or excess material on it, the first weapon to be made entirely of metal and plastic and to be laid out for mass-production by methods far removed from traditional gunsmithing techniques. It is uncertain how many MP38s were made, but it is known that production of the MP40 amounted to 1,047,000—over 700 a day for four years.

The Russian approach to the sub-machine gun was also weighed heavily on the side of production facilities, and as a result the Red Army's weapons represent the most crudely manufactured guns ever placed into the hands of troops. But for all their crudity they worked surprisingly well; they were reliable in every extreme of Russian weather, they were simple to teach, simple to make, simple to operate, and they killed the enemy just as dead as the most expensive Thompson could.

One minor mystery of the Soviet sub-machine gun scene is that the best weapon, the one affording the most advantageous combination of cheapness, simplicity and effectiveness, was never put

into large-scale production; one reason might have been that having organized production for two weapons, the authorities were reluctant to change horses in mid-stream and begin production of a third. But another intriguing suggestion has been put forward that since this third weapon was developed in Leningrad during the siege, and since the Leningraders tended to get a bit above themselves afterwards, the gun's suppression was as much political as economical. It is certainly a fact that almost the entire stock of this model was disposed of to satellite states as soon as the war was over.

The United States had much the same row to hoe as the British; they too had begun with the Thompson, since the US Marines had adopted it in limited numbers as far back as 1928, but in an endeavor to speed up production they considerably modified the mechanism to produce an entirely different gun to that which

Thompson had originally designed. They then began hunting for a simpler weapon, and after testing a wide variety of offerings, including at least one Spanish design, they took the Sten as their example and produced a simple and cheap gun of army design. This had the unusual feature of being able to fire either the US Army's standard .45 pistol cartridge or the universally available 9mm Parabellum cartridge, by simply interchanging the bolt and barrel, a feature which, in fact, appears rarely to have been used.

The Japanese, strangely enough, were lukewarm about the sub-machine gun, which was perhaps just as well, since weapons produced on the Russian scale and placed in their hands would have given the Allies a hard time indeed. But their sub-machine gun production was numbered in the few thousands, and of those produced, relatively few found their way into action.

Italy was the first country ever to adopt a sub-machine gun, in the latter weeks of 1917, though the weapon only qualifies as such by virtue of its blowback action and pistol cartridge. It was actually employed as a light machine gun by mountain troops and as an aircraft machine gun, and in neither employment was it particularly impressive. But somebody saw the light and had the mechanism incorporated into a more handy arm, after which the sub-machine gun was always part of the Italian Army's equipment; strangely enough this seems to have escaped many observers, largely because the weapons were stocked like rifles and carried bayonets, so that unless the distinctive magazine was fitted, most people who saw them assumed they were ordinary carbines. For all that, they were among the best engineered machine carbines ever made, though the Italian Army appear to have made relatively little use of them.

One minor sideline of the sub-machine gun field was the development of silenced weapons for use by raiding parties and guerrilla forces. These weapons were generally standard models with the addi-

tion of a Maxim-pattern silencer on the muzzle which, by means of baffles and acoustic absorbents, reduced the velocity of the emerging gases and thus did away with the noise of the exploding cartridge. Unfortunately this is only part of the business of silencing a weapon; the other part of it lies in silencing the bullet. If the bullet—as is generally the case—is travelling at above the speed of sound, then it pushes the usual sonic wave in front of it, and this is heard as a distinctive crack by people in the target area. In many cases this is more noisy than the discharge of the weapon, and silencing the discharge without silencing the bullet is rather futile. The answer lies in either using a bullet which is ordinarily subsonic—as, for example, the US Army's .45 Auto pistol round—or bleeding gas from behind the bullet as it passes up the barrel so that it emerges at subsonic speed. This was generally done with 9mm weapons such as the British Sten gun, but the Germans and Russians went to a greater degree of complication by developing reduced-charge ammunition; this saved the trouble of designing a gas-bleed system into the weapon, but would have brought a logistic problem in its train of making sure the right ammunition was available when needed. In the event neither of them had much trouble over it, since they do not appear to have produced any silenced weapons for troop use.

An additional problem with silenced weapons was that they could only be fired at single shot; rapid firing at automatic usually built up an excessive pressure inside the silencer which burst the baffles, or else the whole silencer structure would begin vibrating out of line with the travel of the bullet so that the third or fourth round fired would shoot out some of the baffles. Lastly came the problem of silencing the action of the weapon; it was of little use to expensively smother the emergent gas and retard the bullet if the bolt of the weapon crashed back with a noise sufficient to alert every sentry within a quarter of a mile. This problem was never solved.

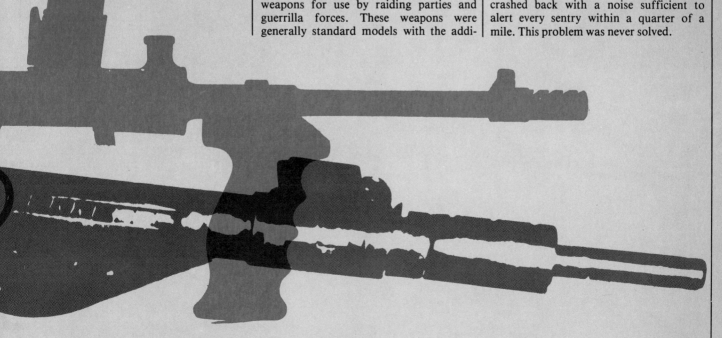

Carbine, machine, Sten, Marks 1–5

(Data for Mark 2)
Caliber 9mm
Length 30.0in
Weight 6lb 10oz
Barrel 7.75in long, 2 or 6 grooves, right hand twist
Feed system 32-round detachable box magazine
System of operation Blowback, selective fire
Rate of fire (cyclic) 550rpm
Manufacturers Royal Ordnance Factory, Fazakerley
Birmingham Small Arms Co., Tyseley
Long Branch Arsenal, Ontario, Canada

A British paratrooper using his Mark 5 during the battle at Arnhem, the first time this model was used in combat

In the summer of 1940 the British Government began to look seriously at the sub-machine gun question, and in August a decision was taken to put into production a copy of the German MP28, an order for 50,000 weapons being contemplated. At the same time an order for 110 million rounds of 9mm ammunition was placed in the USA, since the manufacturing capacity for this caliber in Britain was then negligible. An acceptance trial of the new weapon, known as the Lanchester, was carried out on 28 November 1940 and arrangements for production were put in hand. Then, in the first few days of January 1941, the situation changed. A simplified weapon, designated the 'N.O.T. 40/1' was produced by Major R. V. Shepherd and Mr. H. J. Turpin of the Chief Superintendant of Design's department. It was demonstrated at the Royal Small Arms Factory at Enfield Lock on 10

January 1941 and again on 21 January, whereupon instructions were given for an immediate trial and a rapid decision as to whether the manufacture of the Lanchester should proceed as planned or whether its production should be curtailed in favor of the new design. As the Ordnance Board pointed out the following day, 'the most important consideration at the moment seems to be to get some form of machine carbine acceptable to all three services into production as quickly as possible.'

The N.O.T.40/1 was tested and a report submitted on 31 January. The various tests were passed satisfactorily, 5400 rounds being fired without breakages or malfunction. The report concluded by saying, 'This

carbine appears to be fundamentally sound and functions satisfactorily and accurately.' Arrangements were then made to organize production and the first weapons began to come from the factories in June 1941.

The result of all this effort was the Sten Mark 1. While it was a simple weapon, it still had a certain amount of refinement; there was a wooden fore-end and a folding grip for the forward hand, a barrel jacket and protectors for the foresight, and a flash hider-cum-muzzle compensator. A safety slot at the rear of the cocking

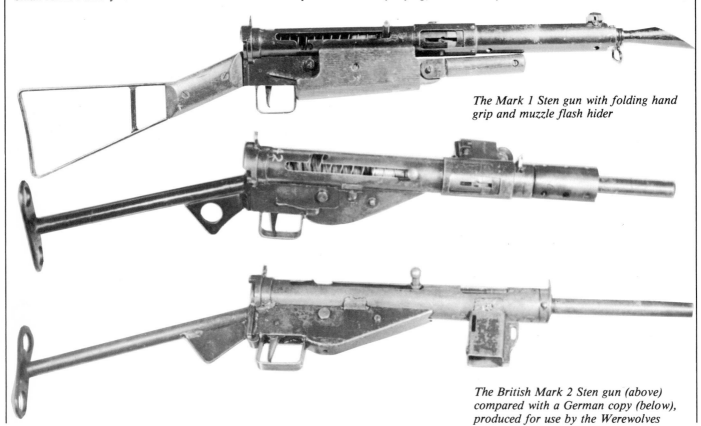

The Mark 1 Sten gun with folding hand grip and muzzle flash hider

The British Mark 2 Sten gun (above) compared with a German copy (below), produced for use by the Werewolves

handle slot allowed the lever to be turned down and locked as a rudimentary safety measure.

Once production began it was appreciated that some of this refinement could be shorn off, thus both speeding production and lightening the gun. The flash hider and fore-grip went, and the wooden fore-end replaced by a sheet metal cover over the trigger mechanism. This became the Mark 1*. But further simplification was possible, and a Mark 2 version, probably the most common of all the Marks, soon entered service. This dispensed with the barrel jacket, retaining the barrel by a large perforated sleeve which doubled as a forward hand grip; the magazine housing was modified so that it could be swung down through 90 degrees to close the feed and ejection openings against dirt; and the safety slot was repositioned at the top rear of the cocking handle slot, since turning the handle up to lock was an easier movement than turning it down. Over two million of this pattern were made, and at one stage they were being turned out at a rate of over 20,000 a week from one factory alone, and the price of manufacture was down to £2.87 per gun. The Mark 2 was first used in action during the Dieppe raid of August 1942, and though the raid was a fiasco there were no complaints about the part the Sten gun played in it.

Next came the Mark 3; even easier to manufacture, this dispensed with the removable barrel and movable magazine housing, containing everything within a welded steel tube with a stiffening rib along the top which also aided quick sighting. A Mark 4, intended for Airborne troops was next designed but never put into production, and in 1944 the Mark 5 was issued. This was rather more carefully made than the previous marks and had a wooden butt and pistol grip. The muzzle and front sight were of the same pattern as those of the Number 4 rifle, allowing a bayonet to be fitted. This model was first issued to Airborne troops and had its baptism of fire at Arnhem, after which it became the standard issue model and gradually replaced the earlier versions. A silenced version of the Mark 2, known as the Mark 2S was developed for Commando use, and there was also a silenced version of the Mark 5, the Mark 6.

The Sten was a highly successful weapon; its introduction was greeted with some reserve by soldiers who were accustomed to more elegant products, but its

performance in battle showed that looks count for little, and the initial misgivings soon died away. It was not without its defects; perhaps the worst was the design of the magazine, which was never entirely satisfactory and unless carefully looked after was prone to deformation of the lips and consequent misfeed. But in spite of this it was one of the most effective sub-machine guns of the entire war, and countless thousands are still in existence around the world. It was copied extensively; resistance and partisan groups in Europe manufactured their own versions, using a parachute-supplied Sten as their pattern; the German Army copied it, with some slight modification, calling it the MP3008; and perhaps the most remarkable of the wartime copies was a German forgery, complete even to the Enfield inspector's stamps, intended for issue to German guerrilla forces intended to harass the Allied troops in Germany. Since the war laudable copies have been seen from China, Kenya, the Northwest Frontier of India, Cyprus and Indonesia, all made in primitive conditions by irregular forces. Imitation, after all, is the sincerest form of flattery.

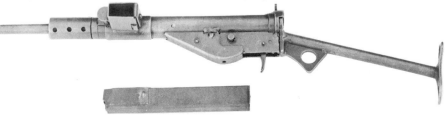

Owen sub-machine gun

The odd but effective Owen gun

Caliber 9mm
Length 32.0in
Weight 9lb 5oz
Barrel 9.75in long, 7 grooves, right hand twist
Feed system 33-round detachable box magazine
System of operation Blowback
Rate of fire (cyclic) 700rpm
Manufacturer Lysaght's Pty, Port Kemble, NSW.

The Owen gun was the principal sub-machine gun of the Australian Army, and in spite of its odd appearance was most effective and highly popular with everyone who ever used it. Its birth was due to the fact that in 1940 the British could not supply Australia with sub-machine guns, since they had none of their own, and the Americans had only the Thompson to offer, and that in small numbers. As a result, it became necessary to look for a local design, and Lieutenant Evelyn Owen produced the prototype of the Owen gun in 1940. Pre-production models in a variety of calibers were made for troop trials, and on 20 November 1941 the 9mm version was authorized for production and issue. Over 45,000 of the Mark 1 model were made before production ceased in September 1944.

The most prominent feature of the Owen was, of course, the top-mounted magazine. This configuration was less cumbersome in practice than it might appear, and it also allowed the assistance of gravity to promote a reliable feed. The magazine was a two-column type, much easier to fill than that of the Sten, and had the ejector machined as an integral part of the magazine mouth, a novel feature. The mechanism was of blowback type, but the bolt travel was remarkably short, $2\frac{5}{8}$ inches as against, for example, the $5\frac{1}{8}$ inches of the Sten, and this made the action rather more violent than most. The bolt was carefully sealed in to prevent dirt entering the action, and the cocking handle was isolated from the bolt for the same purpose. An odd form of construction was used in which an inserted ring in the rear of the gun body acted as a stop to the breech block's travel; this meant that to dismantle the weapon it was necessary to remove the barrel in order to take the bolt out through the front of the action body, and to make this easier a quick-release plunger on top of the body held the barrel in place.

Manufacture was by traditional methods of machining, which led to production figures being modest, and the gun is generally agreed to be unnecessarily heavy. An interesting report, in view of the weapon's eventual success and popularity, was made in February 1942 after a specimen had been sent to Britain for assessment. After discussing the various features of the gun, the report stated, 'the tests carried out on the Owen are the standard tests . . . and we consider it passed them satisfactorily. The accuracy is well within acceptance limits but the rate of fire is unfavorably high.' It then gave the conclusions of the examiners: 'The Owen gun . . . has very few genuine new features to recommend it. Most of the parts which are novel are poor in design and have not been studied from the production angle. We anticipate, before this gun comes from the factory in large quantities, much development work will be required and many teething troubles will be experienced which will involve radical re-design.'

The Owen remained in service, substantially unchanged, until 1962.

Variants
Mk 1/42 The basic model, described above. Had cooling fins on the barrel and a frame-type buttstock. Later models had holes cut in the frame behind the pistol grip to lighten the weapon.
Mk 1/43 The first of these were identical with the later 1/42s, but then the barrel cooling fins were omitted in favor of a plain barrel. This version had a wooden buttstock.
Mk 2/43 A rare model. The frame behind the trigger guard was removed and a new design of wooden buttstock secured beneath the gun body by a knurled screw. Fitted with a bayonet which slid over the muzzle compensator. Apparently about 200 were made early in 1943.
Mk 1/44 Generally the same as the 1/43, but later models had a bayonet lug on the barrel.

Austen sub-machine gun

Caliber 9mm
Length 33.25in
Weight 8lb 12oz
Barrel 7.75in long, 6 grooves, right hand twist
Feed system 28-round detachable box magazine
System of operation Blowback, selective fire
Rate of fire (cyclic) 500rpm
Manufacturers Diecasters Ltd., Melbourne
W. J. Carmichael & Co., Melbourne

While the Owen was a sound and serviceable weapon, the fact remained that it was not designed for mass-production, and consequently in 1941 a fresh design was called for. Shortly thereafter the first supplies of Sten guns arrived in Australia and this was taken as the basis of the new weapon which became known as the Austen, from 'Australian Sten'. The barrel, body and trigger mechanism of the Mark 2 Sten were copied, but the bolt mechanism was copied from the German MP38, using a telescopic cover over the return spring and a separate firing pin. The buttstock was also copied from the MP38 but with a slight alteration to the locking system which was, in fact, an improvement on the German pattern. The magazine was also basically Sten, though of a lesser capacity. A front pistol grip was a useful addition.

The result was a sound and reliable gun with but one small defect; the buttstock was too long for most people to handle in comfort. Whether this small, but important, feature was the cause is hard to say, but the fact remains that the Austen was never popular and the Australian soldiers preferred the Owen gun. Although specifically intended for mass production, no more than about 20,000 were manufactured between mid-1942 and early 1945.

In 1944 an improved version was designed; this was called the Mark 2, but the differences between it and the Mark 1 are so radical that it could well have been

The Austen gun; the Aussies preferred the Owen

given a different name. The basic configuration remained much the same but the gun body was of very light metal, merely serving as a guide for the bolt, and was retained in position by two aluminum castings fitting together to form a rigid framework and housing for the action. The butt was slightly modified, and the bolt now used a fixed firing pin, similar to that of the Sten, instead of the more complicated separate arrangement of the original. This model was put into production late in 1944 but few were made before the contract was terminated in 1945, and it is quite rare today.

USA

Thompson sub-machine gun, M1928

Caliber .45in
Length 33.25in
Weight 10lb 2oz
Barrel 10.5in long, 6 grooves, right hand twist
Feed system 20 or 30-round detachable box magazine, or 50 or 100-round detachable drum magazine
System of operation Delayed blowback, selective fire
Rate of fire (cyclic) 800rpm
Manufacturers Colts Patent Firearms Co. Savage Arms Co.

The Auto-Ordnance Corporation was founded in America in 1916 with the intention of developing a variety of weapons; they may well have done so, but only one has survived, the Thompson sub-machine gun. Named for General John T. Thompson, the company's design director, the first models were built in prototype form in 1919. The first production models appeared in 1921 and from then on manufacture was small but continuous throughout the 1920s and 1930s. The first official military recognition came when the United States Marine Corps were issued with a number of the 1927 model, which were officially named the M1928.

The Thompson gun is rather different from most other sub-machine guns in that it uses a delaying system in the action, to hold the bolt closed for a fraction of time while the cartridge clears the barrel. This was achieved by a device called the 'H-piece', from its shape, which served to lock the bolt to the receiver at the moment of firing. The H-piece was set at a carefully

Top: The Tommy gun in Burma
Above: The Thompson M1, a simplified model which used only box magazines

calculated angle, and the inventor claimed that this angle was so critical that when the maximum pressure of the explosion pressed against it, the result was to lock bolt and receiver securely together. Then, as the pressure dropped, the friction of the inclined faces lessened until the H-piece was able to slide and so unlocked the bolt. This system, known as the 'Blish system' from its inventor, was accepted as the gospel when the gun was first introduced, because a breech lock seemed to be a logical thing on any gun. But with more experience of sub-machine guns as time went on, the effect and desirability of this locking system began to be questioned. Eventually some experimentation showed that the removal of the H-piece made no difference to the functioning of the gun, except to increase the rate of fire.

In 1939 the Thompson was the only sub-machine gun in production outside

Europe, and as a result the government of Britain, France and Sweden hurriedly placed orders. Shortly afterwards the US Army also ordered a large quantity. But the Thompson was a difficult gun to manufacture; the engineering processes were numerous and complicated and the materials used were of the best quality, a fact which was reflected in the price—almost £50. By the end of 1940 orders for over 318,000 guns had been placed; previous production had been by the Colt Company under licence from the Auto-Ordnance Corporation, but now Auto-Ordnance built their own factory and by late summer of 1941 were producing guns. The Savage Arms Co. were also given a licence to manufacture, and between these two plants over one and a quarter million Thompson guns were produced during the war.

In order to make production easier the

The M1928 Thompson, which could be used with box or drum magazines

gun was re-designed in 1941; the H-piece was discarded and the weapon became a simple blow-back gun. The facility of using a drum magazine was also discarded and a 30-round box became the standard. Various other simplifications were made, notably the abandonment of the carefully made front grip and its replacement by a simple wooden fore-end, and the resulting weapon was standardized by the US Army as the M1 sub-machine gun in April 1942. This was later modified into the M1A1 by making the firing pin integral with the bolt, and dispensing with the hammer.

The Thompson had a lot of drawbacks; it was difficult to make; it was expensive, even in its simplified form; it was heavy. But for all that, it had one great virtue in the eyes of soldiers—it was reliable. Trouble with a Thompson was a rare event, provided it was properly cared for. It was a favorite weapon with British Commandos and US Rangers throughout the war and for many years afterwards. One remarkable thing is that in spite of the complication of the H-piece locking system, the Chinese were sufficiently impressed with it to manufacture their own copies (without benefit of licence) as early as 1930 and all through World War II.

USA

US sub-machine gun, M3

Caliber .45in (or 9mm—see text)
Length 30in
Weight 8lb 15oz
Barrel 8.0in long, 4 grooves, right hand twist
Feed system 30-round detachable box magazine
System of operation Blowback
Rate of fire (cyclic) 450rpm
Manufacturer Guide Lamp Division of General Motors, Anderson, Indiana, USA

As we have already seen, when the United States entered the war the only sub-machine gun available was the Thompson, and there were not many of those. Numerous potential designs were examined and tested without producing one which showed any marked superiority, and in October 1942 it was decided to start with a clean sheet of paper and design a completely new weapon. The design was inaugurated by the Small Arms Development Branch of the US Ordnance Corps Technical Division, and right from the start the importance of simplicity of production was well to the forefront. The first proto-type, the Machine Pistol T15 was capable of single shot or automatic fire, but the single shot facility was dropped to turn it into the T20. This was tested in Late November 1942 and found favor in the eyes of potential users, so that on Christmas Eve 1942 it was formally approved as the Sub-machine gun M3.

The design was relatively simple, and from its shape it came to be called 'The Grease Gun'. The barrel projects from the front cap of a cylindrical body, the ejection port is covered by a hinged flap, the pistol grip is, as the rest of the weapon, of steel, and a simple collapsible wire stock is fitted. Cocking was performed by a crank on the right side and was one of the less successful features; another was the design of single-column magazine which inevitably gave stoppages and misfeeds throughout the gun's life. One very ingenious feature was the provision of a conversion kit of barrel, bolt and magazine adapter whereby the normal .45 gun could be rapidly converted to fire 9mm Parabellum ammunition, feeding from a standard Sten magazine.

For all its faults—which were really minor—the M3 did what it set out to do—provide a cheap and efficient weapon which could be stamped out by the thousand in a short time. Over 606,000 of them were made at an average cost of about $25 (£5.30 at the then-current rate of exchange) each.

Variant
M3A1 In January 1944 there were complaints from various users that the cocking crank mechanism was beginning to exhibit defects due to wear, and an investigation showed that the whole of this complicated apparatus could be done away with by adopting an outstandingly simple system. Instead of the usual lever or knob, a large hole was drilled in the bolt into which the firer inserted his finger and pulled the bolt back. To permit this, the ejection port and its cover was extended rearwards. Other small refinements to aid production were incorporated and the resulting weapon entered service in December 1944 as the M3A1. Over 15,000 were produced before the war ended, at a cost of $22 each, and in later years another 33,000 were made.

USA

Reising sub-machine gun, Model 50

Caliber 0.45in
Length 35.75in
Weight 6lb 12oz
Barrel 11in long, 6 grooves, right hand twist
Feed system 12 or 20-round detachable box magazine
System of operation Retarded blowback
Rate of fire (cyclic) 550rpm
Manufacturer Harrington & Richardson Arms Co., Worcester, Mass.

This weapon was designed by a Mr. Eugene Reising and patented in June 1940. After testing by various authorities it was put into production, and a quantity estimated to be in the region of 100,000 of this and the similar Model 55 (see under 'Variants' below) were produced before manufacture ceased in 1945.

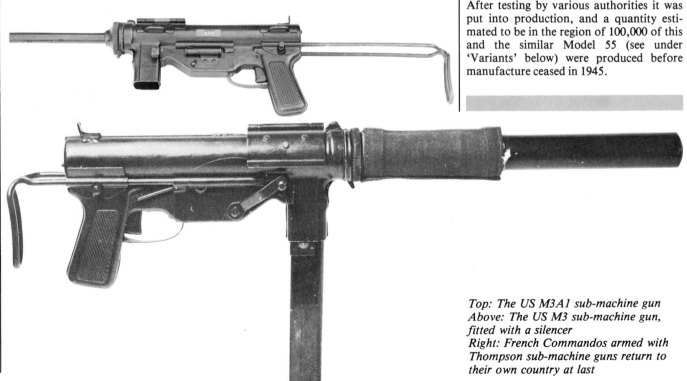

Top: The US M3A1 sub-machine gun
Above: The US M3 sub-machine gun, fitted with a silencer
Right: French Commandos armed with Thompson sub-machine guns return to their own country at last

Top: The US Reising Model 50 as used by the US Marine Corps
Above: The Reising Model 55 for use by airborne troops

The Reising was a rather unusual weapon in that it fired from a closed bolt at all times and the bolt was locked to the receiver before the round was fired. Upon firing the recoil of the cartridge case forced the bolt back, but opening was delayed while the bolt was unlocked and lowered by cams working in paths in the gun body. The bolt then recoiled in the usual way, returning under spring pressure to chamber a fresh round and then being cammed back into the locked position. A hammer was then released to strike the firing pin and fire the next round.

One might justifiably expect trouble from overheating and cook-offs of rounds in the chamber, but there do not appear to have been any complaints on that score. This may have been because they were drowned out by the complaints about other defects, principally of jamming and failure of the bolt to lock when the weapon was dirty, lack of interchangeability of parts and weakness of the springs.

The greater part of the production of the Reising sub-machine gun was taken by the United States Marine Corps and it was extensively used by them in the campaigns in the South Pacific. A small number of weapons was also purchased by the British Government for issue to the Canadian Army and for supply to the Soviet Government, which in view of the Red Army's predilection for sub-machine guns and their voluminous production, must be the armament equivalent of sending coals to Newcastle.

Variant
Model 55 This is mechanically the same as the Model 50 but dispensed with the muzzle compensator and had a wooden pistol grip and a folding wire stock. It was primarily intended for airborne use.

USSR

PPD 1940G

Caliber 7.62mm
Length 31in
Weight 8lb 2oz
Barrel 10.5in long, 4 grooves, right hand twist
Feed system 71-round detachable drum magazine
System of operation Blowback, selective fire
Rate of fire (cyclic) 800rpm
Manufacturer State Arsenals

PPD means 'Pistolet Pulyemet Degtyarev' or Machine Pistol designed by Degtyarev, and the term is qualified by the date, since he designed a number of weapons from 1934 onwards. It is doubtful whether very many were made before 1937, but after that a small number appeared in Spain, where they proved their usefulness, whereupon quantity production began. The original model was based very much on the German Bergmann design of 1928 but used a peculiar drum magazine which had a box-like extension which slipped into a magazine housing on the underside of the fore-end. There were a number of small variations of this model, known as the 1934/38, but in 1940 it was decided to

The Soviet PPD 1940G sub-machine gun

re-design it to a form more suited to mass production. The peculiar drum was changed for the Finnish Suomi pattern of drum and the weapon altered to allow the drum to be pushed into place from the side, rather like the Thompson drum. The earlier rather fussy cooling slots in the barrel jacket were simplified into a few long cuts, and one or two other small changes were made for the convenience of the manufacturers, who were not accustomed to this model.

Like all Soviet sub-machine guns the barrel was internally chromium-plated, a refinement rarely found in weapons of any other country, even today, but one which makes the barrel more resistant to wear and more tolerant of the lick-and-promise cleaning that sub-machine guns sometimes suffer from in war. The caliber is 7.62mm Soviet Pistol, a cartridge derived from the German 7.63mm Mauser round and is one of the few bottle-necked cartridges used with sub-machine guns. Of smaller caliber than the average sub-machine gun round, it compensates to some degree by having a rather higher velocity than average.

The number of PPD sub-machine guns produced is not known, but it was probably small by Russian standards. Production only lasted from the autumn of 1940 to late 1941, after which it was replaced by the PPSh model, and photographs of it in action are few and far between. While it was a very good weapon, and relatively simple to make, it still was not simple enough for the volume of production the Soviets needed to combat the German advance in 1941–42.

USSR

PPSh-1941G

Caliber 7.62mm
Length 33.10in
Weight 8lb
Barrel 10.5in long, 4 grooves, right hand twist
Feed system 71-round detachable drum or 35-round detachable box
System of operation Blowback, selective fire
Rate of fire (cyclic) 900rpm
Manufacturer State Arsenals

Pistolet Pulyemet Shpagin was developed in 1940–41 as a replacement for the PPD-40 model, since although the PPD was good it was not entirely suited to fast production in huge quantities, which was the Soviet's primary concern in 1941. The PPSh used stamped steel for the body and jacket, although the barrel was still chromium lined and the weapon still used a wooden stock. An interesting economy was the utilization of old and reserve Mosin-Nagant rifle barrels to provide barrels for the sub-machine gun; one rifle barrel could be cut up to make two sub-machine gun barrels with a considerable saving in time and machinery. The entire assembly was by pinning and welding, and the barrel jacket extended beyond the

Above: The well-known Soviet PPSh sub-machine gun
Below: Russian partisans armed with PPSh sub-machine guns

muzzle to act as a muzzle brake and compensator to divert some of the gases upwards and thus counteract the tendency, common with all sub-machine guns, for the muzzle to creep upwards during automatic fire. The first models had an optimistic and luxurious tangent sight, but this was soon discarded for a simple peep-sight.

The 71-round drum magazine adopted for the PPD was retained, since production of this item was well established and it gave the firer a good reserve of ammunition, no bad thing considering the high rate of fire of this weapon. The mechanism was simple blowback, a bolt with fixed firing pin and a return spring being almost the only components apart from an agriculturally simple firing mechanism. It was robust, simple to use, and cheap to make, and something like five million were made during the war.

In addition to the 71-round drum a 35-round box magazine was later made for this weapon, but it was much less common than the drum pattern. Large numbers were captured by the German Army on the Eastern Front, so large in fact that they found it worth their while to convert them to fire 9mm ammunition, altering the

magazine housing to take the standard MP-38 magazine.

The PPSh sub-machine gun came to be almost the badge of the Red soldier, much as the MP38 was that of the German, Whole divisions were armed with nothing

else, since it was a weapon which well suited the Soviet tactics and spirit. With this sort of weapon, you cannot hide in a hole and snipe; the only way to use it effectively is to get out of the hole and go after the enemy, and this they did.

USSR

PPS-42

Caliber 7.62mm
Length 32.25in
Weight 7lb 6oz
Barrel 10in long, 4 grooves, right hand twist
Feed system 35-round detachable box
System of operation Blowback, automatic only
Rate of fire (cyclic) 700rpm
Manufacturer State Arsenals

This was the third standard sub-machine gun adopted by the Red Army during the war, and was designed by A. I. Sudarev. In view of the Soviet system of selecting

one design and mass-producing it to the exclusion of every other, it is unusual to find this weapon being apparently produced at the same time as the PPSh, but this was due to the exigencies of war. When the city of Leningrad was besieged by the German Army in 1941–42, weapons were in short supply, and the PPS was designed and put into production inside the besieged city, being sent straight from the factory to the nearby front line. It was a remarkable production, entirely stamped from steel except for the barrel and bolt, and spot-welded together. The only non-metal parts are the wooden grips and a small piece of leather acting as a buffer for

the bolt. Finish is non-existent, rough welds and grinding marks being apparent all over, and it must be the cheapest weapon of any type ever produced. But for all that it works well and reliably, and many thousands were turned out, both in its original form (PPS-42) and in a slightly modified form (PPS-43), which is substantially the same.

The perforated barrel jacket extends beyond the muzzle to act as a muzzle brake and compensator, as in the PPSh; a curved box magazine is fitted; and the skeleton steel butt folds across the top of the gun body. A simple safety catch is fitted in the front edge of the trigger

The PPS43, born during the siege of Leningrad

A variety of Soviet sub-machine guns on display at the capture of Harbin

guard, and there is no provision for firing single shot.

The weapon is so much cheaper and simpler than the PPD or PPSh models that the question arises of why it did not entirely replace them. The authoritative answer will never be known, but a clue is given by the official treatment meted out to Leningrad after the siege. During the siege the heroic defenders became national heroes, and, in the eyes of the hierarchy in Moscow, got a bit above themselves. When the siege was over most of the more prominent figures were quietly removed from the public eye and the whole affair was considerably played down. It seems likely that this attitude spread to the weapon born of the siege, for it never went into full mass-production and it is believed that production was stopped before the war ended. Most of the PPS models were removed from Soviet service and given to satellites immediately after the war; certainly they were more common in Korea in 1951–52 than any other model of Soviet sub-machine gun.

Maschinenpistole 28

Caliber 9mm
Length 32.0in
Weight Weight 8lb 12oz
Barrel 7.75in long, 6 grooves, right hand twist
Feed system 32-round detachable box
System of operation Blowback, selective fire
Rate of fire (cyclic) 500rpm
Manufacturer C. G. Haenel Waffenfabrik, Suhl

The Bergmann Maschinenpistole 18 was among the first sub-machine guns to come into use, and after World War I it was retained by the German police. It had some minor defects, and in the 1920s Hugo Schmeisser redesigned it to become the MP28. The principal differences were that the weapon now had selective single shot or automatic fire instead of automatic only; the bolt had a separate firing pin; a new rear sight was fitted; and the magazine entered the left side at 90 degrees instead of 45 degrees as on the MP18.

The Model 28 was developed as a commercial product; a puzzling point is the question of how Haenel were able to produce and sell this weapon when Rheinmetall had to go to considerable lengths of subterfuge to have their comparable design developed in Switzerland and marketed from Austria. In any event, the MP28 was available in virtually whatever caliber the customer desired, and was turned out in 7.63mm Mauser, 9mm Parabellum, 9mm Bergmann-Bayard, .45 Colt and 7.65mm Parabellum. It was also made under licence in Belgium by the Ancien Etablissment Pieper of Liège, and in Spain. As a result of this latter manufacture it saw widespread use in the Spanish Civil War, one of the factors leading to the re-evaluation of sub-machine guns by Germany and Russia prior to the outbreak of World War II.

Its use in the German Army was principally in the early part of the war, since it was a 'traditional' weapon, manufactured by time-honored methods of milling and machining, and not amenable to mass-production, and it was soon replaced by weapons of more modern construction. However, it deserves credit for being the gun selected by Britain in 1940 to be the standard British sub-machine gun, and it was copied to make the 'Lanchester', used by the Royal Navy; it would have seen even wider service had the Sten gun not appeared at the eleventh hour.

Below: Bergmann MP28, an improved version of the World War I Bergmann 'Musquete,' the original sub-machine gun

Top right: Hand grenades and sub-machine guns were the two weapons which best suited the aggressive instincts of the Red Army soldier
Right: German troops at Stalingrad with Machine pistols MP40

The Solothurn S1-100 in Austrian guise as the MP 34(ö) or Steyr-Solothurn

Germany

Solothurn S1-100

Caliber 9mm
Length 33.5in
Weight 8lb 8oz
Barrel 7.75in long, 6 grooves, right hand twist
Feed system 32-round detachable box magazine
System of operation Blowback, selective fire
Rate of fire (cyclic) 500rpm
Manufacturers Waffenfabrik Solothurn AG, Solothurn, Switzerland
Waffenfabrik Steyr, Steyr, Austria

This weapon, used by the German Army among many others, has a tangled history. It was originally designed in 1924 by Herr Louis Stange of the Rheinmettal Company of Dusseldorf. Since, by the terms of the Versailles Treaty, Rheinmettal were forbidden to develop or manufacture such a weapon, they acquired a moribund Swiss company called Solothurn AG in 1929 and used these nominees to produce the prototypes and do the development engineering. But Solothurn were not equipped to produce in quantity, so Rheinmettal now took a controlling interest in the Waffenfabrik Steyr, an old-established Austrian company, and arranged for the weapon to be put into production as the 'Steyr-Solothurn' sub-machine gun. It was widely sold throughout the world in a variety of calibers, and is still in service with the Portuguese National Guard, who purchased the last weapons made in 1940.

The S1-100 is generally considered to be the 'Rolls-Royce' of sub-machine guns, made of the finest available materials and finished to the highest possible standard. Its mechanism is quite simple, the usual bolt having its return spring housed in the wooden buttstock, and the firing pin being separate. It fires from an open bolt in the usual blowback mode. One of the most unusual features is the incorporation of a magazine loading device in the magazine housing. The first specimens of this weapon were generally made in 7.63mm Mauser caliber or 9mm Steyr, and ammunition of these types was always supplied in pre-packed 10-round chargers for use in the pistols. So that these chargers could be used for loading the sub-machine gun magazine, the magazine housing has a slot in top and bottom; the empty magazine could be withdrawn from its housing and slipped into the bottom slot. Chargers of cartridges were then inserted into guides in the top slot and the rounds stripped down into the magazine, one of the easiest and quickest systems of magazine loading ever devised.

The S1-100 was first adopted by the Austrian police in 9mm Steyr chambering and then by the Austrian Army as their MP34, chambered for the powerful 9mm Mauser 'Export' cartridge. When Austria was incorporated into the Third Reich the weapon was taken into German Army service as the MP34(ö) (ö for Österreich) and extensively used. The unusual thing about this is that the Germans were apparently quite happy to leave it chambered for the 9mm Mauser instead of (as with most other weapons taken over) re-chambering it for the more common 9mm Parabellum round.

Germany

Maschinenpistole 34 and 35

Caliber 9mm
Length 33.0in
Weight 8lb 15oz
Barrel 7.75in long, 6 grooves, right hand twist
Feed system 32-round detachable box magazine
System of operation Blowback, selective fire
Rate of fire (cyclic) 650rpm
Manufacturers Carl Walther Waffenfabrik, Zella-Mehlis
Junker & Ruh AG, Karlsruhe

The MP34 (not to be confused with the MP34(ö)) is the only sub-machine gun ever designed by Bergmann, in spite of the fact that his name is attached to numerous other designs, and the convolutions behind these are not without interest. The Machine Pistols 18 and 28 were actually designed by Schmeisser and manufactured by a company known as Theodor Bergmann Waffenfabrik AG of Suhl. In 1932 Theodor Emil Bergmann, the son, designed this sub-machine gun, and had the prototype built by Schutz & Larsen of Otterup in Denmark, at that time a well-known firm of development engineers with considerable experience in armament work. In 1934 T. E. Bergmann, together with a Herr Stahl, formed a new company, Theodor Bergmann GmbH in Berlin, with the intention of exploiting the patents of the elder Bergmann, Theodor Emil's father. Further work was done on the prototype sub-machine gun, but due to the new company's lack of facilities, manufacture was contracted out to Carl Walther of Zella Mehlis.

The production weapon, taken into use by the German police in the first instance, was the MP34. It was wooden-stocked and had a barrel jacket perforated with long slots and with a built-in compensator at the muzzle. The cocking handle resembled a rifle bolt and protruded from the rear of the receiver end cap. An unusual feature was that the magazine fed from the right, ejection being to the left, and instead of the magazine protruding at 90 degrees to the axis of the weapon, it was slightly angled forward. A double trigger of peculiar form was fitted; pulling the front trigger gave single shots, but further pressure caused it to bear on the secondary trigger to give automatic fire.

The MP34 was in production for about a year, something like 2000 being made, and in mid-1935 a small number of changes were made in order to simplify production. This revised model was known as the MP35. It was available with long or short barrels, the long barrel models often being fitted for a bayonet. In subsequent years these guns were sold in fair numbers to Spain, Sweden, Poland and Ethiopia. In 1940 the Waffen SS adopted the weapon as their standard sub-machine gun, and from then on the entire production (which was now contracted out once more, this

The Bergmann MP 34

time to Junker & Ruh, leaving Walther to get on with more important things) went to the Waffen SS units. It appears to have been mostly used on the Eastern Front, and the few MP35 specimens which appear in the West generally have SS runes engraved on them.

Maschinenpistole EMP

Caliber 9mm
Length 35.5in
Weight 9lb 2oz
Barrel 10.0in long, 6 grooves, right hand twist
Feed system 25- or 32-round detachable box magazine
System of operation Blowback, selective fire
Rate of fire (cyclic) 500rpm
Manufacturer Erfurt Maschinenfabrik B Giepel GmbH (Ermawerke), Erfurt

The Ermawerke company entered the sub-machine gun field about 1930, making a gun designed by Herr Heinrich Vollmer and Herr Berthold Giepel and known as the Vollmer sub-machine gun. After some commercial success with this weapon it was slightly redesigned and marketed as the 'Erma' Maschinenpistole Modell 35. This had a long barrel and was fitted to take a bayonet. Then came a shorter model without bayonet fittings, and another with a rifle-type fore-end replacing the front pistol grip of the two earlier designs.

The second model—short barrel and forward pistol grip—was produced in the greatest number and was adopted by the German Army in small numbers about 1936 when they were still approaching the sub-machine gun with some caution. This model has a barrel jacket with long slots, a magazine entering from the left, and, its most easily recognized feature, a wooden buttstock, the front end of which is formed into a pistol grip. The mechanism uses a simple bolt but has the return spring carried in a telescoping tube, the unique Vollmer patented design which reappeared on the MP38 and MP40.

The EMP remained in production from about 1932 to mid-1938 when the Ermawerke factory was turned over entirely to the production of the MP38. Quite a large number of these weapons were used during the Spanish Civil War. In German service they were largely replaced in the Army by the MP38 and MP40, and some reports point to it having been issued to some of the SS 'Foreign Legions', probably including the 'SS Lettische Freiwilliger Division' (Latvian Volunteers) and the 'SS Pg Division Nederland', which operated against Yugoslav partisans in 1943.

Maschinenpistole 38

Caliber 9mm
Length 32.75in
Weight 9lb
Barrel 9.75in long, 6 grooves, right hand twist
Feed system 32-round box magazine
System of operation Blowback, automatic only
Rate of fire (cyclic) 500rpm
Manufacturer Erfurter Maschinenfabrik B. Giepel GmbH, Erfurt

In the section on the MP34 it was noted that the sub-machine guns usually called Bergmann were in fact designed by Schmeisser; this one was designed by a team from the Ermawerke factory using various patents of Heinrich Vollmer, under the general direction of Berthold Giepel, the owner of Ermawerke. How Schmeisser's name ever got involved with this weapon is one of the minor mysteries.

In 1938, having contemplated the trends and tactics of the Spanish Civil War, the German Army decided that a sub-machine gun was needed; not, apparently, convinced that any of the contemporary designs available were what they wanted, they instructed Herr Giepel to produce one to their specification. As it happened, Giepel had been working on a design for some time, and with a few slight changes

The German MP38 in use on the Russian front. The Wehrmacht assisted the Red Army in their scorched earth policy

this was accepted as the MP38. It broke new ground in weapon design by having no wood anywhere in its construction and by having a folding stock. The bolt was driven by a return spring contained in Vollmer's telescoping tube and it carried a spring-retracted firing pin. The muzzle was threaded to take a blank-firing attachment or a combined muzzle cover and cleaning rod guide, and beneath the barrel was a hook-like steel bar which was to prevent damage to the barrel when firing through the gun-port of an armored vehicle and which was designed to prevent the gun being pulled inadvertently inboard during firing should the gunner lose his footing.

For all its innovations the MP38 was still largely made by conventional methods, and while the Army were pleased with it, they demanded a weapon more easily mass-produced. The MP38 was therefore critically examined and redesigned to make the maximum use of stampings and welded assemblies. The result was known as the MP40 and replaced the MP38 as the standard sub-machine gun, becoming virtually the German Army's trademark. The principal changes were that the body was of stamped sheet steel, formed and

The Erma 'EMP' Machine pistol

welded; the magazine housing was ribbed instead of plain; while the body top was plain instead of ribbed. The cocking handle was redesigned so that it could be pressed inwards when the bolt was forwards so as to engage an enlarged portion of the handle in a slot milled in the receiver, thus locking the bolt forward and preventing inadvertent discharge should the gun be dropped on its butt.

Variants

MP38/40 A modification of the MP38 to bring it up to the safety standard of the MP40 by fitting it with the MP40s cocking handle and cutting a suitable slot in the receiver.

MP40/1 The first model of the MP40 had a smooth-surfaced magazine housing and the cocking handle of the MP38. When these were changed by a retrospective modification to use the cocking handle of the MP40 and the ribbed magazine housing, the official designation became the MP40/1.

MP40/2 During the Russian campaign the German troops complained that the Russian soldier with a 71-round drum on his sub-machine gun had a considerable edge over the German with a 32-round box magazine. As a result, a special magazine housing was produced which allowed two magazines to be inserted side by side; one was aligned with the barrel and fired, after which the second could be slid across into alignment and fired. The device was cumbersome and only produced in limited numbers; its principal drawback was that the weapon with two loaded magazines weighed over 12lbs, while the Russian weighed somewhat less and still had seven shots in hand.

MP41 This weapon was produced in very small numbers and there is some doubt as to whether it was ever officially used by the Army. It was basically the body and barrel of the MP40 fitted to the wooden butt and firing mechanism of the MP28; it is difficult to understand why it was made in the first place.

Top: The MP 40 with muzzle cover
Above: The MP 41 with a wooden stock

Sub-machine gun, ZK383

Caliber 9mm
Length 35.5in
Weight 10lb 8oz
Barrel 12.75in long, 6 grooves, right hand twist
Feed system 30-round detachable box magazine
System of operation Blowback, selective fire
Rate of fire (cyclic) 500 or 700rpm
Manufacturer Czeskoslovenska Zbroyowka, Brno

The ZK383 was developed in Czechoslovakia in the early 1930s and went into production in 1933. Early models are reported to have had a front pistol grip, but this was soon abandoned for the wooden fore-end pattern. It is unusual in that it was provided with a bipod for steadying it when fired in the prone position, and was thus apparently conceived as a sort of squad light machine gun rather than the usual hip-fired hosepipe role of the sub-machine gun. Another unusual feature for this class of weapon was the provision for quick-changing the barrel, pointer to the squad automatic role.

The mechanism is a simple blowback, with the return spring housed in a tube in the butt, the bolt having a connecting link pinned to its rear end to press against a cap on the return spring. As it stands the bolt weighs 1lb 9oz and the gun fires at 500rpm, but a removable section of the bolt, weighing six ounces, can be taken out to lighten the bolt and thus increase the rate of fire to 700rpm.

The ZK383 was widely sold abroad in the

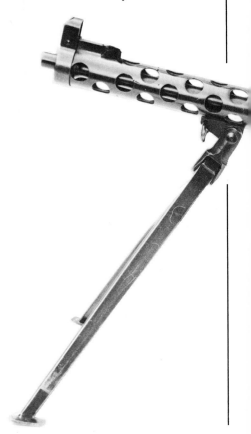

years before the war and was adopted by the Bulgarian Army, although there is no indication available of how they used it, either as a light squad weapon or as a conventional sub-machine gun. When the Germans occupied Czechoslovakia, the CZ factory was taken over and re-organized as the Waffenwerke Brunn AG. Production of the ZK383 was continued, the entire output being taken by the SS and used in battle on the Russian Front. The weapon continued in production after the war, the factory having reverted to its original ownership and name, production finally ending in late 1948. Numbers of this weapon are still in use in South America.

Sub-machine gun, Model 39M and 43M

Caliber 9mm
Length 41.25in
Weight 8lb 3oz
Barrel 19.65in long, 6 grooves, right hand twist
Feed system 40-round detachable box magazine
System of operation Delayed blowback, selective fire
Rate of fire (cyclic) 750rpm
Manufacturer Danuvia Waffen- und Munitionsfabrik AG, Budapest

The Model 39M sub-machine gun was designed by P. D. Kiraly of the Danuvia Company during the late 1930s. Kiraly had been concerned in the design of a number of other automatic weapons, and the 39M shows some affinities with a Swiss weapon in which he had a hand. It is of interest to note that one of the first versions of the 39M was offered to the British Government in May 1939; BSA Ltd. were licensed to manufacture and actually produced a small number for trials, with the assurance that they could be turned out for about £5 ($25) each in quantity. It performed well in trials, though some modifications were desirable before it could have been accepted as a service weapon, but for some reason interest lapsed and it was heard of no more in Britain.

However, Kiraly obviously took note of the comments, since most of the suggested changes appeared in the 39M. It is an unusually bulky weapon for a sub-machine gun, fully stocked like a rifle and taking the standard Hungarian Army bayonet. The magazine can be folded forward to lie in a housing slot cut within the wooden fore-end, and when so folded a spring-loaded cover snaps across the feed entry to keep out dirt. The bolt is of two-piece design with an intermediate rocking arm which engages in a recess in the gun body. When fired, the cartridge case sets back against the front, light, section of the bolt, which begins to move to the rear but which must rotate the rocking arm before it can transmit movement to the rear, heavy, section of the bolt and thus allow the whole assembly to begin movement to the rear. This system is necessary on this weapon, since it is chambered for the powerful 9mm Mauser cartridge, and some form of delay is essential in order to allow breech pressure to drop in such a long barrel.

The 39M was invariably excellently manufactured of the highest quality materials and was a reliable and accurate weapon. Although called the '39' it appears that production did not get under way until late 1940 and the first issues were made to the Hungarian Army in 1941. The Hungarians fought against the Russians and were roughly handled, so that most of these weapons fell into Soviet hands and they are quite rare today.

Variants
Model 39A Made in very small numbers, it resembles the 39M but has the buttstock hinged behind the trigger guard so as to fold sideways and lie alongside the receiver. It is believed to have proved unsatisfactory in service.
Model 43M Mechanically much the same as the 39M but has a skeleton folding stock similar to that of the MP38 which folds beneath the gun. The magazine is slightly altered, having a distinctive forward rake, and a pistol grip is fitted. Numbers of these weapons were used by German troops on the Eastern front under the nomenclature MP43(ü).

Top: The Hungarian Model 43
Above: The Hungarian Model 39 sub-machine gun

Above: The Czech ZK383 sub-machine gun
Left: German paratroops in Rome, 1944, with MP40 sub-machine guns

Sub-machine gun, OVP

Caliber 9mm
Length 35.5in
Weight 8lb 1oz
Barrel 11in long, 6 grooves, right hand twist
Feed system 25-round detachable box magazine
System of operation Delayed blowback, selective fire
Rate of fire (cyclic) 900rpm
Manufacturer Officina di Villar Perosa, Villar Perosa Italy

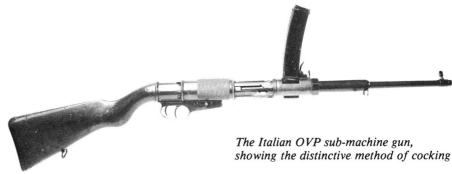

The Italian OVP sub-machine gun, showing the distinctive method of cocking

The Italians were the first army ever to adopt a sub-machine gun, or, more correctly, a light automatic gun firing a pistol cartridge; this was the Villar Perosa, but since this ceased to be a service weapon in 1918 it need not concern us further. Nevertheless the mechanism of the VP was a sound design, and shortly after the end of the war the manufacturers of the VP were asked to produce a more practical weapon which became known as the OVP.

Basically it is little more than the barrel and action of the VP attached to a wooden buttstock and provided with a trigger and some small refinements. Although formally classed as a delayed blowback, the delay is minimal and certainly has little practical effect, as might be deduced from the high rate of fire. The mechanism is the usual one of bolt and return spring, but the bolt is controlled by a track in the receiver body which causes the bolt to rotate 45 degrees as it closes. The striker carries a lug bearing on the receiver track which also bears on a cam face on the bolt, so that the firing pin, driven by the return spring, cannot go forward to fire the cartridge until the bolt has rotated. When the gun is fired, recoil of the cartridge case moves the bolt back, causing it to rotate to the unlocked position, during which movement the pin is withdrawn by the action of the bolt's cam surface. Once unlocked, the bolt is free to recoil and complete the firing cycle.

An unusual feature of the OVP which was not on the original VP gun was the use of a cylindrical sleeve surrounding the receiver for cocking the weapon. This was grasped and pulled to the rear to retract the bolt and then pushed forward again to remain in the forward position during firing. Another oddity, this time carried over from the VP, was the provision of a slot in the rear edge of the top-mounted magazine which allowed the firer to see how many rounds remained inside it; this, of course, also allowed dust and dirt to enter the magazine, so perhaps it wasn't such a good idea after all.

The OVP was issued in the early 1920s, and by the time of World War II had been largely replaced by the various Beretta models. However, it saw use in the Italo-Abyssinian War and was used in small numbers by some Italian units in the Western Desert in 1941, but after this it appears to have been withdrawn from service, and specimens are relatively uncommon today.

Beretta, Model 1918

Caliber 9mm
Length 43.0in
Weight 7lb 3oz
Barrel 12.0in long, 6 grooves, right hand twist
Feed system 25-round box magazine
System of operation Retarded blowback, automatic only
Rate of fire (cyclic) 900rpm
Manufacturer P. Beretta, Brescia

The Beretta 1918, like the OVP, is little more than the Villar Perosa mechanism presented in a more convenient form. Beretta were approached at the same time as OVP with the request to convert the cumbersome VP into a more practical weapon.

The Model 1918 was designed by Tullio Marengoni and was his first introduction to the sub-machine gun field; he has since designed many more weapons and is still a consultant engineer to the Beretta Company, although he retired from the post of Chief Designer in 1956.

The modifications consisted of fitting a new trigger mechanism based on that of the standard Italian service rifle of the day, a long wooden stock, with an ejection slot beneath, and a folding bayonet similar to that used on Italian service carbines. The result was a most practical and handy weapon. The mechanism remained unchanged, still using the rotating bolt system, and the slotted, curved magazine fits into the top of the action.

In order to manufacture the weapon in quantity, since it was preferred to the OVP, the majority of existing Villar Perosa machine guns, together with their spare parts stock, was passed to Beretta and used to build Model 1918s, which is one reason for the scarcity of specimens of the Villar Perosa today.

The Model 1918 was issued to the 'Ardite' regiments of the Italian Army early in 1918 and thus became the first sub-machine gun to be a standard issue, since they predate the German issue of the Bergmann by a few weeks. They remained in service until World War II, but due to their carbine-like appearance they were frequently unrecognized for what they were; one early writer on the subject actually criticized the Italians for not developing automatic weapons and preferring to arm their troops with, 'theatrical carbines with folding bayonets', failing to distinguish between the Model 1918 and the contemporary Mannlicher-Carcano carbine. Numbers were used in the Spanish Civil War and the Italo-Abyssinian

The Beretta M1918; though not apparent, this uses the same mechanism as the OVP model but in the guise of a carbine

War and were frequently encountered in the early phases of the Libyan campaign in 1941.

Variant

Model 18/30 Rarely used as a military weapon, this was derived from the 1918. A 15-round magazine was mounted below the gun, ejecting at the top; cocking was by a ring-shaped handle at the rear end and the mechanism was altered to allow single shot firing only. Intended as a police weapon it was not produced in very large numbers.

Beretta, Model 1938A

Caliber 9mm
Length 37.5in
Weight 9lb 4oz
Barrel 12.5in long, 6 grooves, right hand twist
Feed system 10-, 20-, 30-, or 40-round detachable box magazines
System of operation Blowback, selective fire
Rate of fire (cyclic) 600rpm
Manufacturer P. Beretta, Brescia

This weapon originated as a semi-automatic carbine in 1935, but was then reworked to become a selective-fire weapon and went into production in 1938. A highly successful weapon, it underwent various minor modifications during its life but remained in production until 1950 before being superseded by more modern designs.

The first model was fully stocked, similar to the Model 1918, but had the magazine below the weapon, had a folding bayonet of special design, and had a cooling jacket with long slots surrounding the barrel. It also had an entirely new firing mechanism with two triggers; the front trigger for firing single shots, and the rear trigger for firing automatic. The front end of the barrel jacket was formed into a rudimentary compensator with two large holes in its top.

Although quite a serviceable design, this was only produced in small numbers during 1938 and was soon replaced by the second version, which has no distinctive model number. This version added a fire selector lever in the shape of a cross-bolt locking bar behind the rear trigger which, when pushed in, prevented the rear trigger being depressed and thus restricted fire to single shots. The barrel jacket had smaller, circular holes, but the compensator and bayonet of the first model were retained.

A third version was designed at the end

of 1938 and went into mass production in 1939 concurrently with the second version; the difference lay in the removal of the bayonet and a change in the design of the compensator to give four upward-facing slots.

The two mass production versions were turned out in large numbers for the Italian, German and Rumanian armies until 1944, after which production lapsed for some time until taken up again when the war was over. The original design called for machined components throughout, an expensive and slow business, and in 1940 slight changes were introduced in order to facilitate more rapid manufacture. The barrel jacket was formed from stamped sheet metal, rolled and welded, while the design of the bolt was simplified by adopting a fixed firing pin instead of a separate unit, which had been a legacy from the Villar Perosa.

While this weapon was originally intended for 9mm Glisenti ammunition, it could fire the German 9mm Parabellum

Italian partisans in 1944 with Beretta sub-machine guns in evidence 'liberated' from Italian Army stores

round equally well, and in order to extract the utmost performance from it a special cartridge known as the 9mm M38 was issued for it; identified by a green surround to the cap, it was issued in ten-round chargers which could be loaded into the magazine by use of a special loading tool.

The 1938A was widely used throughout the war; it saw much service in North Africa and Russia with the Italian Army, and was adopted by the German Army as the 'Maschinenpistole (Beretta) 38(i)'. As to its use by the Rumanians we have no information.

Variants

Model 38/42 The move to simplify manufacture of the 1938A was taken further by the development of the Model 38/42. While it was basically the same weapon as the 1938A, the body and magazine

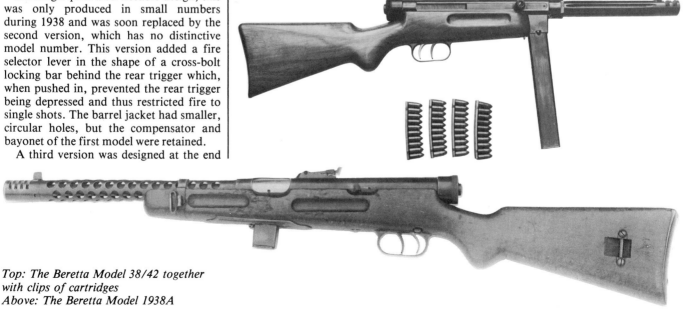

Top: The Beretta Model 38/42 together with clips of cartridges
Above: The Beretta Model 1938A

housing were of metal stampings, the barrel jacket was discarded, and the compensator reverted to a two-slot model. The first version had the barrel milled with longitudinal grooves for cooling, but this was found to be superfluous and was soon abandoned in favor of a smooth barrel. The stock was also shortened and ended in rear of the magazine housing.

Model 38/43 Sometimes used to distinguish later, smooth-barrelled, 38/42s.

Model 38/44 Much the same as the 38/43 but with a slight change in the design of bolt and return spring, as a result of which the receiver end cap is plain, whereas the 38/42 and 38/43 models had a raised center on the cap to act as an anchor for the return spring.

Italy

FNAB–43 sub-machine gun

Caliber 9mm
Length 31.15in
Weight 8lb 12oz
Barrel 7.8in long, 6 grooves, right hand twist
Feed system 20- or 40-round detachable box magazine
System of operation Delayed blowback, selective fire
Rate of fire (cyclic) 400rpm
Manufacturer Fabrica Nazionale d'armes, Brescia

This little-known weapon was designed and developed in Italy during the war and manufactured during 1943 and 1944. It is believed that not more than about 7000 were made, and they were all issued to Italian and German units fighting in Northern Italy.

It was an unusual weapon, one of the more remarkable things about it being that its design was such as to call for expensive and time-consuming methods of precision engineering at a time when the general tendency was to make weapons—particularly sub-machine guns—as cheap and simple as possible. This doubtless accounts for the small production figures; nevertheless it was a well made and efficient weapon.

The action is a delayed blowback of

unique design, firing from the closed bolt position. The bolt is a two-piece unit with a pivoted lever interposed between bolt head and body. On firing, the bolt head moves back and begins to rotate the lever, the toe of which is abutting against a lug in the body; this lever is pivoted so as to delay the opening movement by operating at a mechanical disadvantage, allowing the bullet to leave the barrel and breech pressure to drop before the lever has completed its rotation. The movement of the lever then presses the free end against the bolt body and accelerates the bolt to the rear; the toe of the lever pulls clear of the lug and the whole bolt unit can recoil as one component in the usual way. On returning, the lever engages once more with the body lug and pivots forward, and in doing so removes an interlock which allows movement of the firing pin only when the bolt is fully forward. This unusual and complicated system allows the rate of fire to be kept down to very practical limits without using a heavy bolt or strong spring.

Other features of this weapon included a muzzle brake and compensator built into the barrel casing in the manner of some Russian weapons, and a magazine housing which is hinged so that the magazine can lie beneath the barrel. The stock, a single metal bar, also folds, so that the weapon can be carried as a very compact unit.

Italy

Sub-machine gun, TZ–45

Caliber 9mm
Length 33.5in
Weight 7lb 3oz
Barrel 9in long, 6 grooves, right hand twist
Feed system 40-round detachable box magazine
System of operation Blowback, selective fire
Rate of fire (cyclic) 550rpm
Manufacturer Tonone et Zorzola, Gardone-val-Trompe, Italy

This is another Italian wartime design produced in small numbers by a small company. No more than 6000 were made during 1944–45.

In comparison with the FNAB-43, the TZ-45 is much more the sort of weapon one would expect in that place and at that time. It was cheaply made from metal stampings, welded together in parts, and the finish is rudimentary. For all that, it worked, and managed to exhibit one or two interesting features. The action is simple blowback, but the return spring is assembled around a guide rod which is in two pieces and telescopes as the bolt returns. A muzzle compensator is fitted, and the shoulder stock is formed of steel rods which slide alongside the receiver when retracted. Two separate safety systems are fitted; the fire selector lever has a 'safe' position which locks the bolt in either the forward or rearward positions, while a grip safety is fitted behind the magazine housing. Unless the weapon is held properly and this grip compressed, the bolt cannot move in either direction to cock or to fire.

The entire issue of the TZ-45 appears to

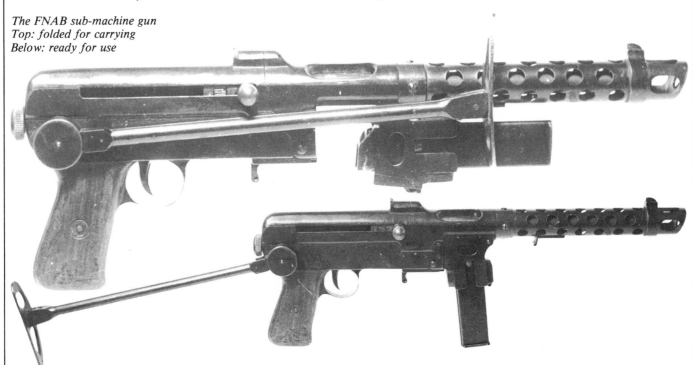

The FNAB sub-machine gun
Top: folded for carrying
Below: ready for use

The TZ-45 sub-machine gun

have gone to various units of the Italian Army operating against guerrilla forces in the mountains. It was offered to the British and United States armies after the war and evaluated by them, but the general opinion was unfavorable; it emerged from the war with a poor reputation for reliability and the style of manufacture and finish were not liked. However the manufacturers managed to sell it to the Burmese Army, where it was later manufactured as the BA-52.

Sub-machine gun, Type 100/40 and 100/44

Caliber 8mm
Length 35.0in
Weight 8lb 8oz
Barrel 9.0in long, 6 grooves, right hand twist
Feed system 30-round detachable box magazine
System of operation Blowback, selective fire
Rate of fire (cyclic) 450rpm
Manufacturer Atsuta Ordnance Factory, Nagoya Arsenal, Japan

Sub-machine gun development in Japan was curiously neglected until about 1935, after which an experimental model was produced and tested. But there appears to have been little enthusiasm for the weapon, which, considering that Japan was by then engaged in a war with China and preparing for war throughout the East, is most surprising. The sub-machine gun would have been an ideal weapon for them, and the thought of the Japanese Army armed with a cheap and simple sub-machine gun such as the Russian PPSh is quite terrifying; the combat in the Far East would have been a good deal more bloody, and one or two touch-and-go affairs might well have gone the other way.

The Type 100, Model 1940, was issued in 1941–42 in limited numbers. Although far from perfect its performance was good enough to stimulate interest in the weapon, and this led to development of an improved version, the Model 1944, but work began too late and was carried out too slowly to allow stocks to be built up.

The Model 40 came in two patterns, one for infantry use with a solid stock and one for Airborne troops using a hinged folding stock. Both were fitted with bayonet bars under the barrel, and the interior of the barrels was chrome plated. The infantry models were sometimes fitted with a small bipod. Mechanically there was little of note; they were simple blowback weapons working on familiar principles.

The only recorded use of these weapons in combat was in the Japanese parachute attack on the Dutch oilfields in Java in 1942, when they were reported to have been highly effective. There is no record of their appearance against US forces in the South Pacific nor against British troops in Burma. It is believed that less than 10,000 of both models were produced.

Variant
Type 100/144 Mechanically the same as the 100/40, this had a weaker recoil spring which increased the rate of fire to 800rpm. The bayonet bar was removed and bayonet attachment was by two lugs on the barrel casing. The muzzle was formed into a compensator by drilling two lateral holes. There were other small changes intended to make the weapon easier to manufacture. It is reported that about 7000 were made in the last year of the war, but none of them appear to have reached the hands of troops.

The Japanese 100/40 with bayonet bar

Suomi, Model 1931

Caliber 9mm
Length 34.25in
Weight 10lb 5oz
Barrel 12.5in long, 6 grooves, right hand twist
Feed system 20- or 50-round box, 40- or 71-round drum
System of operation Blowback, selective fire
Rate of fire (cyclic) 900rpm
Manufacturer Oy Tikkakoski AB, Sakara, Finland

This weapon was one of the designs of the Finnish firearms expert A. J. Lahti, responsible for many other weapons, including a particularly fine pistol. He produced his first sub-machine gun in the early 1920s and gradually improved and refined the design until this model, which was issued to the Finnish Army in 1931; it was not patented until 1932 and is thus, therefore, often referred to as the Model of 1932.

For many years the Suomi was the standard to which other sub-machine guns were referred; it was exceptionally well made, and was extremely reliable and accurate. It was unusual in being provided with a means of quickly changing the barrel. As well as being made in Finland, it was also manufactured under licence in Sweden, Denmark and Switzerland, and adopted by the armies of those countries. It was widely sold throughout the world and was used in large numbers in the Spanish Civil War.

The operation of the Suomi is by the usual blowback system, firing from an open bolt. The cocking handle is rather oddly positioned beneath the rear cap of the receiver and is so designed that it remains still while the gun is firing. Of the various magazines provided for the weapon, the 71-round drum was adopted by the Soviets as their standard pattern after that had first-hand experience of the effectiveness of the Suomi in the Winter War of 1940–41. After this affair the Suomi turned up in the hands of Soviet troops in the Leningrad area when the German Army besieged the city. It was also used by elements of the Norwegian Army in their brief campaign against the Germans in 1940.

The Finnish Suomi

MACHINE GUNS

The twentieth century has seen the rise of the machine gun from its first employment almost as a piece of artillery to its development in lightweight form to become the pivotal weapon of the infantry section. The original type of weapon, exemplified by the Maxim, Vickers and Browning water-cooled guns, were weapons of position more than of maneuver, to be carefully sited to defend locations, to deliver long-range sustained fire to break up enemy formations, and notably to be sited 'in defilade', that is, firing across the front so as to sweep down a line of advancing infantry and thus achieve the maximum effect for the minimum of fire. It was this sort of employment which earned the machine gun its fearsome reputation during World War I, but shortly after that

war had begun it became obvious that these heavy guns were not the best answer for all circumstances. What was needed was a lightweight weapon which could be carried forward in the attack, emplaced rapidly and inconspicuously, to add to the volume of fire delivered by the riflemen. In this way the light machine gun was born. Few of the light guns developed during the war were particularly good; some, indeed, were quite disgraceful and can only be excused by the pressure of events. In consequence the postwar years saw much research and design effort expended in developing a more suitable light gun. The requirements were not particularly easy to meet at first; rapid firing soon heats up gun barrels, and hot barrels wear out very quickly, therefore the prime demand was

some efficient method of cooling which weighed very little—at least less than the conventional two or three gallons of water. The rate of fire was a delicate matter too; too fast led to overheating, too slow to inefficiency and a heavy weapon. The feed problem also had to be faced; some method of getting the cartridges into the gun which was light, efficient, and not prone to derangement by the dust and dirt of the battlefield.

The final solution took on a fairly common form; a gas-operated weapon firing from a bipod, controlled by one man, using a magazine holding thirty or so rounds, and usually with a barrel that could be rapidly changed for a spare so that it could be allowed to cool down before the wear problem became serious.

The French were the first to produce a new weapon along these lines, no doubt due to the fact that during the war they had been cursed with the worst light machine gun and the most inconvenient cartridge. At the same time the Czechoslovakian company Czeskoslovenska Zbroyowka produced the first of a series of excellent designs which came to be used all over the world in subsequent years, and one of which was to achieve fame as the British Bren gun, probably the best light machine gun ever made.

The German Army, although among the first to appreciate the need for a light machine gun, were curiously dilatory in developing one; this was partly due to the Versailles Treaty which restricted the activities of the gunmakers, and it was also partly due to a certain amount of re-thinking which the German Army were doing on the whole subject of machine guns. Eventually they adopted a variety of light guns as stopgaps, none of which was particularly outstanding, but placed their main reliance on a totally new concept —the 'General Purpose Machine Gun' as it is known today. Here the same weapon was intended to fill both roles, that of a light machine gun and a medium machine gun. In the light role it was used with butt and bipod; in the medium or heavy role

with tripod and optical sight. But in both roles it was the same gun, air-cooled and belt fed—and that in itself was a new departure for a light weapon —but due to excellent design and an ingenious barrel-changing system the problem of over-heating in sustained fire was overcome. This had advantages all round; one gun to supply, one weapon to train on, one type of ammunition supply, and complete interchangeability of role depending on what the tactical requirement happened to be at the time. The lesson was assimilated but slowly by the rest of the world, and indeed the 'GPMG philosophy' is not entirely accepted even yet.

Undoubtedly the advent of the automatic rifle had a lot to do with attitudes to the light machine gun, and there are voices to be heard today assuring us that the days of the LMG are numbered. The first effects of this can be seen in the United States Army during the war; with the infantry section completely equipped with rapid-firing automatic rifles there was a less pressing need for the light machine gun's additional firepower, and as a result the US Army never had a decent LMG throughout the war. The Browning Automatic Rifle, which filled the slot, was neither one thing nor the other; and when, at last, the Infantry Board decided to

produce something to replace it, the best they could come up with was to add some fittings to the standard Browning Medium Machine Gun and hope that the soldiers could be persuaded that the result was a light machine gun; they weren't.

Japan and Italy were notably ill-served in the matter of machine guns; between them they fielded some of the most abysmal designs ever to see daylight, and both armies compounded the mischief by attempting, on the eve of war, to change calibers in the hope of improving matters. Neither managed any improvement, since the change of calibers was swamped by the demands of wartime production, and all they managed to achieve was a nightmare for their supply officers. Their machine guns were all modifications of modifications of designs which should have been scrapped years before; only the fact that their inter-war activities had been against unsophisticated enemies allowed such armament to survive. One must give credit where credit is due; and in this case the credit is due to the soldiers of the Italian and Japanese Armies who, with this unprepossessing collection of antiques, still managed to make them work and give the Allies a hard time in the process.

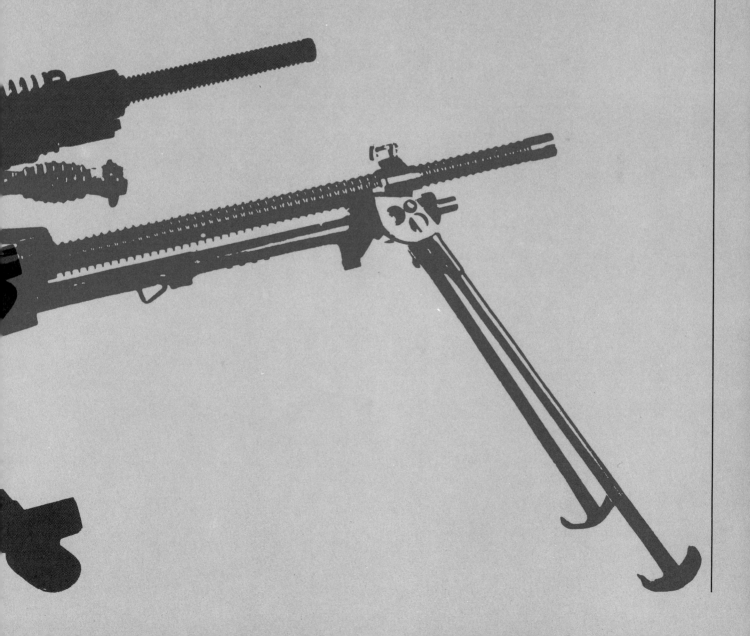

Gun, machine, Bren

Caliber .303in
Length 45.25in
Weight 22lb 5oz
Barrel 25.0in long, 6 grooves, right hand twist
Feed system 30-round detachable box magazine
System of operation Gas; tipping bolt
Rate of fire (cyclic) 500rpm
Manufacturer Royal Small Arms Factory, Enfield Lock, Middlesex

The Bren Gun is spoken of with affection by every British soldier who ever used one, and with good reason. Beyond any doubt it was—and still is—the finest light machine gun ever adopted in quantity by any army. It was reliable, robust, simple and accurate, and beyond that no one has a right to ask.

It is fairly well known that the design came from Czechoslovakia, but some doubt was thrown on its real parentage and an interesting theory advanced by the late Lt. Col. R. K. Wilson, a noted authority on automatic weapons. In his *Textbook of Automatic Pistols* published in 1943 and largely written before the war, he included a chapter on light machine guns, and after discussing the French Chatellerault went on to say, 'Since . . . the Great War, Czechoslovakia has been the most faithful of France's allies, and the connection between the French War Office and the Czech Ministry of Defense has been of the closest. One result of this has been the manufacture of the Chatellerault at the Czech government arsenal at Prague, and its sale as a commercial weapon under the name ZB . . . It has recently been extensively tested by the British Army . . . and now seems likely (1935) to be adopted . . .' There is certainly some similarity of outline between the Chatellerault and the ZB26, but more recent research has revealed the existence of a ZB24 model, produced before the Chatellerault was revealed, so it looks as if the ZB was, after all, a native Czech product. In view of the disastrous record of explosions and other malfunctions suffered

An unusual Bren gun, with a reversible barrel; below, the standard Mark 1 Bren Opposite: British airborne troops in North Africa with a Bren Mark 1

by the Chatellerault during its first few years of service, this is probably just as well.

The ZB26 was succeeded by a slightly improved model the ZB30, and this was taken to England in the early 1930s and demonstrated. The British Army were looking for a light machine gun to replace the Lewis, and expressed interest, provided the gun could be made to work satisfactorily with the British .303 cartridge. In a surprisingly short time the Czechs were back with a specially-produced model, the ZB33 of which only a handful were made, solely as demonstration and trials weapons; they were ZB30 guns redesigned for .303 with the barrel shortened, the gas port repositioned and

The Bren machine gun in action, supporting the rifle squad in its assault

the sights graduated in yards. If nothing else, the production of these weapons showed a high degree of salesmanship.

The other weapons under consideration at the time were the Danish Madsen and the Vickers-Berthier, and the latter was almost at the point of being accepted when the ZB33 appeared. Subsequent comparative trials showed the superiority of the ZB design, and it was put into production as the Bren Gun Mark 1, formally introduced into service on 4 August 1938. This model was a direct copy of the ZB33, and had a drum-pattern rear sight, a strap which passed over the firer's shoulder, and a grip

for the firer's left hand beneath the butt. The magazine was curved, due to the demands of feeding the British rimmed cartridge; the original Czech design, using rimless 7.92mm ammunition, had a straight magazine.

The Bren gun served everywhere during the war, and many and varied were the deeds performed with it. Representative of many, though perhaps just that little bit more daring than most, was the action in Italy, 18 September 1944, when Rifleman Sherbahadur Thapa of the 1st/9th Gurkhas, seized a Bren gun and charged a German machine gun post, killing the machine-gunner. A German infantry section counter-attacked at once . . . and Rifleman Sherbahadur Thapa drove back the attack with his Bren gun, and then ran to the crest of a ridge where, lying in the open, he poured fire into a German company preparing to counter-attack the Gurkhas. Rifleman Thapa was killed shortly afterwards while attempting to rescue a wounded comrade under fire, and for these activities he was awarded the Victoria Cross.

Variants

Mark 2 The Mark 1 gun was luxurious by wartime standards, and in order to simplify manufacture some modifications were made. The butt fittings were discarded, the drum sight replaced by a simpler tangent sight, the telescopic bipod replaced by a simpler fixed-length pattern, the cocking handle no longer folded, and certain lightening grooves on the body were omitted, resulting in the weight going up to 23¼lbs. This mark was introduced on 6 June 1941.

Marks 3 and 4 Introduced 18 July 1944; were identical with the Marks 1 and 2, except that the barrel was 22.25in long.

Vickers-Berthier LMG, Mk 3

Caliber .303in
Length 46.5in
Weight 22lb
Barrel 23.5in long, 5 grooves, right hand twist
Feed system 30-round detachable box magazine
System of operation Gas; tipping bolt
Rate of fire (cyclic) 600rpm
Manufacturer Royal Ordnance Factory, Ishapore, India

The Vickers-Berthier machine gun was the invention of a French designer, M. Adolphe PVM Berthier, who patented the essential details as early as 1909. The gun was completed in the early 1920s, and in 1925 the manufacturing rights were purchased by Vickers of England, who thereafter offered it commercially. The early models were purchased in small numbers by several countries, and in 1933 the Indian Government adopted it as their standard light machine gun. At the same time it was extensively tested in Britain when it was edged out by the Bren gun.

At a casual glance there seems little difference between the V-B and the Bren, but a closer examination shows small differences in contour of the barrel, barrel handle, pistol grip and other components. The action is very similar, both weapons using a tilting bolt driven by a gas piston and feeding from a curved magazine mounted above the gun.

The V-B was to be found with Indian Army divisions throughout the war, though in many cases battle losses were replaced by Bren guns where the logistic situation made this quicker and easier than providing new V-Bs from India. Due to the similarity between the two weapons there seems to have been little problem in retraining the troops. Unfortunately, due to its similarity to the Bren gun it is uncommon to find any references to it in reports, but one or two of the many feats of gallantry performed by Indian soldiers which were reported in the newspapers as having been done with a Bren gun were, in fact, done with a Vickers-Berthier.

Vickers, Mark 1

Caliber .303in
Length 45.5in
Weight 40lb
Barrel 28.5in long, 4 grooves, right hand twist
Feed system 250-round belt
System of operation Recoil; Maxim toggle lock
Rate of fire 450rpm
Manufacturer Vickers, Son & Maxim, Crayford, Kent
Royal Ordnance Factories

The British Army originally adopted the Maxim as their standard medium machine gun, and this was produced by the Maxim Gun Company, the chairman of which was Albert Vickers. Later the company became Vickers, Son & Maxim, and it was in their Crayford factory that the Maxim design was re-worked to produce the Vickers Gun. The principal change was to invert the Maxim lock mechanism so that the toggle broke upwards. The gun was also lightened and sundry small modifications incorporated, which made production a little easier. The Mark 1 gun was introduced into service on 26 November 1912 and it was eventually followed by a further ten marks, though all of these were for either aircraft or tank use and the Mark 1 remained the standard infantry gun until it was declared obsolete on 24 April 1968, having outlived all the others by a considerable margin.

The mechanism of the Vickers reflects the era in which it was designed; it was a complicated engineering solution to a difficult problem, that of feeding a rimmed cartridge from a fabric belt. Consequently it was built the hard way, with expensively machined and precisely fitted components made of critical materials. In spite of this

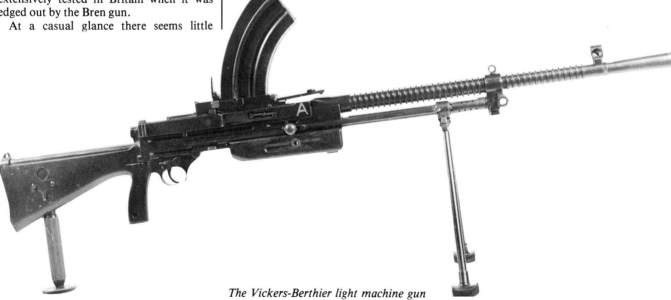

The Vickers-Berthier light machine gun

The Vickers machine gun, showing the tell-tale plume of steam from the condenser

—or possibly because of it—the Vickers gun became synonymous with reliability. Failure in action was almost unheard of; it could—and did—jam sometimes, and there are some 25 different types of stoppage noted in the drill book as being possible, together with involved descriptions of the symptoms; if the gun stopped with the crank handle in such-and-such a position, then so-and-so was at fault, all of which demanded a good memory and a cool head in an emergency. But such stoppages were brief and did not affect the long-term reliability. During both World Wars, though more so in the First due to the tactics prevailing, Vickers guns fired for phenomenal lengths of time in support, the most often-quoted case being that of ten guns on the Somme in 1916 which between them got rid of a million rounds in twelve hours, using up a hundred barrels and untold quantities of water in the process. One gun actually averaged 10,000 rounds an hour for twelve hours. There were no failures, and all the guns were serviceable when the affair was over. *That* is reliability, and one is entitled to doubt whether today's stamped metal and wire spring wonders could do half as well.

USA

Johnson, M1941

Caliber .30in
Length 42.0in
Weight 14lb 5oz
Barrel 22.0in long, 4 grooves, right hand twist
Feed system 20-round detachable box magazine
System of operation Recoil; rotating bolt head
Rate of fire (cyclic) 300–900rpm
Manufacturer Cranston Arms Corp., Providence, R.I., USA

Melvin M. Johnson was a Captain in the US Marine Corps Reserve and a noted authority on automatic weapons. In the middle 1930s he had designed an automatic rifle (described elsewhere) and from this began developing a light machine gun. Like the rifle, the machine gun operated by recoil, not a common system with such a light weapon and one which demanded a high standard of manufacture for reliable working. Although the design was mechanically sound, it was insufficiently robust to stand up to the rigors of campaigning. It was tested by the US Army but with little real interest since they were satisfied with the Browning Automatic Rifle, had sufficient of them, and were not keen on making a major change. Numbers were purchased by the Dutch Government for their forces in the East Indies, but with the Japanese invasion of that area the

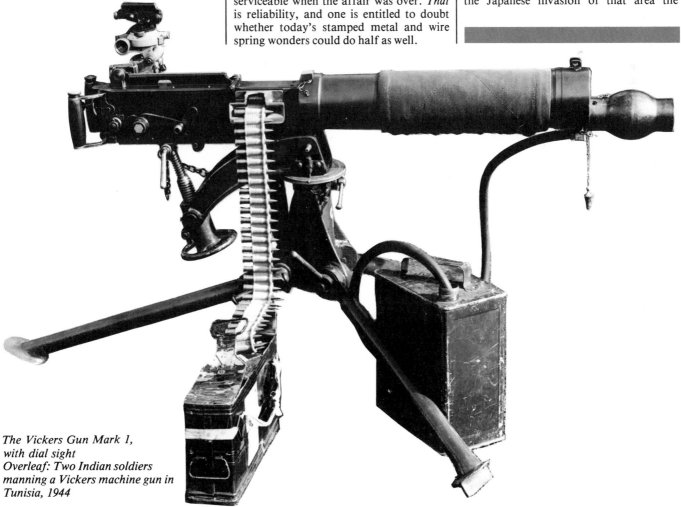

The Vickers Gun Mark 1, with dial sight
Overleaf: Two Indian soldiers manning a Vickers machine gun in Tunisia, 1944

The Johnson M1941 machine gun

contract lapsed. Production continued throughout the war for the US Marine Corps and US Rangers, but the total production was relatively small.

The weapon possessed a number of interesting features. When fired in the single shot mode the bolt closed and locked before each shot, but in the automatic mode it fired from an open bolt, ensuring that no cartridge was ever loaded into a hot chamber and allowing air to flow through the barrel between bursts in order to cool it. The magazine fed from the left side, which helped the silhouette but gave rise to problems of balance, and could be 'topped up' from the right side of the action from the standard five-round Springfield clip. An interesting bonus was that even with a full magazine fitted, a further five rounds could be fed into the action from a clip. The rate of fire was adjustable between wide limits by varying the setting of the recoil buffer.

The Johnson was an original and interesting design and, had it appeared at a more propitious time, might have become much better known. Its wartime activity was almost entirely restricted to the South Pacific area in the hands of the US Marines, though it is reported that some were used in Italy by the US Army's First Special Service Force. It is of interest that a slightly improved design was manufactured in postwar years for the Israeli Army under the name 'Dror', but this too was only made in small numbers.

Variant
M1944 This was the same basic weapon as the M1941 and differed only in having a tubular monopod instead of a bipod; a skeleton steel butt with wooden side fillers was also fitted. The redesign appears to have been solely a matter of production convenience.

Browning M1917A1, M1919A4, M1919A6

	M1917A1	M1919A4	M1919A6
Caliber	.30in	.30in	.30in
Length	38.64in	37.94in	53.0in
Weight	32.6lb	30.75lb	32.5lb
Barrel	23.9in	24.0in	24.0in
	All models 4 grooves, right hand twist		

Feed system All models 250-round fabric belt
System of operation All models recoil, vertical sliding breech lock
Rate of fire 450–600rpm 400–550rpm 400–450rpm
Manufacturers Remington Arms-UMC
Winchester Arms Co.
Westinghouse Inc.
Colt's Patent Firearms Co.

John Moses Browning began work on a machine gun design as early as 1889 and patented his first model the following year. This early idea was built by the Colt Company and became known as the Colt M1895; it was gas operated. In 1900 Browning decided that recoil operation offered more possibilities than did gas, and he began work on a completely new design. He took out his first patent the following year but it was not until 1910 that he produced a prototype. He could raise no interest in the US Army at that time, but in February 1917, with war looming closer, the US War Department woke up to the fact that it had virtually no machine guns, and Browning was finally able to demonstrate his new weapon. No decision was made, and in April the US went to war. The following month saw Browning demonstrating his gun once more, giving spectacular proof of the gun's efficiency by firing 20,000 rounds non-stop. Contracts were forthwith placed for the manufacture of 45,000 guns and the Browning M1917 entered US service. After the war some few changes were made, a new bottom plate, various components of steel instead of bronze, an improved water cooling system and the weapon became the M1917A1.

The mechanism of the Browning relies on the recoil of the barrel; this moves to the rear, carrying the bolt with it. After a short recoil a vertically sliding lock is withdrawn by cam surfaces in the gun body,

Landing on Iwo Jima, a Marine carries a Browning M1917 machine gun
Opposite: Troops of the First French Army firing a Browning .300 machine gun at Belfort, 1944

unlocking the bolt. The final movement of the barrel's recoil causes an accelerator, a curved steel claw, to swing back and, due to leverage gain, flip the bolt backwards very rapidly against a return spring. This movement of the bolt also drives the belt

Browning M1919A6 'light' machine gun

*Above: The Browning Automatic rifle
Left: A Browning .5 M2 on a half-track, Rome 1944. In this case the basic ground weapon is being employed for air defense*

feed mechanism which moves the belt, strips rounds from it and positions them in front of the bolt.

In addition to ground requirements the Browning was wanted as an aircraft gun, but water-cooling was neither necessary nor desirable in this role and an air-cooled model was developed, known as the M1918. From this stemmed the M1919, also air-cooled but with a heavier barrel and intended for use in tanks. During the

1920s it was found that this air-cooled weapon worked well as a ground gun, and eventually the M1914A4 was issued, tripod-mounted, to supplement and later largely replace the water-cooled M1917A1 model.

We have already commented on the US

Army's reluctance to adopt a good light machine gun. One attempt to provide something better than the Browning Auto Rifle was the Browning M1916A6; this was little more than the 1919A4 gun with a shoulder stock, carrying handle, pistol grip and bipod. It was an unfortunate design, which was heavy and cumbersome, it was adopted in February 1943 but sentenced as 'Substitute Standard' and relatively few were issued.

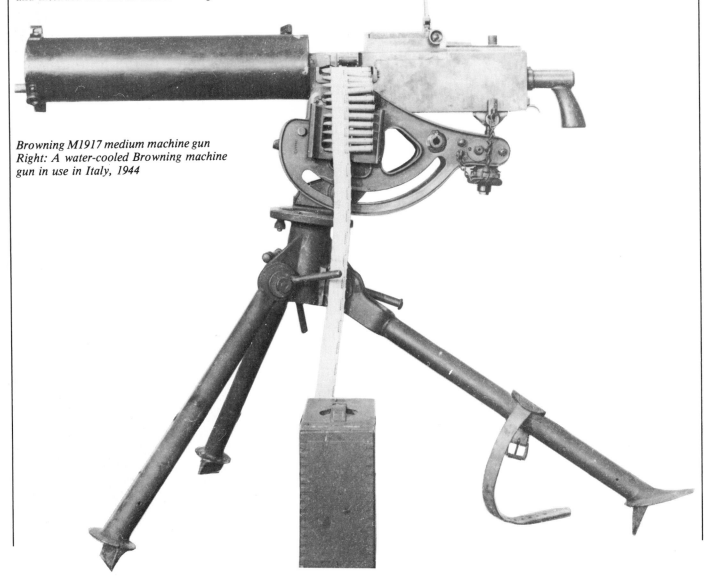

*Browning M1917 medium machine gun
Right: A water-cooled Browning machine gun in use in Italy, 1944*

USSR

Machine gun, DP 1928

Caliber 7.62mm
Length 50.8in
Weight 20lb 8oz
Barrel 23.8in long, 4 grooves, right hand twist
Feed system 47-round detachable drum
System of operation Gas; locking struts
Rate of fire (cyclic) 550rpm
Manufacturer Tula Arsenal

Vasily A. Degtyarev was one of the foremost Soviet gun designers, and he began work on this machine gun in 1921. By 1926 it was perfected and submitted for trial, and in 1928 it was adopted by the Soviet Army as their standard light machine gun. It was a very good design, particularly well suited to the Soviet Army: it had but six moving parts, and did not demand highly skilled labor or complex machinery to make it, it was simple to operate and it was extremely robust. Two slight disadvantages later showed up as a result of long use in war; the drum magazine was of thin sheet steel and liable to distort if dropped or roughly handled, and the return spring surrounding the gas piston was located beneath the barrel, in which position it was heated by radiation during prolonged firing and was apt to lose its temper (speaking metallurgically, of course). Nevertheless the DP was produced in enormous numbers.

The operation of the Degtyarev was rather unusual, though not original. The system was based on a patent of one Friberg, taken out in 1872 and improved by Kjellman in 1907. After this, one or two designers played with it, but Degtyarev was the first to put it to practical use. Two side-swinging struts are carried in the side of the bolt, pivoting outwards into recesses in the gun body. As the striker moves forward to hit the cartridge, shoulders force the struts out so that the breech must be positively locked before the round is fired. As the gas piston moves to the rear after firing, cam surfaces force the struts inwards, disengaging them from the body and unlocking the bolt so that further movement of the piston can open it. When Rolls-Royce decided to design a machine gun in 1941 they selected this system of locking.

Variants
DT (Degtyarev Tankovii) A modification of the DP for use in tanks. The magazine was deeper and carried 60 rounds; the barrel was heavier and not quickly changeable; a telescopic butt and pistol grip were fitted. A bipod was provided as an accessory so that the weapon could be used as a ground machine gun if the need arose.
DPM (DP Modified) The war in Russia revealed minor defects, as noted above, and in 1944 the gun was modified in order to improve matters. The return spring was

Opposite: Soviet sub-machine gunners protect the squad machine gunner as he operates his Degtyarev DP machine gun

Above: Soviet partisans train with the DP machine gun
Below: the Degtyarev DP machine gun

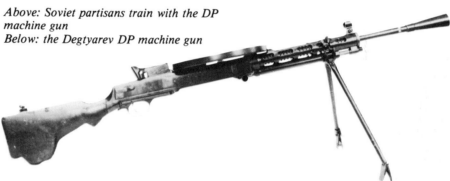

moved to a tube at the rear of the gun body, protruding over the butt. This made it difficult for the gunner to hold the gun in the usual way, so a pistol grip was fitted. The bipod was strengthened and attached to the barrel instead of the gas cylinder.

USSR

Maxim 1910

Caliber 7.62mm
Length 43.6in
Weight—Gun 52lb 8oz
—**Mounting** 110lbs
Barrel 28.4in long, 4 grooves, right hand twist
Feed system 250-round fabric belt
System of operation Recoil; Maxim toggle lock
Rate of fire 550rpm
Manufacturer State Arsenals

There is a lot to be said for settling on a good design and then sticking with it, which is just what the Russians did with the Maxim gun. Hiram Maxim himself demonstrated the weapon at St. Petersburg in 1887, and eventually the Tsar's army was provided with British-made Maxims. In 1905 manufacture began at Tula Arsenal in Russia, and from then until 1945 the weapon was in more or less continuous production. The original model had a cast bronze water jacket, but in 1910 this was replaced by a steel jacket and slight improvements were made to the feed mechanism, and with that the design was settled for evermore. The only minor changes made subsequently were the fitting of a corrugated water jacket during World War I and the fitting of a much larger filler cap, reputed to be originally designed for a tractor petrol tank, during World War II.

The mechanism was, of course, the basic Maxim toggle lock operated by recoil; not the simplest mechanism ever made but certainly one of the most reliable. Where the Russian weapons were unique was in the matter of weight. The British Vickers, more or less the same gun, weighed 32½lbs, and the German Maxim 1908, which was virtually the same gun as the Russian 1910, only 40½lbs. Doubtless the massiveness of the Russian construction contributed to its reliability but it certainly made it a difficult proposition to move. As a result the Russians developed their unique wheeled 'Sokolov' mounting, a tubular steel trail into which the gun was mounted and which acted both as a carrying cart and a firing mounting. Early models had two extra legs which could be extended forward to raise the gun for firing over parapets, but this was abandoned during World War I. A more con-

Soviet Maxim M1910 on Sokolov mounting

ventional tripod mounting was also provided but in smaller numbers than the Sokolov mount and it was rarely seen. The wheels of the Sokolov could be removed in the winter and replaced with a pair of sledge runners, when the whole affair could be towed by ski-troops. While ingenious, the result was an equipment weighing 162½lbs without water or ammunition, which was no sort of joke, even for a husky Russian.

The Maxim 1910 was widely used in both World Wars, in the Revolution, in the Spanish Civil War and, after 1945, when replaced in Soviet first-line service, it was given to many satellite countries. Its last appearance in combat was in the Korean War 1950–53, but there are undoubtedly large numbers still in existence and it would not be safe to say that their day is done.

USSR

Machine gun, DShK 1938

Caliber 12.7mm
Length 62.5in
Weight 78lb 8oz
Barrel 42.0in long, 4 grooves, right hand twist
Feed system 50-round belt
System of operation Gas; hinged locking struts
Rate of fire 550rpm
Manufacturer State Arsenals

Degtyarev first developed a heavy machine gun, the DK, in 1934 but it was only made in prototype form and underwent further development before being adopted in 1938 as the DShK. The initials indicate the appearance of a second designer, Georg S. Shpagin, later a Lieut-General of the Red Army and designer of the PPSh submachine gun. Degtyarev laid out the general design and basic mechanism, while Shpagin was responsible for the feed mechanism. Special attention to the feed was demanded by the fact that the weapon was designed to use the large 12.7mm cartridge, and the weight of a full belt of this placed a considerable strain on the feed system. Shpagin's solution was to mount a rotary 'squirrel-cage' block above the bolt; the belt was fed into the gun, the cartridge withdrawn from the belt into a

recess in the block, and the block indexed round. This process was repeated until the drum was almost filled and the first cartridge had moved around to the lowest position, from which it could be stripped by the forward movement of the bolt. Each subsequent stroke of the bolt loaded one cartridge from the drum, and at the same time took another from the belt and loaded it into the drum. The idea was not entirely original, having been used by Maxim in his first design of 1883, but Shpagin was the first to make it work successfully in or out of the Soviet Union.

The remainder of the mechanism was pure Degtyarev, using his well-tried system of hinged struts to lock the bolt by the movement of the striker, unlocking by movement of the gas piston. The long barrel was heavily finned to aid cooling and a single-baffle muzzle brake used to try and abate the recoil force. The mounting was a tripod which, for transport, folded and took on a pair of wheels so that it resembled the Maxim's 'Sokolov' mounting. This tripod could be erected some five feet high so that the weapon could be used as an anti-aircraft machine gun, a role in which it was very prominent during World War II.

At the end of the war it was modified by removing the rotating drum feed and replacing it with a simple swinging-arm pattern which had been developed for a postwar gun, and as the DShKM it remains in service today. Numbers of DShK were supplied to various satellite countries, and it was particularly prominent as an anti-aircraft weapon during the Korean War.

USSR

Machine gun, Goryunov SG 43

Caliber 7.62mm
Length 44.1in
Weight 30lb 4oz
Barrel 28.3in long, 4 grooves, right hand twist
Feed system Metallic link belt
System of operation Gas; side-moving bolt
Rate of fire 600rpm
Manufacturer State Arsenals

In the early 1940s it became apparent that the Maxim 1910 was feeling its age and was not really suited to modern warfare, and the Red Army demanded something to replace it. With the war in Finland just over, and a war with Germany not unlikely, a modern machine gun was urgently required by the Soviets. Peter Maximovitch Goryunov produced the answer which was introduced into service in 1943.

There is some evidence that Goryunov was working on a design for a tank machine gun at the time of the demand, and simply modified it to produce the ground gun. The barrel is much heavier than might be expected in this role, but it does lead to long life and is probably due to tank influence. The mechanism was entirely new, representing the first Soviet departure from Degtyarev's designs. The bolt locks by moving sideways into a recess in the gun body, operated by a conventional gas piston. The feed system is unusually complicated since it has to withdraw the rimmed cartridge from the belt, move it forwards in front of the bolt, and then move it sideways into line with the chamber. In spite of the complexity the system is reliable and foolproof and will continue to work irrespective of the gun's attitude—upright, on its side, or even upside down—though this is more in the nature of a mechanical curiosity than a useful combat feature.

Another feature of the SG is the extreme simplicity of its mechanism; there is, for example, only one large spring in the gun. It has been acclaimed by one authority as the most successful air-cooled medium ma-

The Soviet DShK 12.7mm machine gun on a wheeled mount with split trail. A sledge could replace the wheels in winter in order to travel over snow and ice

The Goryunov SG43 machine gun

chine gun ever made with the exception of the American Browning. Certainly the Soviets were satisfied with it, and although it never replaced the Maxim during the war since production could not keep up with the demand, in postwar years it became the standard medium gun and also went back to its origins to become the standard tank machine gun.

Germany

Maschinengewehr 15

Caliber 7.92mm
Length 52.5in
Weight 28lb
Barrel 23.5in long, 4 grooves, right hand twist
Feed system 75-round detachable saddle drum magazine
System of operation Recoil; rotating bolt
Rate of fire (cyclic) 850rpm
Manufacturer Rheinmettal AG, Dusseldorf

As outlined earlier, the German Rheinmettal company established a subsidiary in Switzerland in 1929, known as the Waffenfabrik Solothurn AG, which was to act as their proof and experimental unit for designs which could not be produced in Germany. Shortly after its opening, Solothurn offered an aircraft machine gun and later superseded it by an improved design known as the MG30. In 1932 a modified version of this weapon was produced by Rheinmettal for the German Air Force, and this was the original MG15.

The action is by short recoil and the mechanism inside is rather involved; as the

barrel and breechblock move back, the block is rotated by two rollers riding in tracks in the gun body. This rotation unlocks the breech lugs from the barrel and the last part of the recoil movement actuates an accelerator which throws the breechblock to the rear. Feed was from a double-drum magazine which fitted saddle-wise across the body and fed from both sides alternately, thus keeping the weight evenly balanced. The net result was a very sound gun for its purpose; the mass of the barrel tended to absorb a lot of recoil, but the lightweight breechblock and accelerator gear gave quite a high rate of fire. As an aircraft gun it was very successful.

As the war progressed, the MG15 was superseded in aircraft by heavier caliber weapons, and at the same time there was a continual demand from the Army for more machine guns. As a result the MG15 was taken into infantry service in 1944. It was fitted with a bipod and a simple buttstock and a carrying handle; as a ground gun it had one good feature, that the stock was in line with the action, which meant very little tendency to rise and a stable gun when firing. But that is about the only good thing that can be said of it. The data table above tells the rest of the story; no infantry LMG ought to be 52in long and weigh 28lbs when empty. The Bren, which was no lightweight, was 46.5in and 22lbs. The MG15 was too cumbersome to be a successful infantry weapon. Numbers were used, because they had to be used, but they were never liked, although they were accurate and reliable.

The German MG 15 with saddle magazine

Germany

Maschinengewehr 34

Caliber 7.92mm
Length 48.0in
Weight 26lb 11oz
Barrel 24.75in long, 4 grooves, right hand twist
Feed system Belt, or 75-round saddle drum magazine
System of operation Recoil; revolving bolt head
Rate of fire 850rpm
Manufacturers Mauserwerke AG, Berlin
Stey-Daimler-Puch AG, Austria
Waffenwerk Brünn (Brno), Czechoslovakia

In 1930 the Solothurn Company of Switzerland produced a machine gun known as the MG30, which they offered to the German Army. It was a very advanced design which used barrel recoil to drive back the bolt which was rotated by two rollers running in cam tracks in the receiver. It was probably the first 'straight line' design, the butt being in prolongation of the barrel axis, and it incorporated an ingenious quick-change method for the barrel in which the butt was twisted through 90 degrees and pulled off; the bolt and barrel could then be quickly withdrawn through the gun body and the barrel replaced. About 5000 of these guns were made, most of which were bought by Austria and Hungary, and doubtless a number were used during the war. But the German Army were less impressed and passed the gun across to Mauserwerke with the request that they improve it.

This Mauserwerke did. They jettisoned the side-feeding box magazine of the MG30 and made the new design a belt-fed weapon which, by quick substitution of a different feed unit, could also use the 75-round saddle drum of the MG15. The bolt locking system was changed so that only the bolt head revolved, locking by interrupted threads; an additional recoil impulse was given to the barrel by adding a muzzle gas trap. Barrel changing was simplified by hinging the gun body to the rear end of the barrel casing; unlatching allowed the gun body to be swung sideways and the barrel pulled straight out of its bearings.

The most far-reaching feature of the MG34 was tactical rather than mechanical; it was the first example of what is known today as the 'General Purpose' machine gun. Fitted with a bipod it functioned as the squad light automatic; on its tripod, which incorporated a sprung cradle to reduce the recoil and vibration and thus make continuous fire less fatiguing for the gunner, it functioned as a medium machine gun; and on a different pattern of light tripod and fitted with the saddle-drum magazine, it made a good anti-aircraft weapon. It was the first belt-fed weapon to be used as a light machine gun in quantity and it proved that the concept was valid; previously it had always been considered that the feed system of the light machine

gun had to be one to which riflemen could contribute in an emergency, and this argued some form of easily-filled box magazine. The MG34 showed that provided the supply organization was efficient, belt feed was perfectly acceptable in this role, even if it did mean the gun crew going about the battlefield festooned with belts of ammunition.

The MG34 only had one real defect; it was too good. The quality of design and workmanship meant long and extremely precise manufacturing processes, and eventually five factories were doing nothing but turn out MG34s as hard as they could, plus a number of manufacturing parts. By 1941 this was obviously impractical and a new design was sought; but in spite of this, the MG34 remained in production and use until the war ended.

Variant

MG34s, MG34/41 These are virtually the same weapon, the 34s being the prototype of the 34/41. It was originally intended as a replacement for the MG34, and has various simplifications in order to speed up production. The ability to fire single shot was removed; the bolt locked by lugs instead of on an interrupted thread; the replacement feed unit to allow use of the 75-round saddle drum was dropped; the barrel was shortened so as to speed up the rate of fire by reducing the recoiling mass. While all these measures were successful, the advent of the MG42, which was both a better weapon and a simpler manufacturing design, stopped the intended production of the 34/41, and only a handful were made.

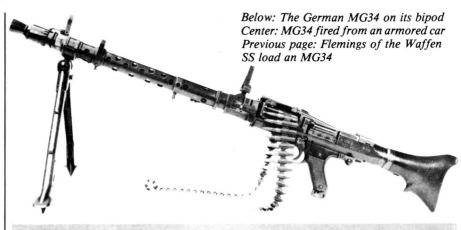

*Below: The German MG34 on its bipod
Center: MG34 fired from an armored car
Previous page: Flemings of the Waffen SS load an MG34*

Germany

Maschinengewehr 42

Caliber 7.92mm
Length 48.0in
Weight 25lb 8oz
Barrel 21.0in long, 4 grooves, right hand twist
System of operation Recoil; roller locking
Feed system Belt
Rate of fire 1200rpm
Manufacturer Mauserwerke AG, Berlin

When the production of MG34 models was obviously insufficient for the German Army's needs, a new design of weapon was begun, one which would be easier to mass-produce. For the first time the design was not left entirely in the hands of gunmakers; a Doktor Grunow of the Johannes Grossfuss Metall und Lackierwarenfabrik of Döbeln, experts in pressing and stamping metal, was called in to advise at an early stage in design. As a result the final design was specifically laid out to suit stamping and pressing processes, with welding and riveting used for assembly.

The action of the MG42 was modified to use a non-rotating bolt locking into a barrel extension by two rollers cammed outwards. Unless the rollers were out, locking the breech, the firing pin could not pass through the centre of the bolt. On recoil the barrel, bolt and barrel extension re-

Below: The German MG42 in its light machine gun role. Right: top cover opened to show the feed mechanism

coiled locked together until cam tracks in the gun body moved the rollers inwards to release the bolt.

Movement of the bolt drove a feed arm mounted in the top cover of the gun which in turn operated pawls to feed the ammunition belt; the design was most ingenious and fed the belt smoothly and reliably and has been widely copied in other weapons since its original appearance in the MG42.

One of the results of the re-design was to raise the rate of fire to an astonishing 1200rpm, much higher than any other contemporary machine gun and a rate which has only rarely since been exceeded. As a result the barrel had to be designed for quick-changing—every 250 rounds was the recommended figure—and this was done by unlatching the breech end and swinging it out through a long slot in the right-hand side of the barrel casing; a fresh barrel could be fitted in five seconds.

As with the MG34, the MG42 was used on a bipod as a light machine gun or on a tripod as a medium gun, though the high rate of fire made it difficult to control on a bipod. It was extremely reliable, highly resistant to dust and cold conditions and was extremely popular with the Wehrmacht—and understandably less popular with their enemies. Its first use in action is said to have been by the Afrika Korps at Gazala in May 1942. It has been reported that 750,000 MG42s were made before the war ended. At the war's end many countries who seized stocks of the guns adopted them into their own armies, among them France and Yugoslavia, and when the German Bundeswehr was reconstituted and required a machine gun they simply put the MG42 back into production in 7.62mm NATO caliber as the MG1. An interesting point about this is that the original engineering drawings were destroyed at the end of the war, and the draughtsmen had to obtain an MG42 from a museum in the USA, strip it, and produce fresh drawings to guide manufacture.

Left: Italian troops with a German MG42. A large number of German weapons were taken into use by the Italian Army, often renaming them in the process

Czechoslovakia/Germany

Machine gun, VZ37

Caliber 7.92mm
Length 43.5in
Weight 41lb
Barrel 26.7in long, 4 grooves, right hand twist
Feed system Belt
System of operation Recoil and Gas; tipping bolt
Rate of fire 500 or 700rpm
Manufacturer Ceskoslovenska Zbrojovka, Brno

This weapon may also be met under the designation VZ53, its factory nomenclature and that under which it was exported; in the Czechoslovakian Army it was the Kulomet VZ37, in the German Army it was the Maschinengewehr 37(t) and in the British Army it was the Besa machine gun. Whatever name it was travelling under it was still the same gun, developed in the early 1930s and put into production in 1937.

The mechanism was a peculiar mixture of recoil and gas operation, but it bore distinct resemblance to the light machine gun designs (for example the Bren) which came from the same company. The barrel had an extension into which the bolt locked by having its rear end lifted to abut against shoulders. On recoil the whole unit moved rearward, and then the gas piston functioned in the usual way to unlock the bolt. The weapon was extremely reliable, and, certainly in British service, was renowned for its accuracy.

In the British Army the gun was used as a tank machine gun and need not be further considered. In the German Army, however, it was used in its original guise as

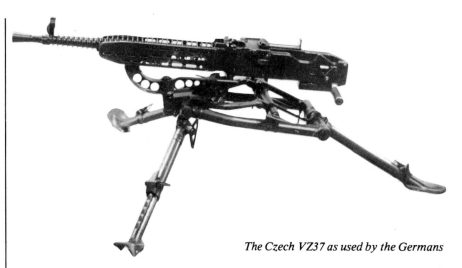

The Czech VZ37 as used by the Germans

an air-cooled medium machine gun, in which its adjustable rate of fire was an unusual asset. It was provided with a tripod of somewhat complicated aspect.

Germany

Knorr–Bremse MG35/36

Caliber 7.92mm
Length 51.48in
Weight 22lb
Barrel 27.25in long, 4 grooves, right hand twist
Feed system 20-round detachable box magazine
System of operation Gas; tipping bolt
Rate of fire (cyclic) 500rpm
Manufacturer Knorr-Bremse AG, Berlin-Lichtenberg

This machine gun originated in Sweden and was designed by Lauf and Przkalla in 1932–33. Known as the LH33 it was in 6.5mm Swedish caliber and used the magazine of the Browning Automatic Rifle. It was offered to various nations, being tested in Britain shortly before the war, but it was turned down in all cases.

. Lauf then sold the patents to a German company, Knorr-Bremse, who until then had concerned themselves solely with the manufacture of automobile brakes. Probably attracted by the prospect of a large military contract to the expanding Wehrmacht, Knorr-Bremse decided to enter the arms business and, making some slight alterations, produced the weapon as the MG35/36. However, the German Army were no more impressed than anyone else and turned the weapon down. Numbers

The Swedish-designed and German-made Knorr-Bremse light machine gun

There is no record of how many VZ37s were manufactured, but large numbers of them are still in use throughout the world, notably in a number of African countries.

were sold to the Waffen SS who used them principally as training weapons until they had a sufficiency of standard machine guns, whereupon the MG35/36 were off-loaded on to the various Foreign Legions of the SS which were, by then, fighting in Russia.

The Knorr-Bremse is a fairly conventional gas-operated light machine gun which fed from a box magazine on the left side. The barrel could be quickly changed by a quick release nut on the breech end, and, for some unknown reason, the last three inches of the barrel at the muzzle were smooth-bored. A flash hider was fitted to the muzzle and a bipod was attached to the gas cylinder above the barrel. One dangerous feature was the safety catch; if carelessly applied it could hold the bolt three-quarters cocked without the sear being engaged, so that subsequent release of the safety catch with a magazine in place would release the bolt and load and fire the gun. The butt was also a source of trouble, since its attachment to the gun was too weak to withstand the firing vibrations and thus the butt tended to come loose and fall off while the gun was firing; which is upsetting to the firer, to say the least.

Schwarzlose, Model 07/12

Caliber 7.92mm or 8mm
Length 42.0in
Weight 44.0lb
Barrel 20.75in long, 4 grooves, right hand twist
Feed system Belt
System of operation Delayed blowback
Rate of fire 400rpm
Manufacturer Osterreichische Waffenfabrik Gesellschaft, Steyr

The Schwarzlose machine gun was an elderly design which nevertheless remained in service with the Austrian, German, Hungarian and Italian Armies throughout World War II. It was one of the heaviest weapons ever to use the delayed blowback system of operation and one of the more successful ones into the bargain.

The mechanism was rather unusual, relying partly on the inertia of an unusually heavy breechblock and partly on a toggle mechanism which Schwarzlose originally patented in 1900 as part of an automatic

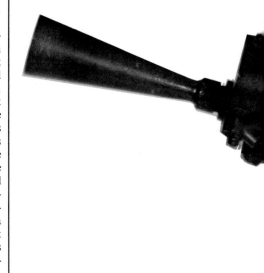

pistol design. The toggle actions of the Parabellum pistol and the Maxim machine gun are the most well-known applications of the toggle lock, wherein the toggle lies straight to resist movement until the centre joint is made to lift and thus allow the toggle to fold. In Schwarzlose's design the toggle is folded to begin with, very tightly, and the action of the breechblock is to unfold it into a straight line. Obviously there is no longer any positive lock, but the operation is at a severe mechanical disadvantage due to the way the toggle is folded, and thus there is a delaying action to the initial movement of the breech.

In spite of the delaying action, extraction was still violent, and the original design included the inevitable oil pump to lubricate the cartridges. In later models the pump was abandoned and the breechblock made even heavier in order to give more resistance and thus extract more slowly.

Although obsolescent after World War I, large numbers of Schwarzlose guns remained in use. The Italian Army took several thousand as postwar reparations from the Austrians, and many more remained. All these were put back to use during the war, and a large number were re-barrelled to use the standard German 7.92mm cartridge, after which they were used by the German Army as the MG7/12(ö).

Norway/Germany

Madsen machine gun

The standard Madsen light gun

Caliber 7.92mm
Length 45.0in
Weight 20lb
Barrel 23.0in long, 4 grooves, right hand twist
Feed system 25-, 30- or 40-round detachable box magazines
System of operation Recoil; rising block
Rate of fire (cyclic) 450rpm
Manufacturer Dansk Rekylriffel Syndikat AS 'Madsen', Copenhagen

The Madsen was one of the most unusual machine guns of all time, using an action totally unlike any other, produced in virtu-

ally the same model for fifty years, used in almost every war from the Russo-Japanese to Vietnam, and yet never officially adopted in quantity by any major power. It was designed by a Dane called Schouboe, and was probably the only one of his many weapon designs which was a success. It was then adopted by the Danish cavalry and named 'Madsen', after the Danish Minister of War who had been particularly enthusiastic about its adoption. After that it was bought in small numbers by almost

The Austrian Schwarzlose Model 07/12

every nation and evaluated both in peace and war. It rates its mention by virtue of being the Norwegian Army's light machine gun in 1940, being used in the brief campaign against the German invasion.

The action of the Madsen is based on recoil of the barrel, which transmits movement to a pivoting breechblock similar in concept to that of a Martini rifle. Since the block is working in a vertical arc, a separate rammer is needed to insert the cartridge and a separate extractor to remove the fired case. In spite of its undoubted mechanical perfection, the action is open to criticism on the grounds that the cartridge is slightly distorted or bowed as it is forced into the chamber. This appears to be borne out by the fact that jams frequently occur when the weapon is used with rimmed ammunition or with slightly

over-size cases. It seems to work well enough with rimless cartridges, however, and the majority of Madsens have been built for this type. One major innovation of the Madsen design was the top-mounted curved magazine, widely copied after its introduction on this gun.

As well as being in use in Norway, Madsens were to be found in Estonia, Lithuania, Latvia, Poland and many other European countries, many of which found

their way into German service. As well as employing them as they stood, the Germans developed an ingenious conversion unit which allowed the use of the standard German Army machine gun belts instead of the box magazines. Bearing in mind the complexity of the Madsen's mechanism, this is technically on a par with operating two lifts in one shaft.

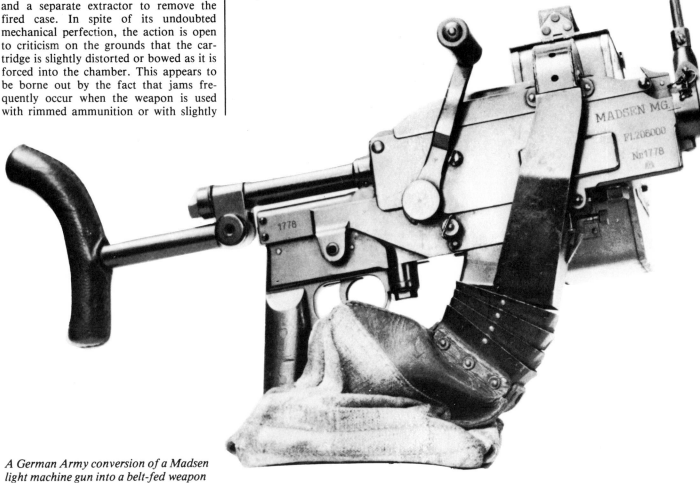

A German Army conversion of a Madsen light machine gun into a belt-fed weapon

Italy

Fiat–Revelli, Model 1914

Caliber 6.5mm
Length 46.5in
Weight 37lb 8oz
Barrel 25.75in long, 4 grooves, right hand twist
Feed system 50-round strips
System of operation Blowback
Rate of fire (cyclic) 400rpm
Manufacturer FIAT SpA, Turin

The Model 1914 bears some resemblance to its contemporaries the Maxim, Vickers and water-cooled Browning, but this is entirely superficial and the weapon is not in the same class. In spite of its manifold defects, however, it remained a part of the Italian Army's equipment from its introduction in 1914 until the close of World War II.

The weapon was a delayed blowback using a mechanism long perpetuated in Italian gun designs. The barrel and bolt

recoiled a short distance, held together by a swinging wedge; as this swung out of engagement so the bolt was freed to be blown back by the recoil of the spent case. Like most blowback designs this led to extraction difficulties and an oil reservoir

and pump were installed to lubricate the cartridges before being loaded.

The feed mechanism was also unusual. A magazine of ten columns of five rounds was entered into the left side of the gun. As each column was emptied, the maga-

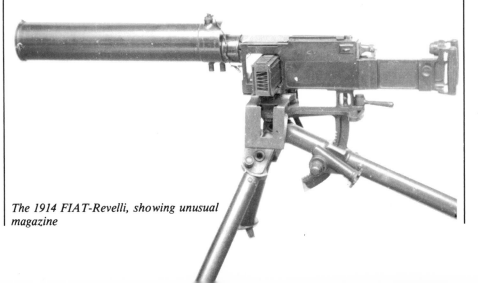

The 1914 FIAT-Revelli, showing unusual magazine

zine was indexed across to bring the next column into line, until finally the empty magazine was ejected from the right side of the gun. As may be imagined, the mechanism required for this operation was rather complex and its functioning was not improved by the oil and dust coating it acquired during firing; it was notoriously prone to jamming.

Finally, an operating rod forming part of the bolt structure protruded from the rear of the topmost portion of the receiver and recoiled with the bolt, passing across the top of the gun and striking a buffer unit placed just in front of the operating handles. Oscillating back and forth at 400 times a minute, it was a constant hazard to the gunner's fingers as well as being a highly effective device for pumping grit and dirt into the mechanism. Taking one thing with another, the Revelli (FIAT came into it only as manufacturers) was not a particularly outstanding design, not unlike many Italian models.

Breda, Model 1930

Caliber 6.5mm
Length 48.4in
Weight 22lb 8oz
Barrel 20.5in long, 4 grooves, right hand twist
Feed system 20-round attached box
System of operation Delayed blowback
Rate of fire (cyclic) 475rpm
Manufacturer Societe Anonyme Ernesto Breda, Turin

The Breda company were a heavy engineering firm specializing in railway locomotives, and they came into the weapons business by being given contracts to manufacture FIAT machine guns during World War I. After the war they decided to retain their foothold in this new business and set about designing a light machine gun. With the utmost respect, they would have served the Italian Army better by remaining in the locomotive business exclusively.

The first design was the M1924, of which the Italian Army bought 2000. It was then replaced by the M1930, a slight modification, and this became the standard Italian light machine gun. With the best will in the world, it is difficult to find something good to say about it; there is an old engineering maxim to the effect that if a thing looks right it generally is right; the M1930 looked wrong, was wrong, and invariably went wrong.

To start with it was a blowback gun, working on similar lines to the FIAT-Revelli. This is acceptable in low-velocity cartridges, but even though the Italian 6.5mm was relatively weak, it was too powerful for this system. In blowback weapons firing heavy charges there is a tendency for the neck of the case to be tightly expanded against the chamber while the bolt is opening, leading to the body of the case stretching as the base moves out with the bolt. To overcome this the Breda incorporated an oil reservoir and pump which sprayed a small quantity of oil on to each cartridge as it was being entered into the chamber, thus lubricating it so that it could be extracted more easily. In a dusty environment this meant that the weapon soon acquired an internal coating of oil, grit and carbon fouling.

The magazine was a permanent fixture on the right side and could be hinged forward to allow it to be re-loaded by either pushing in a 20-round clip or re-loading from rifle chargers. In theory this is a good idea, since it means that the magazine lips, which are critical for correct feeding, are machined within the gun body and thus are less liable to accidental damage. But in fact it meant a low rate of fire due to the need to re-load instead of simply changing box magazines.

The final drawback was that the quick-change barrel lay on a recoil slide, since it had to move about 4mm to the rear before the breech opened. As a result the sights were on the gun body and not on the barrel; this, plus the fact that the barrel support bearings soon showed signs of wear, led to considerable inaccuracy.

The Breda 30 was, in spite of all its faults, the only light machine gun available to the Italian Army, and it was extensively used in the Libyan campaign, although reports speak more frequently of its troubles than of its feats of arms.

Variant
Model 1938 In 1938 the Italian Army began to introduce a 7.35mm cartridge, and a small number of Model 1930 machine guns were re-chambered for the new round. Such conversions were known as the Model 1938, but few were issued.

Below: The Italian Breda Model 1930
Center: The Breda 1930 in use by Italian mountain troops

Italy

Fiat–Revelli, Model 1935

Caliber 8mm
Length 50.0in
Weight 40lb
Barrel 25.75in long, 4 grooves, right hand twist
Feed system Belt
System of operation Blowback
Rate of fire 500rpm
Manufacturer FIAT SpA, Turin

The Italian Army, feeling the need of an improvement on the 1914 model, developed this Model 1935. The principal changes from the 1914 were firstly to improve its hitting power by adopting a new 8mm cartridge; secondly to make it more convenient to use by dispensing with the water-cooling arrangements and making it air-cooled; and thirdly removing the remarkable magazine feed of the 1914 and replacing it with a more conventional belt feed. At the same time the barrel was arranged for rapid changing, doubtless because it was rather underweight for sustained fire.

In spite of these very laudable improve-

The FIAT in use as an anti-aircraft weapon

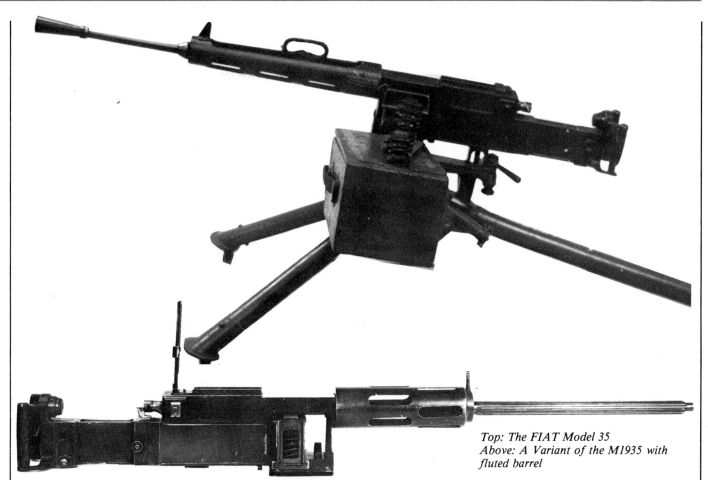

Top: The FIAT Model 35
Above: A Variant of the M1935 with fluted barrel

ments, there was still enough of the 1914 model left to damn the design. The oil pump was discarded, but since the mechanism was still the same delayed blowback, extraction was still a problem, and it was overcome by fluting the interior surface of the chamber so as to float the case out on gas, but this rarely seemed to work the way it was intended, and a large number of guns actually had the oil pump of the M1914 replaced as a modification. For the rest, the cartridges were greased as they were put into the belts, which was an even worse solution.

Probably the worst feature of the design was that the mechanism had been altered to make the weapon fire from a closed bolt, presumably in the interests of improved accuracy. As a result, when firing stopped a cartridge was chambered but not fired. Since the chamber of the thin barrel was invariably hot, this led to frequent cook-offs, with all the attendant hazards.

To sum up; it seems fair to say that the 1935 was actually a worse design than the weapon it was intended to replace.

Breda, M1937

Caliber 8mm
Length 50.06in
Weight 43lb
Barrel 26.75in long, 4 grooves, right hand twist
Feed system 20-round strip
System of operation Gas; vertical sliding lock
Rate of fire (cyclic) 450rpm
Manufacturer Ernesto Breda SA, Turin

The Breda 37 was a final attempt to produce a reasonably satisfactory medium machine gun for the Italian Army; while it had its own oddities, it was certainly an improvement on the Revelli designs and was well liked by its users as a reliable weapon. It might also be said that since producing their Model 1930 light gun, the Breda company had redeemed themselves by producing some first-class aircraft machine guns.

The mechanism is a simple gas piston type, but no opportunity was taken to design it so that the bolt began opening by a slow movement to start the empty case

The Breda Model 1930

out of the chamber. The same violent operation as every other Italian gun occurred, which, inevitably, led to extraction problems and equally inevitably to oiled cartridges and all the troubles they brought in their train.

The design of the rest of the gun was straightforward enough, and it was mounted on a simple and robust tripod, but the whole effect was ruined by the adoption of the most remarkable feed system ever seen. The designer, basically, took the old and well-tried Hotchkiss system in which a light metal strip holding twenty rounds is fed into one side of the gun. As the gun fires, the rounds are pulled from the strip and the strip moved across, until eventually the empty strip falls from the other side of the gun. The designer of this weapon went one better, however, and arranged the machinery so that when the empty case was extracted from the chamber it was replaced in the strip before the strip was moved across.

Whatever advantage this system may have—and the only one which presents itself is a desire to keep the gun position tidy—it possessed the grave disadvantage that, unless the gunner had a supply of loaded strips handy, his unfortunate assistant had to spend time shelling the empty cases out of the ejected strips before he could begin to re-load them with live rounds, not the happiest of activities in the face of an advancing enemy.

Variant
Model 1938 Presumably somebody in the Italian Army had words to say on the matter of this peculiar feed system, for in the following year the Model 1938 was produced; this merely changed the feed system to use a twenty-round detachable box mounted on top of the gun. A pistol grip at the rear end replaced the spade grips of the Model 37, but beyond that there was no other change. It appears that few of this model were made.

The Breda Model 1937 in action providing long-range supporting fire

Japan

Machine gun, Taisho 11

Caliber 6.5mm
Length 43.5in
Weight 22lb 8oz
Barrel 19.0in long, 4 grooves, right hand twist
Feed system 30-round hopper
System of operation Gas
Rate of fire (cyclic) 500rpm
Manufacturer State Arsenals

The Japanese were very quick to appreciate the potential of the machine gun and by 1902 had purchased manufacturing rights to the French Hotchkiss Gun M1897 and were issuing it to their army. It was used with considerable success in the Russo-Japanese War, and, as a result, the Hotchkiss design was retained as the basis of further developments.

The Taisho 11 gun was introduced in 1922—the 11th year of the Taisho Era—

and was designed by Colonel Kirijo Nambu, the noted Japanese firearms expert. The basic Hotchkiss gas-operated system was retained, but a unique feed system was introduced: a square hopper on the left of the gun accepted six standard five-round rifle chargers lying on their sides. As the gun fired so the rounds were stripped from the bottom charger, the empty charger being discarded and the next full one falling into place. In theory this system allowed any rifleman to provide ammunition for the squad weapon, but in practice it was found that the standard rifle round was too powerful for the smooth working of the gun, and led to the rate of fire being too fast for the rather complicated feed mechanism. As a result, a special cartridge, loaded with a slightly less powerful charge, had to be provided for the machine gun, which rather negated the designer's intentions.

Japanese Taisho 11 light machine gun

The Taisho 3rd Year (1914) heavy machine gun, a modified Hotchkiss design of gas-operated weapon, which remained in first-line service until 1945

Another fault of the weapon was that the action was so built that the bolt opened suddenly and jerked the empty case out of the breech; there was no period of slow opening with powerful leverage to give what is called 'primary extraction'. This led to separated and split cases, and the solution to this was to add an oil reservoir arrangement which lubricated every round as it entered the chamber. Like every other lubricated-feed design, this gave good results under ideal conditions but in the dust of battle it simply meant that the round was coated with grinding paste as it entered the breech, leading to rapid wear of the chamber.

The sights and butt on the Taisho 11 were offset to the right, giving the weapon a peculiar appearance, and the barrel was extensively finned in order to assist cooling. The gun was widely used during the Manchurian and China campaigns of the 1930s, but by the time of World War II it was about to be replaced by improved models. However, the manufacturing capacity of Japan was never capable of producing the new weapons in sufficient quantity, and so the Taisho 11 remained in service until 1945.

Japanese troops line up for their sake ration; in the foreground, a Taisho 11 light machine gun with its notoriously inefficient feed hopper invented by Colonel Nambu of Nambu pistol fame

Type 92, heavy machine gun

Caliber 7.7mm
Length 45.5in
Weight 61lb
Barrel 29.5in long, 4 grooves, right hand twist
Feed system 30-round strip
System of operation Gas; vertical sliding lock
Rate of fire (cyclic) 450rpm
Manufacturers Nambu Armament Mfg. Co. Tokyo
State Arsenals

When it came to equipment the Japanese Army were among the most staunchly conservative; it took an age for them to adopt anything new, but once they did, and it worked, they stayed with it for evermore. As a result, most of their machine guns were Hotchkiss guns. The Model 92's parentage is strongly apparent from its appearance, but sufficient small changes were made internally by Nambu to make sure that it was not, in fact, as good as an untouched Hotchkiss would have been. It had actually begun as the Taisho 3 Model of 1914, which in its turn was a copy of the French Model 1914 Hotchkiss. The Taisho 3 barrel was more prominently finned, and two spade grips placed at the rear, but the principal difference was a slight change in the connection between the gas piston and the breechblock. This

Right: The Type 92 machine gun in use
Below: The Taisho 3 medium machine gun, known as the 'Woodpecker'

was made to give efficient operation with the lower-powered Japanese 6.5mm cartridge, and because of this alteration the extraction was violent and, as usual, the cartridges had to be oiled before loading.

In 1932 the Army began changing to 7.7mm caliber and the machine gun was again re-designed by General Nambu to suit the characteristics of the new cartridge. The main external change was the addition of a flash hider to the muzzle and a new pattern of firing grip at the rear which resembled two pistol grips hanging beneath the gun. The internal mechanism was basically unchanged and oiling remained a necessity. Perhaps the most

unfortunate feature was its weight—122lbs when on its tripod; as a result the tripod, like that of the earlier Taisho 3, had two sleeves on the front legs into which carrying poles could be slipped for two men, while the third member of the gun team attached a yoke, resembling overgrown bicycle handlebars, to the rear tripod leg. In this way three men could carry the whole equipment fairly rapidly about the battlefield without dismantling it.

The Type 92 was the most common medium machine gun of the Japanese Army throughout the war, and its slow and distinctive rate of fire earned it the nickname 'Woodpecker' among Allied troops.

Machine gun, Type 96

Caliber 6.5mm
Length 41.5in
Weight 20lb
Barrel 21.7in long, 4 grooves, right hand twist
Feed system 30-round detachable box
System of operation Gas; rising lock
Rate of fire (cyclic) 550rpm
Manufacturer State Arsenals

This weapon was introduced in 1936 (year 2596 in the Japanese calendar, hence Type 96) with the intention of replacing the Taisho 11 model. In the event the production never kept up with the demand so that it never completely ousted the earlier gun from general use.

Although still based on the same action as the Taisho 11, it is obvious that a number of ideas had been taken from the Czechoslovakian ZB designs, probably from guns captured from the Chinese. The most important feature was that the com-

plicated hopper feed of the Taisho 11 was replaced by a more usual form of top-mounted detachable box magazine; unfortunately this did not do away with the troubles due to the full-power rifle round, and the reduced-charge cartridge was still necessary.

The offset butt and sights were abandoned in favor of a more conventional form of butt and a drum-set rear sight copied from the ZB design. The quick-change barrel was heavily ribbed throughout its length and, somewhat incongruously, a bayonet boss on the gas cylinder allowed a large sword bayonet to be attached. One of the approved doctrines with this weapon was to sling it from the shoulder so that it could be fired from the hip during the assault, and in this role the bayonet was usually fixed. It was probably quite useless as an offensive weapon, but it may have served to hold the muzzle down and thus make the gun easier to control.

Another change from the Taisho 11 was

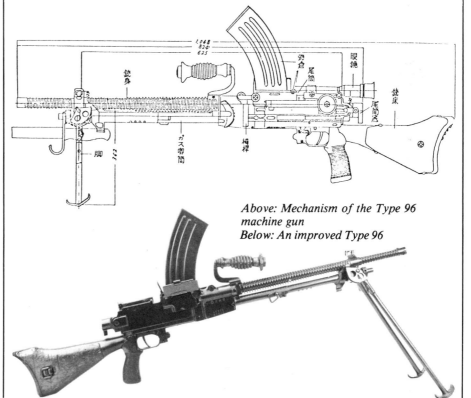

Above: Mechanism of the Type 96 machine gun
Below: An improved Type 96

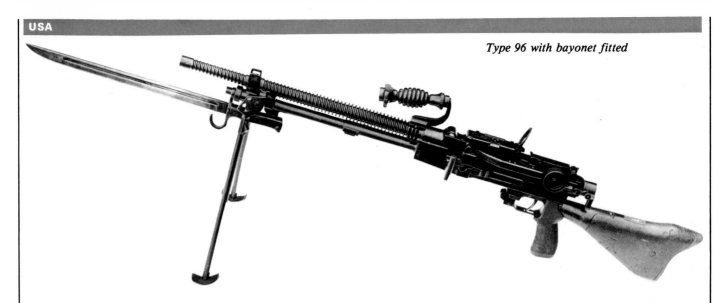

Type 96 with bayonet fitted

the removal of the cartridge oiling system. But since the action was the same, the rounds still required lubrication and this was now done by a combination oiler and magazine loading tool; if anything, this led to a worse state of affairs, since the gun team now ran around with magazines full of oily cartridges which attracted dust and grit like magnets. It comes as no surprise to find that the gun handbook lists 26 different types of stoppage or malfunction as being likely.

One unusual feature of the Type 96 is that it was often found fitted with a low-power sighting telescope. Sighting telescopes are extremely uncommon on light (or any other) machine guns, and there is no satisfactory explanation for it, since the degree of accuracy of this class of gun did not warrant the fitting of such a sight.

Machine gun, Type 99

Caliber 7.7mm
Length 42.0in
Weight 20lb
Barrel 21.65in long, 4 grooves, right hand twist
Feed system 30-round detachable box
System of operation Gas; rising lock
Rate of fire (cyclic) 800rpm
Manufacturer State Arsenals

After using 6.5mm ammunition since 1897, the Japanese Army decided in 1932 as part of their program to expand their East Asian empire in China and Manchuria to change to something more powerful, and after studying various types developed a 7.7mm round more or less copied from the British .303. After this quite logical step, they threw logic to the wind and produced three different cartridges, one rimmed and interchangeable with British .303, one rimless, and one half-way between the two, a semi-rimmed round. There has never been a satisfactory explanation of the reasoning which produced such a logistic horror.

The Type 99 machine gun used the rimless 7.7mm round and was introduced in 1939 with the new ammunition, the rimmed and semi-rimmed types having been put into service in 1932. It was intended to issue the weapon in place of the Models 11 and 96, but production never approached demand and all three guns remained in service, the Type 99 only appearing in relatively small numbers.

Its appearance is virtually the same as the Type 96, since it was little more than a 96 in a new caliber. But one or two internal changes were made, the most important being that at last the need for adequate primary extraction had been appreciated, the breech was designed to give a slow initial opening movement, and at long last the Japanese Army had a machine gun which did not need to have its cartridges oiled. As a result it was one of the most reliable weapons they ever produced. Another addition, this one of doubtful utility, was the addition of a monopod beneath the butt in order to provide a firm base for firing on fixed lines at night.

Type 99, a change in caliber and a slight improvement on the Type 96

Lahti–Saloranta, M1926

Caliber 7.62mm
Length 46.5in
Weight 19lb
Barrel 22.3in long, 4 grooves, right hand twist
Feed system 20-round detachable box or 75-round detachable drum
System of operation Recoil
Rate of fire (cyclic) 500rpm
Manufacturer VKT (Valtion), Jyvaskylo, Finland

Aimo Lahti was a well-known Finnish designer and this light machine gun is one of the better inter-war designs. Although it was purchased for evaluation by many countries only the Finns adopted it in quantity, but it is of interest that a modified version for use by aircraft observers was tested by the Royal Air Force in 1934.

The Lahti was one of the few recoil-operated light weapons to achieve success, and deserves credit for being probably the only one to be successful in combat—though that may be due to the particular combat. It was used in the Russo-Finnish Winter War of 1939–40, in conditions of extreme dry cold for the most part; it is open to doubt whether it would have been so successful in a different environment—the Libyan desert, for example. However it must be said that Lahti's designs all exhibit a concern for protecting the weapon from dust and dirt; the question must remain hypothetical.

The Lahti action relies on the recoil of the barrel on firing; this carries both barrel and breechblock to the rear, locked together until the chamber pressure has dropped to a safe level. At this point the barrel stops, the block is unlocked and allowed to continue rearwards to complete the loading and cocking cycle. While there is much more mechanical movement going on than in the ordinary gas-operated light machine gun, the action is rather more smooth and thus the disturbance of aim is no worse than with other systems.

Little is known of the use or effects of the Lahti during the Winter War, but since the Finns put up a good fight, in spite of the fact that the Soviet Army outnumbered the Finnish Army by an enormous ratio, and since they retained the Lahti in service until the late 1940s, it appears to have been satisfactory.

Chatellerault, M1929

Caliber 7.5mm
Length 42.6in
Weight 20lb 4oz
Barrel 19.7in long, 4 grooves, right hand twist
Feed system 25-round detachable box magazine
System of operation Gas
Rate of fire (cyclic) 500rpm
Manufacturers Manufacture d'Armes de Chatellerault
Manufacture d'Armes de St. Etienne

The French Army were, to say the least, unfortunate in their light machine guns during World War I, and their first priority afterwards was to get rid of the egregious Chauchat and equip themselves with something a good deal better. They had received a number of Browning Automatic Rifles from the US Army and, impressed with the mechanism, decided to develop a machine gun based on a similar action.

The first step, however, was more basic. They had to redesign their ammunition. The 8mm Lebel cartridge was ill-suited to automatic weapons due to its awkward shape, and its ballistics were out-of-date in any case. After some trials, a new cartridge based on the Swiss Army 7.5mm round was adopted, and with this settled, the design of the machine gun proceeded. An early model, the M1924, had been produced for one of the earlier trial cartridges, but this had an unfortunate history of explosions and other misfortunes. The improved design, for the new cartridge, was the Model 24/29 or M1929 and this remained the standard light machine gun until the middle 1950s.

While using the basic Browning automatic rifle action, the bolt being locked by a bolt lock engaging in a shoulder in the roof of the receiver, the whole layout was changed by using a top-mounted magazine instead of the Browning's bottom-mounted pattern. The gas was tapped close to the muzzle and a shock-absorber fitted in the butt, giving a rather less violent action than that of the Browning. One of the more obvious features of the weapon is the provision of two triggers, the front one being for single shots and the rear for automatic fire, thus removing the need to manipulate a change lever.

Supply of the M1929 was slow, but by about 1938 it had completely replaced all earlier machine guns. After the collapse of France in 1940 large numbers were captured by the German Army and put to use by them, notably in arming their occupation forces and coastal defenses in France and the Channel Islands. These defenses were strong in places but remarkably weak when taken as a whole, and in the event they were scarcely used except on 6 June 1944.

Variant
Model 1931 This model used the same basic mechanism but fed from a peculiar side-mounted 150-round drum. It was intended for use in fortresses and other fixed defenses and was also used as a tank gun.

The French Chatellerault Model 24/29

MORTARS

The mortar is generally considered to be the infantry's own artillery, though in fact large mortars—those of over 12cm caliber—have usually been manned by artillery personnel in those few countries which have employed them. It might be opportune to point out here that the word mortar does not always mean what you might expect; the word is one of strict definition. A mortar is a piece of ordnance which fires projectiles at angles of elevation between 45 and 90 degrees. A gun, on the other hand, fires only between zero and 45 degrees, and a howitzer between zero and 90. Thus, on reading that the US Coast Artillery had a 12-inch mortar emplaced in several forts in the latter years of the 19th century, one should not assume that these were smooth-bore muzzle-loaders firing finned bombs. They were quite conventional breech-loading rifled guns firing normal shells, but since they only fired at angles of elevation over 45 degrees they were rightly termed mortars. It is notable that when these same weapons were mounted on railway trucks to be used as heavy artillery in the field, since they could then fire at angles below 45 degrees they were re-named howitzers.

But the infantry mortar is nothing as complicated as that; it is derived from the prototype which Sir Wilfred Stokes put together in 1915 and, indeed, has changed very little since then. Basically it is a smooth-bore tube, closed at the bottom, sitting in a baseplate and supported by a bipod. Some form of elevating apparatus is generally (but not always) provided so that the angle of elevation can be changed in order to alter the range, and a limited amount of traverse is also provided. For greater movements of traverse it is no particular hardship to lift the bipod legs out of the ground and heave them around a little.

The projectile is generally a tear-drop-shaped bomb with fins at the rear to give stability in flight and to ensure that the bomb noses over at the top of its trajectory and descends nose first so that the fuse strikes the ground and detonates the contents of the bomb. Propulsion is by means of a cartridge lodged inside the tail in such a position that when the bomb is dropped tail-first into the muzzle of the mortar and allowed to slide down the barrel, it strikes against a firing pin in the base. This fires the cartridge and the evolved gas blows the bomb out of the barrel. Such a cartridge is the 'primary' cartridge; greater propulsive effort can be provided by the addition of 'secondary' cartridges arranged around the tail so that they are ignited by the explosion of the primary. These secondary cartridges take many forms; generally celluloid containers held in place by springs or rubber bands or by being shaped so that they could be lodged between the bomb fins. In some cases the secondary took the form of sheets of smokeless propellant stitched together;

individual sheets could be torn off to adjust the charge, after which the remains of the bundle were lodged in the tail fins before the bomb was loaded.

Small mortars generally dispensed with secondary cartridges and also had to use another method of firing, since the light bombs and short barrels of this class did not allow the loaded bomb to attain sufficient force to fire a cartridge cap by simply falling on it. In these weapons a trip mechanism was provided, in which the bomb was dropped in and then, when it had settled, a lanyard or lever was pulled to drive a firing pin into the cartridge cap.

Generally speaking the Russians were the greatest mortar enthusiasts, and this, of course, comes back to their great love of keeping things simple. Mortars are cheap and easy to make, their ammunition is cheap and less difficult to manufacture than normal artillery ammunition, they are easy to operate, and for their caliber they deliver a much larger load of explosive on the enemy than a gun. This is due to the fact that mortars are less highly stressed; their chamber pressures are less, there is no rifling to demand strength in the shell side-walls, and the rate of acceleration of the bomb is lower. All this means that the bomb can, in the first place, be made of lower-grade metal; it can be made thinner in section, and thus it can hold more explosive than a gun shell of the same caliber and weight. Then too, the trajectory of the mortar leads to the bomb arriving at the target in a steep fall and standing almost on its nose when it detonates, ensuring a much more even distribution of fragments and blast than can be achieved by an artillery shell. To use the modern jargon, the cost-effectiveness of the mortar is high. There is also another fundamental point about the mortar which attracted the Soviets; it is there, under the hand of the infantry commander, when he needs it. With the Western armies, who had far better communication networks and more highly developed command systems for their artillery, the infantry commander could call for, and get, artillery support from the divisional artillery or from higher artillery formations in a very short time indeed; a British divisional artillery regiment could be brought on to one target in less than a minute, and the whole of the divisional artillery could be brought in in less than three minutes in the latter stages of the war.

The Soviets had nothing like this degree of availability or command of their artillery, and thus the infantry commander in need of fire support looked first to his own mortars. This, by the way, is not to denigrate Soviet artillery—they had far more of it than anybody else and they used it highly effectively, but their system of organization and employment differed considerably to that of the British or American armies, and Soviet artillery was

not freely available at a moment's notice to all and sundry. As a result of all this the Soviets employed vast numbers of mortars, but by far the majority of them were actually manned and treated as artillery pieces, which takes them out of our terms of reference.

Britain and the USA used mortars rather less, since, as outlined above, their artillery organization was far more flexible and placed gun power within the reach of any infantry unit. The situation in the German Army was very similar and was also helped by their liberal allocation of infantry guns. As a result the three 'Western' armies relied on mortars solely as instant support for infantry, providing covering fire, and particularly for short range work where guns could not cope, such as dropping rounds steeply behind cover or into village streets.

It must be mentioned here that towards the end of the war both the British and US Armies began experimenting with radar in an attempt to intercept mortar bombs in flight. Due to the relatively small choice of trajectories open to the mortar, it is possible to extrapolate the form of the trajectory if the bomb can be located at two points in its flight, and this allowed the position of the mortar to be deduced and plotted on a map. Once this was done, it was only a matter of minutes before retaliatory fire was opened by artillery. This technique was in its infancy during the closing months of the war in Europe, using radar sets originally built for the detection and tracking of aircraft, but sufficient experience was gained to point to the desirability of such equipment in the future, and after the war much research was done, leading to the adoption of sophisticated radar equipments which can locate a mortar from a single bomb and produce its position before the bomb has landed. Confronted by this, mortar firing rapidly loses its charm.

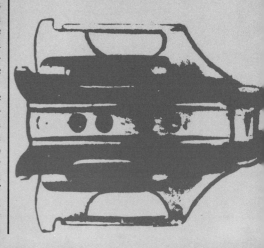

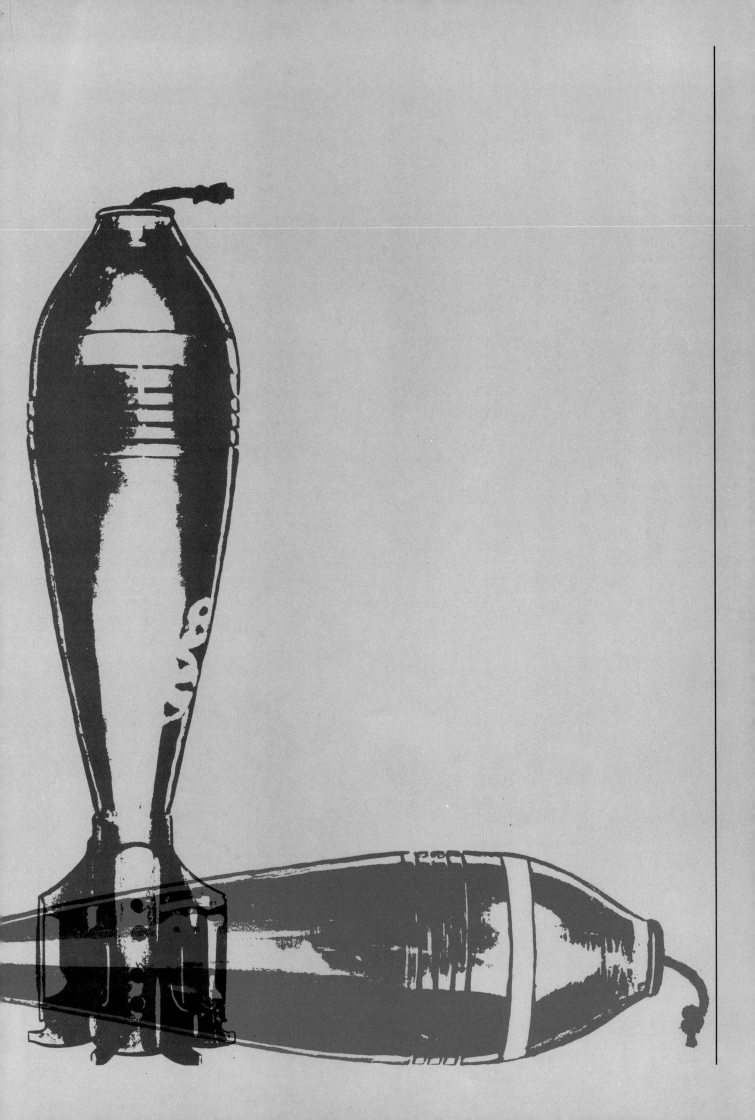

Ordnance, smooth bore, muzzle loading, 2 inch mortar

Caliber 2.0in
Barrel 21in long, smoothbore
Weight in action 19lb (large baseplate); 10½lb (small baseplate)
Firing mechanism Trip
Elevation 45–90 degrees
Traverse
Projectiles & weight HE 2¼lb; Smoke 2lb; Illuminating 1lb 5oz
Maximum range 500yds
Rate of fire 8rpm

During the early 1930s the British Army had engaged itself very industriously in the development of an improved hand and rifle grenade, but the results were disappointing, and eventually it was decided to look into the question of a small mortar or grenade-thrower. A variety of designs was acquired for trial, and the best available appeared to be a Spanish 5cm model made by Esperanza & Cie of Vizcaya. As it stood it was not suitable, and taking this as their starting point, the Armament Research Department finally perfected the 2in mortar. Its trials were so successful that the Director of Artillery, in view of the threatening international situation in 1938, immediately ordered it into production without the usual exhaustive user trials on pre-production models. As a result the weapon was in service in numbers when the war broke out when Germany attacked Poland in 1939.

As originally issued, it was a relatively luxurious weapon, with a large baseplate, a trip firing mechanism, and a collimating sight with elevating and cross-level bubbles. However, wartime experience soon showed that much of the refinement could be dropped; eventually the baseplate shrank to a small curved plate, and the

Firing the British 2-inch Mortar

sight was rarely seen, aiming being done by a white line painted on the barrel to give direction and the firer's experience in estimating the elevation.

The projectile was a simple high explosive bomb with an impact fuse in the nose and a die-cast four-finned tail carrying a single primary cartridge. A smoke bomb of similar outline but without a fuse was also provided, the smoke-producing chemical being ignited through a delay unit by the propellant flash. Later more types of ammunition were provided, including a parachute illuminating bomb, white phosphorous smoke bombs, and a variety of colored smoke signals.

An unusual projectile was a bomb body with a long harpoon-like head with barbs. This was attached to a thin wire and could be fired across suspect areas and dragged back so that the barbs of the harpoon would catch on any trip-wires of mines or booby-traps and thus spring them. Another oddity was a solid bomb with a cable attached which could be fired across a minefield to carry an explosive net which, after landing on the ground, could be detonated so as to set off any mines beneath it by the blast effect.

The 2in mortar formed part of the standard equipment of every infantry platoon throughout the war and was in constant use. In addition it was issued to anti-tank gun detachments to provide them with a way to illuminate their targets at night.

Variants
The 2in went into an astounding number of marks and sub-marks, largely governed by such things as attachments for carriage on various vehicles. The principal types were:
Marks 2*, 2** and 7 Standard pattern with large baseplate.
Marks 2***, 7* Standard pattern with small baseplate.
Mark 8 14in barrel and small baseplate for Airborne troops. The short barrel restricted range to 350yds.

Ordnance, smooth bore, muzzle loading, 3 inch mortar

Caliber 3in
Barrel 51in long, smoothbore
Weight — Barrel 44lb
 — Bipod 45lb
 — Baseplate 37lb
 — In action 112lb
Firing mechanism Drop, fixed striker
Elevation 45–80 degrees
Traverse 5¼ degrees right or left
Projectiles & weight HE 10lb; Smoke 10lb
Maximum range 1600yds (Mk 1); 2800yds (Mk 2)
Rate of fire 10rpm

The 3in mortar was the descendant of the Stokes 3in of World War I, which had been improved in the intervening years. In the 1920s the infantry mortar almost vanished from the British Army, close support being provided by 3.7in pack howitzers of the Royal Artillery, but the questions of manpower and finance raised their heads and the 3.7in howitzer was superseded by this improved mortar.

Since the original Stokes had been the ancestor of all postwar mortars the British 3in was much the same as its foreign contemporaries. It fired a fin-stabilized bomb by means of a charge consisting of a primary cartridge in the tail unit and four secondary cartridges, celluloid tubes containing smokeless powder, tucked between the tail fins and retained by a wire spring. The breech end of the mortar rested on a baseplate, and the muzzle end was supported by a bipod with screw elevating and traversing arrangements. To reduce the effect of firing shock on the mounting, the barrel was free to slide in the yoke of the bipod and was controlled by two tension springs clipped to a barrel band.

As originally developed the mortar had a maximum range of 1600 yards but, like every weapon since the dawn of time, the users were soon asking for more range. By adopting a slightly heavier barrel of stronger steel and a stronger baseplate it was found possible to adopt a six-secondary propelling charge which sent the bomb to 2800 yards, and this Mark 2 model became standard.

Much experimental work was done during the war in an endeavor to obtain even greater range; a barrel in 40-ton steel was developed but with the extra propelling charge necessary to reach the target of 4000 yards, this barrel began to bulge. A fresh design in 50-ton steel was then made, and this withstood firings but the accuracy was far below the standard the users were willing to accept. Eventually, in 1945, it was agreed that trying to extract more performance from this design was a forlorn hope, and work began on the development

Right: Mortar platoon of the Dorset Regiment firing their 3-inch mortar in Normandy, 1944

Mortars

The British 3 inch mortar about to be loaded

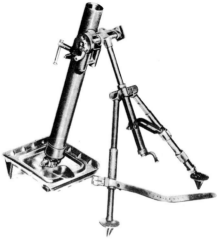

The US 60mm Mortar M2

of an entirely new mortar, work which, after many experimental models in a variety of calibers, resulted in the present-day 81mm mortar.

Variants

As with the 2in mortar, there were a number of minor variations on the 3in which were largely concerned with special clips and brackets to suit particular methods of transportation.

The Canadian Army developed a model with an 81in barrel which, it was hoped,

would give longer range; but the increase was only 300yds, and the weight had gone up by 32lbs, so on balance the change was not worth it and the design was dropped.

The Australians, on the other hand, were more concerned with lightness and portability in the jungle than with extremes of range, and their development was a version with a barrel only 30in long. This led to some difficulty in obtaining accuracy, and eventually special fast-burning cartridges had to be produced to suit this short mortar. It was only made in small numbers and was never adopted outside the Australian Army.

cap and fixed firing pin, while the Mount M2 comprises baseplate and bipod with traversing and elevating mechanisms. Sighting was by the 'Sight, Collimator M4' which carried deflection and elevation scales and was mounted on a special bracket on the mount traversing head.

The ammunition provided included the high explosive shell M49A2 of 2.94lbs, a practice shell M50A2 similar to the HE shell but containing only a small charge of gunpowder to give a smoke puff on impact, and an Illuminating shell M83. This carried a 100,000 candle-power star unit suspended from a parachute, and gave illumination for 25 seconds while falling to the ground. This shell was used in considerable numbers to provide battlefield illumination at night so that machine guns and other squad weapons could see their targets. The mortar was also issued to anti-tank gun detachments for the same purpose.

Variants

Mortar M1 on Mount M1 was the original French-manufactured model, purchased in small numbers for evaluation and later issued for service. It was almost identical with the M2, the only changes in the latter being for manufacturing convenience, ie, the adoption of standard American threads and tolerances.

USA

Mortar, 60mm M2 on mount M2

Caliber 60mm
Barrel 28.6in long, smoothbore
Weight—Barrel 12.8lb
　　　　—Bipod 16.4lb
　　　　—Baseplate 12.8lb
　　　　—In action 42lb
Firing mechanism Drop, fixed striker
Elevation 40–85 degrees
Traverse $3\frac{1}{2}$ degrees right or left
Projectiles & weight HE 2.94lb
Maximum range 1985yds
Rate of fire 18rpm

During the course of World War I the US Army adopted a variety of British and French mortars and rifle grenades, none of which was satisfactory. In the 1920s research began to find some form of light mortar or grenade thrower.

The 60mm mortar was a French design by the Edgar Brandt company, and to all intents and purposes it is no more than a

scaled-down model of their 81mm model. After evaluation of a number supplied by Brandt, a licence to manufacture was obtained and the drawings modified to United States Standards, after which manufacture began in the USA.

The weapon, while similar in tactical use to the British 2in, is heavier and somewhat more complex. It consists of barrel, breech

Left: Burma 1944 and one of Merrill's Marauders cleans his 60mm mortar before going into action
Right: The US 60mm mortar in action

Mortar, 81mm M1 on mount M1

Caliber 81mm
Barrel 49.5in long, smoothbore
Weight—Barrel 44.5lb
   —Bipod 46.5lb
   —Baseplate 45.0lb
   —In action 136.0lb
Firing mechanism Drop, fixed striker
Elevation 40–85 degrees
Traverse 5 degrees right or left
Projectiles & weight HE M43 6.87lb; HE M36
10.62lb; Smoke M57 10.75lb
Maximum range 3290yds (HE M43); 2558yds
(HE M36); 2470yds (Smoke)
Rate of fire 18rpm

The United States Army adopted the
Stokes 3in mortar in 1918 and retained
numbers of them after the war ended. As
the Stokes, in its 1918 guise, was a trifle
primitive, work began in 1920 to improve
it, with particular emphasis on improving
the accuracy of the finned bomb. While
this work was in progress the French company of Edgar Brandt had developed an
81mm mortar based on Stokes' design, and
they offered this model to the US War
Department for test. As it appeared to meet
the specifications stated by the Army, a
number were purchased for evaluation.
Subsequent tests proving successful, the
manufacturing rights were purchased from
Brandt and the weapon entered US service
in the early 1930s.

It was originally provided with two high
explosive bombs, a 'light' and a 'heavy'.
The latter had an unusual type of fin
assembly consisting of four fins, each with
a pair of spring-loaded fins at its outer
edge. These spring units were folded up
and secured by soft rivets until fired, when

Above: Aiming the US 81mm mortar

*The US Mortar Carriage M21, an 81mm
mortar mounted in the back of a half-
track*

the force of the explosion drove a shearing ring forward and cut the rivets, allowing the fins to open out under spring pressure once the bomb had left the muzzle. Once unfolded, the fins were of greater caliber than the bomb, thus they were well out into the airstream to give the bomb excellent stability. While theoretically very sound—indeed, Brandt was some years ahead of anyone else in appreciating the value of super-caliber fins—it was found in practice that the springs tended to lose their tension in storage and the cartridge explosion often bent or warped the fins, leading to unstable or inaccurate flight. As a result this bomb, the M45, was declared obsolete in March 1940 and replaced by the M56 model of the same weight and general appearance but with a cluster of conventional fins.

Variants

There were no variant models of either mortar or mount. However there were a variety of self-propelled carriages provided or proposed which are summarized here:
Mortar Carrier M4 or M4A1 The 81mm mortar installed in the bed of a half-track weapons carrier, firing to the rear.
Mortar Carrier M21 (ex T19) Similar to M4 but firing to the front, over the cab.
Mortar Carrier T27 Project believed to involve a tank chassis; initiated in April 1944 it was closed down shortly afterwards.
Mortar Carrier T27E1 Spin-off from the T27, this was intended to use redundant light tank chassis without turrets. Begun in April 1944 it was closed down about a year later without having shown any results.

USSR

5cm mortars, M1940 and M1941

	M1940	M1941
Caliber	5cm	5cm
Barrel	21.0in long, smoothbore	22.0in long, smoothbore
Weight in action	21.3lb	22.0lb
Firing Mechanism	Drop	Drop
Elevation	both models; fixed 45 or 75 degrees	
Traverse	both models; 9° at 45°, 16° at 75°	
Projectile & weight	both models, HE 1.5lb	
Maximum range	800m	800m
Rate of fire	30rpm	30rpm

The Soviet infantry in the immediate prewar years were confronted with a bewildering variety of small mortars, largely the result of designers trying to tell the Army what it ought to have, rather than the Army telling the designers what they needed. The first 5cm mortar was issued in 1938 and was rapidly withdrawn and replaced by the Model 1939, which in turn was soon discarded in favour of the M1940. This latter model was rather more successful, having been designed with an ear to the Army's complaints about the earlier versions, and it was a much simpler and more effective weapon.

The M1940 was fairly conventional in appearance, using a small baseplate, barrel, and pressed-steel bipod with elevating and traversing screws, but in addition it had a small recoil buffer between the barrel and the bipod yoke, a refinement hardly necessary in such a small weapon. The most interesting technical feature was the system of controlling range. Although the elevation gear allowed setting of any elevation between 45 and 75 degrees, the sights were arranged so that the mortar could only be fired at these two angles, and control of range at each elevation was done by venting a proportion of the propellant gas to the atmosphere, thus reducing the amount available to propel the bomb. The firing pin holder was constructed to act as a spring-loaded poppet valve, the amount of opening of which could be governed by a setting sleeve.

While the 1940 was quite efficient, it was still capable of simplification in the interests of faster production and easier handling, and it was replaced in the following year by the M1941. This dispensed with the bipod and buffer and hinged the barrel to the baseplate. The sights were simplified and the gas system changed to vent through an exhaust pipe below the barrel. The same method of firing at fixed elevations was retained.

Although serviceable enough, and com-

Soviet troops parade carrying their PM41 mortars on manpack carriers, which could be unfolded to form the firing baseplate

parable with the British 2in and German 5cm models, the Soviet 5cm did not see the war through. Its range and effect were satisfactory in a defensive role, but when the Red Army took the offensive its performance was insufficient. In 1941 the infantry division had 84 of these mortars, but by December 1944 there were none, their place having been taken by an increased allocation of 82mm models.

The Soviet 5cm Mortar M1940

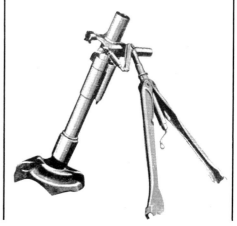

82mm mortar, M41/43

Caliber 82mm
Barrel 48in long, smoothbore
Weight—Barrel 42.9lb
    —**Bipod & wheels** 45.2lb
    —**Baseplate** 41.9lb
    —**In action** 99.2lb
Firing mechanism Drop
Elevation 45–80 degrees
Traverse 3 degrees right or left
Projectile & weight HE 7.4lb
Maximum range 3100m
Rate of fire 15–20rpm

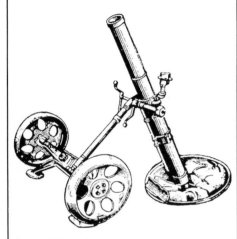

Soviet 82mm Mortar M1943

As with the 5cm model, the Soviet infantry were presented with a rapid succession of 82mm mortars, the Models 1936, 1937 and 1941. The first two were quite orthodox, using the usual baseplate and bipod configuration, and although precise information is unobtainable it seems that their faults lay not so much in their performance as in their design; certainly the M1937 exhibited a baseplate made up from steel stampings welded together and other components showing an eye to mass-production techniques, and it may well be that the successive models merely showed improved constructional methods without changing the performance very much.

The 1941 model replaced all the others and carried the mass-production theme even further; the baseplate was a circular steel stamping, and the twin spring buffers of the 1937 model were replaced by a much simpler single spring pattern contained in a tube beneath the barrel. But the greatest change was in the bipod assembly. Previous designs, indeed all designs based on the normal barrel-bipod-baseplate layout, required that either the three components be carried individually by manpower or that they be carried in some form of vehicle: for example the British 3in was usually carried piecemeal on a tracked Universal Carrier. Neither of these solutions satisfied the Russians; transport was in short supply, and while the soldiers were capable of carrying the component parts, once so loaded they could carry little else, such as their own personal equipment, arms and ammunition. The designers of

this mortar, therefore, adopted a novel solution and formed small stub axles on the lower ends of the bipod legs. On to these axles fitted small pressed-steel wheels, so that the mortar could be trundled along with the barrel and baseplate clamped to the bipod, and brought into action very rapidly without having to re-assemble the whole thing. Once in action the wheels were removed to allow the bipod feet to dig into the ground.

This design was eventually refined by designing the lower section of the bipod so that the wheels remained permanently attached, being so located that they were clear of the ground when the mortar was in action. As well as saving time, this also placed more weight on the bipod and made the mortar more stable when firing. This version became known as the M1943.

The 82mm mortars were the standard rifle division mortars of the Red Army. Originally the division was furnished with 84, but as the 5cm model declined in importance, holdings of the 82mm were increased and by the end of the war the divisional strength was up to 98 mortars.

Granatwerfer 36

Caliber 50mm
Barrel 19.3in long, smoothbore
Weight in action 30.9lb
Firing mechanism Trip
Elevation 42–90 degrees
Traverse 17 degrees right or left
Projectile & weight HE 1lb 15½oz
Maximum range 500m
Rate of fire 40rpm

The 5cm mortar was part of the equipment of every German rifle platoon at the outbreak of war; it was handled by a three-man squad who carried the mortar and 45 rounds of ammunition between them.

The Granatwerfer 36 was typical of the equipment of the prewar Wehrmacht; a well-designed weapon, well-made of the best materials and immaculately finished. The barrel was attached to the baseplate by a locking pin and could be levelled in-

German 5cm Granatwerfer 36

dependently of the baseplate's orientation. A quick-release gear allowed elevation to be set rapidly, and even a cleaning rod formed part of the basic equipment clipped to the baseplate. For long-distance carriage the locking pin was removed and the elevating gear disconnected, so that the barrel and elevating screw became one load and the baseplate and levelling base a second load. For short moves in action the whole assembly could be lifted and carried by a handle provided on the barrel.

The first issues were provided with a collimating sight, but as with the British 2in, this was dispensed with in due course,

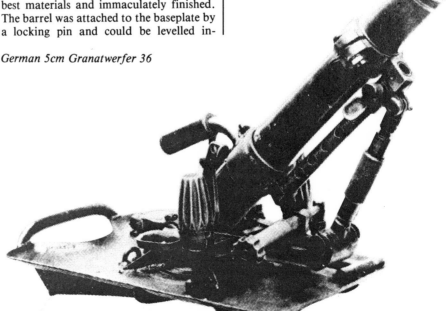

German 81mm Granatwerfer 34

The German GrW 36; steel helmets shield against the muzzle blast

aiming being a matter of the firer's experience. Mortars issued after mid-1938 were never provided with sights.

The 5cm mortar appears to have declined in importance in the German Army much as it did with the Soviets, and it became less used as the war continued, being largely superseded by the Granatwerfer 34.

It is interesting to note that a trial of a captured 5cm mortar was conducted in Britain in 1941, and the report observed that it was, 'well constructed and easy to operate, but the degree of accuracy is unnecessarily high'. This must be one of the few times when a complaint has been voiced that a weapon was *too* accurate.

Germany

Granatwerfer 34

Caliber 81.4mm
Barrel 45in long, smoothbore
Weight — Barrel 40.3lb
     — Bipod 40lb
     — Baseplate 44lb
     — In action 125lb
Firing mechanism Drop
Elevation 40–90 degrees
Traverse 9 to 15 degrees, varying with elevation
Projectile & weight HE 7lb 8oz
Maximum range 2625yds
Rate of fire 15rpm

The 8cm Schwere Granatwerfer 34 was a conventional design of mortar, based much on the Stokes pattern but with a few native variations. It was standard equipment in all rifle companies, two mortars being held

in the 'Granatwerfergruppe'. On the march the mortar was usually carried in a light horse-drawn cart, one member of the detachment being described in the establishment as the 'Pferdführer' or 'horse-leader'. In action the three basic sections were carried by the members of the detachment, together with 21 rounds of ammunition.

The GrW 34 was provided with a range of ammunition which included two remarkable bombs, the Wurfgranaten 38 and 39. These were 'bouncing bombs' which were intended to produce an airburst effect at the target. The 'approved' method of obtaining airbursts is, of course, to provide the bombs with a time fuse, but this means calculation of the necessary time of flight and the setting of each fuse before firing, a time-consuming exercise which has no place in an infantry mortar's operation.

The 'bouncing bomb' resembled a normal bomb in appearance, but instead of the bomb body being a solid casting, the head was separate and pinned to the rest of the body. The body proper terminated in a flat head containing a channel filled with gunpowder, and the space within the head carried a charge of smokeless powder. An impact fuse was fitted in the nose. When the bomb landed at the target, this impact fuse ignited the smokeless powder, which

exploded. The explosion sheared the pins holding the body and head together and blew the body back up into the air; at the same time the flash of the explosion ignited the channel of gunpowder. This filling burned through rapidly and detonated the body of the bomb when it was some 15 to 20 feet above the ground, thus showering the area with fragments.

The rebound action was, of course, highly dependent upon the nature of the ground at the target; if it were soft, the explosion might well blow the nose into the ground instead of sending the body into the air. But on any firm surface it was quite effective. A copy was later developed in Britain for the 3in mortar, but its erratic behavior on soft ground led to the idea being dropped.

Variant
8cm Kurz GrW 42 or 'Stummelwerfer' This was a shortened lightweight version; it used the same ammunition but had the barrel length reduced to 29.4in, and had the baseplate and bipod lightened and simplified. The total weight was reduced to 62lbs and the maximum range dropped to 1200 yards. Originally developed for airborne troops, it was later taken into use by all infantry and largely replaced the standard model. The loss of range was compensated for by easier handling.

Schwere 12cm Granatwerfer 42

Caliber 120mm
Barrel 73.5in long, smoothbore
Weight—Barrel 231lb
         —Bipod 154lb
         —Baseplate 243lb
         —In action 628lb
         —In Transit 1234lb
Firing mechanism Selective drop or trip
Elevation 45–84 degrees
Traverse 8 to 16 degrees, varying with elevation
Projectile & weight HE 34.83lb
Maximum range 6615yds
Rate of fire 15rpm

In the early days of their advance against Russia in 1941, the German Army captured vast quantities of artillery material, much of which was put to use against its former owners. Among this booty were large numbers of the 12cm Soviet Mortar Model 1938; in Soviet hands this was an artillery weapon, but the German Army issued it as an infantry mortar under the nomenclature GrW 378(r). It was successful and well-liked by its new operators, and as a result it was decided to manufacture a German copy, which was issued late in 1942 as the GrW 42. There were some small differences in the German design, both to improve the weapon and to facilitate manufacture by German methods. Thus the maximum elevation of the Russian weapon was only 80 degrees and the traverse 8 to 14 degrees; these were increased. The track of the trans-

Aiming the German 12cm mortar; one man levels the sight while another aims

porter was increased in width for better stability in towing (51cm to 57cm), and the baseplate, bipod and transporter were made rather more robust and thus somewhat heavier—a total increase in weight of about 100lbs in the transit mode.

The design of the mortar was quite conventional. A smooth-bore barrel was locked into a circular baseplate and supported by a bipod with a two-spring shock absorber unit connecting the barrel and bipod together. For movement, a transporter was provided; this was a framework of steel tubing carrying two short axles on which were mounted pressed-steel wheels (perforated in the German model, plain in the Russian) with pneumatic tires. A towing eye at the front end allowed it to be pulled by any convenient vehicle. At the front end of the framework was a circular clamp to hold the mortar barrel, and the rear end was formed into a

A German GrW 42 12cm mortar about to be loaded with a high explosive bomb

U-shape which fitted into two brackets on the baseplate of the mortar.

To bring the mortar out of action, all that was necessary was to lift the bipod out of the ground, bring the mortar barrel vertical and swing the bipod around it so that it lay, folded, at the rear of the barrel, and then push the transporter into position with its frame vertical so that the U-brackets locked into the baseplate. The barrel was then pushed forward until it lay in the barrel clamp, where it was secured, and the bipod feet were strapped to a bracket on the frame. By pulling the towing eye downwards, leverage was applied which would lift the baseplate from the ground and the unit was ready to travel. Bringing the mortar into action was simply the reverse process.

Italy

Brixia mortar, Model 35

Caliber 45mm
Barrel 10.2in long, smoothbore
Weight in action 34lb
Firing mechanism Trip
Elevation 45–85 degrees
Traverse Nil
Projectile & weight HE 1lb
Maximum range 585yds
Rate of fire 25rpm

Italy produced some peculiar weapons during the war, and among them was this mortar, probably the most complicated machine ever devised for throwing 2½ ounces of explosive to less than 600 yards.

To start with the weapon is a breech-loader; it consisted of two concentric tubes, the inner one being the barrel and the outer forming the breech cover, both tubes having a slot in their sides through which, when they were aligned, a bomb could be placed into the barrel. A magazine of propelling cartridges was also attached to the breech assembly, and operation was done by a large 'actuating lever' which lay alongside the barrel. The operator pulled this to the rear, which slid the breech cover rearwards and aligned the two loading ports. The second member of the team dropped a bomb through the port into the breech end of the barrel, whereupon the operator pushed the lever forward, closing the breech and loading a cartridge into a small firing chamber. He then fired by squeezing a trigger with his other hand.

In order to have room for all this mechanical performance, it was necessary to have the mortar suspended on a tripod, leaving room beneath for the breech mechanism and firing trigger and for the movement of the breech cover. Elevation was done by a handwheel operating a toothed arc attached to the barrel, and the sights were simply a barleycorn front and aperture rear similar to those of a rifle. Traversing was done by simply shifting the whole affair about on the ground.

The Italian Brixia Model 35; opening the breech

To add to the complication—and the weight—a padded pack-board was provided, to which the weapon could be attached and then folded up so that it could be carried on a man's back, the padded section easing the burden on his spine. It could be unfolded, still attached to the carrier, whereupon the firer sat on the padded section and operated the mortar rather like, as one description aptly puts it, 'a man on a rowing machine.'

As well as altering the range by changing the mortar's elevation, a gas port was also used; by opening or closing this, gas could be vented and the propelling force altered. With the port fully open the maximum range was reduced to 350 yards.

The projectile was a streamlined finned bomb with a filling of 2½ ounces of TNT-dinitronaphthalene mixture, a winding of steel wire to increase fragments, and a wind-vane-armed fuse which is probably the most complicated design ever seen on a mortar projectile.

All in all the Brixia 35 was one of the less successful mortars. It rarely figures in wartime reports and it is believed that, except for the early part of the Libyan campaign, it was rarely used.

Italy

81mm mortar, Model 35

Caliber 81.1mm
Barrel 45.3in long, smoothbore
Weight—Barrel 47lb
—**Bipod** 39.7lb
—**Baseplate** 44.1lb
—**In action** 129lb
Firing mechanism Drop
Elevation 45–85 degrees
Traverse 5 degrees right and left
Projectile & weight HE (light) 7.2lb; HE (heavy) 15.13lb
Maximum range 4430yds (light) 1640yds (heavy)
Rate of fire 18rpm

The Italian 81mm Model 1935 is virtually the same weapon as the US Army 81mm M1, since both were derived from the same Brandt design. The US model differed slightly from the original, due to changes for manufacturing convenience, but the Italian weapon was substantially Brandt's design. As such, the data above exhibits some differences from the US model; the American barrel was lighter and elevated from 40 degrees; the US bipod and baseplate were heavier; but the Italian model outranged the US by some 600 yards with its light bomb, while the American outranged the Italian by 900 yards with its heavy bomb. The bombs are virtually the same, differences in weight being accounted for by different grades of metal and types of explosive in use by the different countries, and the range difference stems from different composition of the propelling charges and probably, in the case of the light bomb, indicates a somewhat lower factor of safety in the Italian design.

Japan

Mortar, Type 89

Caliber 50mm
Barrel 10in long, rifled, 8 grooves, right hand twist
Weight in action 10lb 1oz
Firing mechanism Trip
Elevation 45 degrees
Traverse Nil
Projectile & weight Grenade, 23oz; HE Shell 28oz
Maximum range 700yds
Rate of fire 25rpm

The Mortar Type 89 was more properly known as a 'Grenade Discharger', and it also received the sobriquet 'The Knee Mortar' which led to considerable misfortune. The weapon was extremely simple but ingenious with it, and was an inseparable part of every Japanese platoon, being much preferred to the other designs of 50mm mortar—which is hardly surprising.

Range control was done by screwing the support rod up into the barrel. This rod carried the firing pin inside, so that when the bomb or grenade was loaded into the muzzle it only dropped as far as the screwed-in rod allowed, being fired from that point. Thus there was a variable chamber space for the propelling gas to expand in; the greater the space to be filled, the less pressure was available to drive the projectile.

The support rod terminated in a very small curved spade, and it was this which led to trouble among Allied troops. During the early part of the war against Japan, the British 2in had the large baseplate, and the small spade of the Model 89 was unusual. It was the habit of the Japanese troops to carry the mortar strapped to the leg of the mortar-man, and from this it appears to have been called the 'Leg Mortar'. An unfortunate translation by an Allied intelligence unit turned this into 'Knee Mortar', and the belief arose that the approved method of operation was to kneel on one knee, place the curved spade on the other thigh, and thus fire the mortar; there appeared to be no other justification for the small spade, and it had just the right curvature. Unfortunately a number of Allied soldiers tried this and suffered broken thighs as a result; after a few such accidents an official announcement was made that 'This weapon is *not* to be fired from the thigh'.

The projectiles were either a shell, designed for the weapon, or the standard Type 91 Hand Grenade. It will be noted from the data given above that the weapon was also unusual in being rifled; the shell was provided with a copper driving band surrounding a propellant container which was perforated at the rear to allow gas to escape for propulsion, and was also perforated radially, beneath the driving band. When dropped into the muzzle the band was of small enough diameter as not to engage the rifling, but when the firing pin was released, it struck a percussion cap in

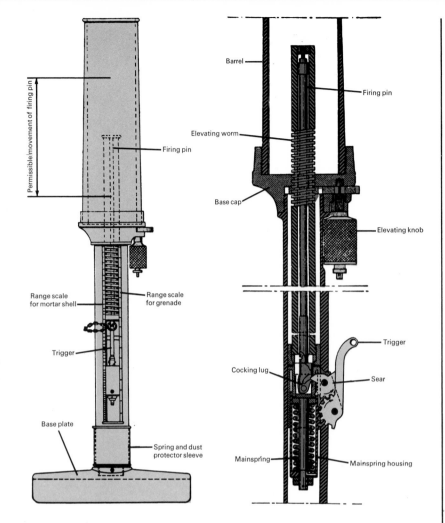

Section drawing of the Type 89 mortar showing the method of range adjustment Japanese troops in Malaya, a 'knee mortar' in the foreground

the base of the shell which ignited the propelling charge. This blew gas through the radial holes and expanded the driving band into the rifling. At the same time the gas escaping from the rear holes filled the chamber area and expelled the bomb.

The hand grenade had, of course, no driving band. A small propellant container with percussion cap was screwed on to the base of the grenade to convert it for this role. Due to the lack of efficient sealing, the maximum range when firing the grenade was much less than that obtained when firing the shell.

Japan

Mortar, Model 98

Caliber 50mm
Barrel 25.6in long, smoothbore
Weight—Barrel 16.3lb
— **Baseplate** 33lb
— **In action** 48lb
Firing mechanism Friction primer
Elevation 40 degrees, fixed
Traverse 10 degrees right or left
Projectile & weight HE 14.1lb
Maximum range 400yds
Rate of fire 5rpm (estimate)

The Model 98 is a surprisingly primitive weapon when one considers it was introduced in 1938; it would have been more at home in 1915, firing jam tins. It seems to have been designed with the intention of providing the most simple and foolproof weapon possible, and yet one with a most devastating effect at the target.

The mortar is a simple construction of barrel, baseplate and bipod; the bipod feet ride in a traversing arc at the front of the baseplate and there is no means of adjusting the elevation which is fixed at 40 degrees. There is a vent-hole at the rear end of the barrel, reminiscent of an old-time smooth-bore cannon, and two hooks protrude at the sides of the barrel-bipod clamp. Around the muzzle is clamped an adjustable range scale in the form of a graduated rod which protrudes beyond the muzzle.

The projectile is most peculiar; a square box holding about 7lbs of Shimose (picric acid) explosive, attached to a stick. In the base of the explosive container are two holes, and into these screwed two friction igniters with pull-cords. The propelling charge was supplied in the form of small silk bags of gunpowder, and one or more of these, depending on the range required, was dropped down the barrel. Then the range scale was set, according to the charge in use, which caused a greater or lesser amount of the scale rod to extend past the muzzle. The stick of the projectile was now entered into the muzzle; due to the projecting range scale, the entry of the stick was stopped when the range scale touched the

Japanese 50mm Type 98 Mortar

Japanese 81mm Type 99 Mortar

base of the explosive container. This, of course, determined the chamber volume and thus the range was controlled.

The strings of the two friction igniters were now looped around the hooks on the barrel clamp. Another friction igniter was inserted into the vent in the breech end, and its string pulled to fire the igniter and ignite the propelling charge, launching the bomb. As the bomb left the mortar, so the two strings on the friction igniters in the explosive charge were pulled free, igniting delay trains in the explosive unit which burned for seven seconds before detonating the 7lb charge.

Obviously this form of fusing meant that for the best results one should adjust one's position and range so that the bomb landed just as the fuses burned through, and this is probably the reason why the Model 89 grenade launcher was more often used. While the 7lb charge gave a very effective result at the target, particularly against defensive works, the weapon was too inflexible.

Japan

Model 99 mortar

Caliber 81mm
Barrel 25.25in long, smoothbore
Weight—Barrel 17.5lb
   —Bipod 16.5lb
   —Baseplate 18lb
   —In action 52lb
Firing mechanism Selective drop or trip
Elevation 45–70 degrees
Traverse 16 degrees
Projectile & weight HE 6.93lb
Maximum range 2200yds
Rate of fire 15rpm

The Japanese Army adopted an 81mm Mortar, the Model 97, in 1937, though it seems that few were used. It was adapted from the familiar Stokes-Brandt model, and except for one or two minor changes it was the same as that used by the United States and Italian Armies. It was in fact known, somewhat confusingly, as the 'Model 97 High Angle Infantry Gun'. But due to its size it was not popular, and in 1939 a shortened version, known as the '99 Model small trench mortar' was introduced. It is remarkably similar to the German 'Stummelwerfer', and it may well be that the Germans adopted the idea after seeing the Japanese weapon.

The 81mm barrel was shortened and a new baseplate and bipod produced to suit the new dimension. The result was efficient and was a handy weapon with good performance. The original Type 97, like the other Brandt designs, was provided with two bombs, light and heavy; documentary evidence suggests that both were made available for the Model 99, but no report can be found which confirms the use of the heavy bomb in service, and it is believed that only the light bomb was ever used with the short model mortar.

The firing mechanism is of interest. The firing pin could be locked in position, protruding from its housing; in this mode the bomb could be drop-fired. As an alternative, the firing pin could be retracted into the housing until its base rested on a conical shaft which passed across the base cap and protruded from the breech end of the mortar at right-angles to the barrel axis. The bomb was now dropped down the barrel until it came to rest with its cartridge cap poised above the firing pin housing. To fire, the end of the cross-shaft was struck with a wooden mallet; this drove the shaft in and, due to its conical section, forced the firing pin up to strike the cartridge cap.

As well as high explosive bombs, the Type 99 could fire a white phosphorous smoke bomb, a green signal flare and a parachute smoke signalling bomb.

Japan

Mortar, Type 94

Caliber 90mm
Barrel 47.8in long, smoothbore
Weight—Barrel 74.5lb
   —Bipod 73lb
   —Recoil system 104lb
   —Baseplate 88.5lb
   —In action 340lb
Firing mechanism Drop
Elevation 45–70 degrees
Traverse 10 degrees
Projectile & weight HE 11.5lb
Maximum range 4050yds
Rate of fire 15rpm

The Type 94 was a heavy and complex weapon, a surprising piece of equipment to find in the Japanese Army where simplicity and lightness were the usual keynotes. But due to its massiveness, and particularly to its very effective recoil system, it was an outstandingly successful and effective

weapon. However, it was relatively uncommon, and there do not appear to have been very large numbers manufactured.

The general design of the weapon was conventional, except for the inclusion of two hydro-pneumatic recoil cylinders. These were attached to a U-shaped yoke which rested on the baseplate. The lower end of the barrel was attached to a crosspiece which in turn was attached to the lower end of the recoil cylinders. The piston rods of the recoil system were attached to the barrel band and also to two spring shock-absorbers at the top of the bipod.

On firing, the barrel recoiled inside the barrel band, forcing the cross-piece down and thus pulling on the recoil cylinders. The cylinders moved rearward relative to the piston rods, displacing liquid and compressing air which, after absorbing the recoil thrust, returned the barrel to the firing position. The total length of the recoil stroke was 5.75in.

Although on the face of it this is an unnecessary complication to add to a mortar, it had the advantage of somewhat reducing the blow on the baseplate, which probably meant the plate was not driven so deeply into the ground when firing and was thus easier to remove when required.

In addition to the customary high explosive bomb, this weapon fired an unusual incendiary bomb containing white phosphorus, carbon disulphide and about 40 pellets impregnated with the incendiary composition. A small explosive charge in the nose served to burst the shell and scatter the contents. This projectile appears to have rarely been used during the war, and was apparently developed for use in China in the 1930s where its effect on Chinese villages would have been most marked.

Bombs for the 90mm Type 99 Mortar

INFANTRY GUNS

The infantry gun is largely a Continental concept, and in its modern form was born of World War I; there had been infantry-accompanying guns in the 17th century, but during the 18th and 19th centuries the establishment of regular artillery concentrated guns into the hands of specialists and left the infantry to get on with their own affairs. During the 1914–18 fighting the German and Austro-Hungarian Armies introduced the practice of giving light artillery pieces, especially mountain guns, to the infantry so that they could carry or drag them forward during the advance and bring them to bear against any unexpected obstacle. The idea was later taken up by the French who introduced a small 37mm Trench Cannon capable of being pulled by two men on a light wheeled carriage or mounted on a tripod for defensive firing from behind cover. This gun was also adopted by the United States Army in 1917.

In the British Army the mortar was con-

sidered quite sufficient, although in 1918 a '1.59-inch Crayford Aeroplane and Trench Gun' was developed by Vickers Son & Maxim. This was accepted for service but was only used in aircraft and never reached the trenches.

During the years between the wars the British Army examined the infantry gun idea and decided against it, relying on the 3-inch mortar, but Germany and other Continental nations decided in favor, considering that direct-fire ability was an asset. At the same time the general adoption of tanks led to numerous trials of lightweight weapons for the infantry, both heavy anti-tank rifles and light cannon. Only in Britain did the infantry rebel; they considered that they had enough on their plate as it was, without being asked to operate anti-tank guns as well, and in 1938 the 2-pounder anti-tank gun was taken from

them and given to the Royal Artillery who found themselves called upon to produce anti-tank regiments overnight. From then on, throughout the war, anti-tank defense with guns was primarily the responsibility of the gunners; a number of infantry regiments did acquire 6-pounder anti-tank guns, and therefore this weapon is included here, but the 2-pounder and 17-pounder remained in artillery hands until after the war. When it was eventually given back to the infantry, the weight of the gun confirmed their worst fears and doubtless accelerated the provision of recoilless guns.

The recoilless gun came into prominence during the war years, and due to its lightness and short range was invariably given to infantry in the first place. Then, as the guns followed the usual tendency to get more complicated and heavier, these larger models were destined for artillery

use, but since none of them ever got past the prototype stage the RCL gun has remained primarily infantry.

As with everything else, the difficulty is to know where to stop; sooner or later during the war, units came into possession of weapons and equipment which they were never meant to have and which never figured on their Table of Organization. Thus we cannot be certain that somewhere on the Russian Front some enterprising German infantry battalion might not have organized a 21cm gun for some private enterprise. But for the sake of space we have had to resist the temptation to include the 'possibles' and confine our attention to the 'probables'. Goodness knows, there are enough of them to make the student wonder where all the men came from to man them.

Ordnance, quick-firing 6-pounder, 7cwt, Mk 2, on carriage, Mks 1, 1A or 2

Caliber 2.244in
Length of barrel 100.95in
Rifling 24 grooves, uniform right hand twist, 1 turn in 30 calibers
Breech mechanism Vertical sliding block, semi-automatic, percussion
Weight in action 2521lb
Elevation From −5 to +15 degrees
Traverse 45 degrees each side of centerline
Projectile & weight Armor-piercing shot, 6lb 4oz
Propelling charge 1lb 13½oz Cordite in brass case. Fixed round
Maximum range 5500yds
Muzzle velocity 2675ft/second
Penetration 74mm at 1000yds at 30 degrees striking angle

The 6-pounder anti-tank gun was originally designed in mid-1938 as a potential replacement for the existing 2-pounder, but the production facilities available at the time were insufficient to allow it to be manufactured, a greater priority being accorded to other weapons. In November 1939 the pilot models were ordered and by August 1940 they had successfully completed firing and travelling trials, but by this time the production prospects were even worse. The vast losses in equipment at Dunkirk had to be made up; production allotted to the 6-pounder would mean taking over factories at present engaged in turning out the 2-pounder, and a 2-pounder in the hand was worth any number of 6-pounders in the future. However, an order for 40 guns was placed by the Army and this was later increased by the Ministry of Supply to 400, to be produced as and when factories could be found. By March 1941 sufficient guns had been made for them to be issued for user trials, as a result of which the traversing mechanism was removed to allow the gun to be freely traversed by the gunlayer pushing and pulling on the breech. By late 1941 issues to units began, and by April 1942 production reached 1500 guns per month.

During 1942 various forms of muzzle brake were tried and in October a single-baffle swaged pattern was approved. At the same time a longer barrel had been designed, and this new barrel fitted with muzzle brake was issued as the Mark 4 gun; the increase in length was 16 inches and this brought with it an increase in muzzle velocity to 3020ft/sec.

Subsequent improvement was in the ammunition; the original armor-piercing (AP) shot was replaced in turn by armor-piercing capped (APC) and armor-piercing capped, ballistic-capped (APCBC) in order to give better performance against the face-hardened armor plate used on the German PzKpfW IV. A composite rigid (APCR) shot with a tungsten core was developed and issued briefly but it was rapidly superseded by the first discarding sabot (APDS) round early in 1944; with this projectile the original penetration performance was doubled.

The 6-pounder was originally intended as the armament for Royal Artillery Anti-tank Regiments, to which the vast majority were indeed sent, but once these units were up to strength a small number were issued to infantry units. They were well-liked, being small and handy but with a respectable performance, and the infantry units made good use of them. Probably the most spectacular action was that of the 2nd Bn The Rifle Brigade who, in the initial battles round El Alamein, destroyed 37 tanks with its 6-pounders, a total so incredible that an official enquiry was held to verify it, and the Commanding Officer received the Victoria Cross.

Variants
There have been 33 different 6-pounder guns in British service since 1885, and the tank and anti-tank guns of World War II must always be referred to as 6-pounder 7-cwt in order to avoid confusion. Of this type, the following marks entered service:
Mark 1 Original development model; only in service for trials
Mark 2 Production model towed anti-tank gun
Mark 3 As Mark 2 but for tank mounting
'C' Mark 3 Mark 3 manufactured in Canada
Mark 4 Improved Mark 2; barrel 16in longer and fitted muzzle brake

'C' Mk 4 Mark 4 manufactured in Canada
Mark 5 Improved Mark 3; barrel 16in longer and fitted with muzzle counterweight
'C' Mk 5 Mark 5 manufactured in Canada
The last 6pr 7cwt guns were declared obsolete in July 1960

Ordnance, QF 95mm infantry howitzer, Mk 2, on carriage 95mm inf how, Mk 1

Caliber 95mm (3.7in)
Length of barrel 74.05in
Rifling 28 grooves, uniform right hand, 1 turn in 25 calibers
Breech mechanism Vertical sliding block, hand operated, percussion
Weight in action 2105lb
Elevation From −5 to +30 degrees
Traverse 4 degrees right and left
Projectile & weight High explosive, 25lb
Propelling charge Three-part cordite in brass case. Separate loading
Maximum range ca 8000yds
Muzzle velocity Ch.1 563ft/s; Ch.2 813ft/s; Ch.3 1083ft/s

The 95mm howitzer was the only infantry gun proposed for the British Army during the war, and its history makes depressing reading. The story opens on 23 January 1942 when the Chief Superintendent of Armament Design proposed a tank or howitzer of 3.7in caliber. There was a grave lack of a suitable support weapon for tanks, and this proposal was well-received. In order to simplify production the barrel was to be made from the standard 3.7in Anti-aircraft gun barrel and fitted with the breech mechanism of the 25-pounder field gun. To simplify fitting it into tanks it was to use the 6-pounder recoil system and fit and balance in the standard 6-pounder turret mounting. It was proposed to use the existing 3.7in mountain howitzer shell, but for various reasons a new shell of 25lbs weight was decided upon instead of the other one proposed.

The British 6-pr in the firing position

Ammunition for the 95mm howitzer. On the left, the cartridge case; center, the propelling charge; right, the 25lb shell

In March 1942 six pilot models of this '3.7in Howitzer Mark 6' were ordered, and in the following month, in order to avoid confusion with the mountain howitzer, the nomenclature was changed to '95mm Tank Howitzer'.

Sometime during the summer of 1942 the idea of an infantry howitzer was born; the records do not show how the thought arose, but a progress summary of 18 November 1942 reveals that two designs of wheeled carriage were being worked on at that time. In April 1943 the pilot models of these carriages were delivered to Woolwich Arsenal to have the howitzer barrels fitted and begin their trials.

These trials showed some serious defects; the recuperator springs in the 6-pounder recoil system were over-stressed and broke frequently, and the gun chambers expanded during firing. A fresh design of spring and a new chamber contour were developed and trials began once more.

These appear to have gone well, since in October 1943 the Director of Infantry accepted the weapon for service. But there were more trials to be done, and in May 1944 it was reported that the wheel track was too narrow and the weapon was unstable when towed across country. At about the same time a conference of infantry commanders was informed of the new weapon, and their response was far

from enthusiastic. The general opinion was that the infantry had enough to do without being called upon to man field guns, and unless the necessary extra manpower came with the guns, the new addition simply was not wanted.

In October 1944 a full report on the development and testing of the weapon was drawn up, which showed that the spring recuperator was still consistently faulty in spite of every effort to find or design springs which would stand up to the work. The Ordnance Board recommended a complete redesign of the recoil system as being the only solution. As a result, on 13 November 1944, the Deputy Chief of the Imperial General Staff minuted, 'In view of the amount of redesign necessary and since, even if redesigned, the equipment will not fully meet the requirements due to the limited elevation, I consider the project should be abandoned.' On 18 April 1945 the 95mm Infantry Howitzer was formally declared obsolete.

In spite of this foregoing history, a surprising number seem to have been built; Ian Hay's *ROF: The Story of the Royal Ordnance Factories* (HMSO 1949) has a photograph taken in Woolwich showing 37 complete equipments ready for issue, and I have seen other photographs of long rows of them parked in open country awaiting the day of battle which never came. Today

only one remains, in a small museum of equipment inside the Central Ordnance Depot at Donington.

Variants
The only proposed variant was put up in October 1943; this was a redesign of carriage to allow elevation up to 70 degrees. It never left the drawing board; action was suspended in April 1944 with the announcement of a new pack howitzer development program which, one might add, also got nowhere.

USA

37mm gun M3A1 on carriage M4A1

Caliber 37mm
Length of barrel 82.5in
Rifling 12 grooves, uniform right hand, 1 turn in 25 calibers
Breech mechanism Vertical sliding block, hand operated, percussion
Weight in action 990lb
Elevation From −10 to +15 degrees
Traverse 30 degrees right and left
Projectile & weight APC 1.92lb; HE 1.61lb
Propelling charge Flashless Nitrocellulose powder in brass or steel case; fixed charge; fixed round
Maximum range 12850yds
Muzzle velocity APC 2900ft/sec; HE 2600ft/sec
Penetration 2.0in 1000yds 0 degrees

During World War I the US Army adopted a 37mm French gun as a trench cannon and anti-tank weapon. As time went on its performance fell behind in the race, until it became necessary to produce something better. The 37mm M3 gun was designed shortly before the war, being frankly based on the successful German PAK 36 design.

The weapon was quite conventional, having a split-trail two-wheeled carriage with small shield, but the breech was entirely hand-operated; semi-automatic operation was much more the rule in anti-tank weapons, and its omission here is quite inexplicable. In spite of this, a skilled detachment could reach a rate of fire of some 20 rounds a minute. In order to increase the stability of the weapon in action, firing segments were attached to the axle; these were lowered to the ground and the gun pulled across them so that the wheels were lifted from contact with the ground and the gun was then supported on the segments and the trail-end spades. While theoretically sound, these devices—popular in American design circles at that time—merely add complication and work, and study of a number of photographs of the gun in action show that the segments were rarely used.

The principal employment of the 37mm gun was in the Pacific theater of war. By the time the United States entered the war the 37mm was outmatched by the tanks it

Overleaf: Australian infantry in the Desert firing the 6-pounder anti-tank gun

would have met in Europe; but the Japanese tanks were smaller and vulnerable to the 37mm throughout the war, so that it retained its usefulness. An interesting point was the provision of case shot for this gun, a shotgun-like round filled with lead balls for close-range anti-personnel firing. It was also found to be an excellent method of clearing away jungle foliage and undergrowth to clear fields of fire and flush out snipers.

Variants

Only the M3 series of 37mm guns were an-ti-tank guns; other models were either anti-aircraft (M1), aircraft (M4) or tank guns (M5 and M6).

Gun M3 Original version.

Gun M3A1 M3 with the muzzle threaded and fitted with a five-port muzzle brake. These brakes were subsequently removed, but guns with threaded muzzles remained known as M3A1.

Carriage M4 Original version.

Carriage M4A1 As M4 but with a clutch built into the traverse mechanism so that the gears could be disengaged and the gun swung freely.

Above: The US 37mm anti-tank gun in firing position
Right: On frozen ground it was necessary for the gunners to lie across the trail legs of the 37mm to prevent it sliding backwards when fired

Gun 37mm T32 on Mount T9

Caliber 37mm
Weight—Barrel section 54lb
  —**Breech section** 52lb
  —**Tripod and elevating mechanism** 52lb
  —**Recoil mechanism and cradle** 68lb
  —**Sleigh and top carriage** 38lb
Elevation From −5 to +12 degrees
Traverse 20 degrees right and left
Length of recoil 10 to 12in

The Mount T9 was based on the tripod of the .50 Browning machine gun. Note that 'Sleigh' above means a connection piece between gun and recoil system, not a method of transportation.

37mm Manpack guns

Although few of these weapons saw service and full specifications for them are not available, the development, like that of the British 95mm, is not without interest, as it shows the measures to which the US Army were prepared to go in order to get firepower well forward in jungle warfare.

The proposal for these weapons seems to have arisen late in 1943, after experience in the Pacific area, and in November 1943 a project was begun to develop a light 37mm gun which could be dismantled easily and quickly to be carried among the members of the infantry squad. The chamber was to take the short (5.69in) cartridge of the M4 aircraft gun, and, working at a chamber pressure of 27,000lbs per square inch, it was predicted that it would be able to fire a high explosive shell at 1500 feet per second. A case-shot anti-personnel round was to be developed, and the entire gun and mount (a modified machine gun tripod) to weigh 250lbs. Within six weeks a pilot model was built; 200 were ordered but the trials of the pilot showed it to be unstable on its mounting, so the order was suspended while a redesign was begun. In January 1944, with the re-design complete, authority was given for the limited procurement of 200 'Guns

37mm T32' as they were now known, with the proviso that further development would depend on what the users thought of it.

By July 1944 155 guns had been sent to the Central Pacific area and the procurement order had been increased to 455 equipments, but that appears to have been the end of development of that model. In June 1945 the procurement authority was cancelled since, 'there have been no Theatre requests for extra consignments' . . . Apparently the users didn't think a great deal of it.

Meanwhile in April 1944 work had begun on a T33 model. This was of similar characteristics to the T32 but much lighter; the gun was to weigh 75lbs instead of the T32's 106lbs. When it was finally built, however, this target was not reached, the weight coming out at just under 100lbs. Twelve guns were made, but by the time they were completed the 57mm recoilless gun was ready for issue; since this delivered a heavier shell and weighed a lot less, the infantry preferred it and the T33 project was terminated in September 1945.

The last project was the T10E1, begun in July 1944 in the hopes of getting the weight of the T33 down to 75½lbs; this was terminated before any results were reached.

Gun 37mm T33 on Mount T10

Weight—Tube section 50lb
  —**Breech section** 48lb

The Mount T10 consisted of two light aluminium tubular trail legs with small spades, joined to a tubular upright resting on the ground and carrying the gun cradle at its top. Handles were provided to allow carriage in one piece by four men. Mount T10E1 was similar, with the addition of two small rubber-tired wheels.

High explosive, smoke and HE Anti-tank (hollow charge) shells were designed. By August 1944 production plans were

issued for 2000 weapons and 600,000 rounds of HE, with 200,000 each of HEAT and white phosphorus smoke. In July 1945 the weapon was standardized and first issues were made to the Pacific theater. Both in the island-hopping campaigns and in Burma it saw action. It is believed that one or two early specimens were sent to Europe just before the war ended, for combat evaluation purposes.

Three methods of firing were recommended; it could be fired from the shoulder; or the shoulder rest and hand grips could be unfolded to make a form of bipod support for firing from a prone position; or it could be fitted to the Machine Gun Tripod M1917A1. There was, as with all recoilless weapons, a triangular danger area behind the gun fifty feet deep and forty feet wide.

Variants

There were an enormous number of development models, of which the most important were:

T15E1 The first design, based on ballistic calculations completed in July 1943. The first gun was fired in November 1943. Development of 100 guns and their ammunition was considered in April 1944.

T15E3 Minor constructional differences from E1; Standardized as M18 in July 1945.

T15E13 A T15E3 with the twist of rifling reduced to 1 turn in 30 calibers in an endeavor to improve the HEAT performance. Design approved in March 1945. The trigger mechanism differed slightly from that of the M18, being cable operated instead of rod-operated. Numbers were made and issued, remaining in service as the T15E13 for several years.

USA

57mm recoilless rifle, M18

Caliber 57mm
Length of barrel 61.6in
Rifling 24 grooves, uniform right hand, 1 turn in 25 calibers
Breech mechanism Interrupted lug, percussion firing
Weight in action 44lb 7oz (shoulder fired); 91lb 4oz (tripod)
Elevation From −28 to +65 degrees on tripod
Traverse 360 degrees
Projectile & weight HE 2.75lb; HEAT 2.69lb
Propelling charge 0.93lb Nitrocellulose powder in perforated steel case
Maximum range HE 4340yds; HEAT 4300yds
Muzzle velocity HE 1200ft/sec; HEAT 1217ft/sec
Penetration 3in

American interest in recoilless guns began with examination of captured German weapons and the Artillery Section of the Research & Development Service began work on a 105mm based on a German design. The Infantry Section attempted to produce the lightest possible weapon for infantry use. It was loosely based on the British 'Burney Guns', using a multi-perforated cartridge case which released gas to an annular space around the chamber, from which it was exhausted to the rear through jets in the breech block unit. In addition, the shell driving band was pre-engraved to match the gun rifling, thus reducing the chamber pressure needed to start the shell moving up the barrel. This kept the pressure at the jet nozzles low, so minor variations in ballistics due to charge temperature or manufacturing tolerances would not upset the recoilless 'balance'.

USA

75mm recoilless rifle, M20

Caliber 75mm
Length of barrel 82in
Rifling Uniform right hand, 1 turn in 25 calibers
Breech mechanism Interrupted screw, percussion firing
Weight in action 165½lb
Elevation From 0 to +20 degrees
Traverse 360 degrees
Projectile & weight HE 14.4lb; HEAT 13.19lb; Smoke 15.05lb
Propelling charge Smokeless powder in perforated steel case
Maximum range HE, Smoke 6955yds; HEAT 7000yds
Muzzle velocity HE, Smoke 990ft/sec; HEAT 1000ft/sec
Penetration 4in (estimated)

The 75mm RCL rifle was developed once the success of the 57mm model was apparent and is, in fact, little more than an enlarged model of the 57mm. It used a similar perforated cartridge case and pre-engraved driving band on the shell, and was also mounted on the Machine Gun Tripod M1917A1. Due to its larger size it was not furnished with shoulder rests or hand grips for shoulder firing.

Early development was split between two proposals; one to fire a pre-engraved driving band shell and one to fire conventionally-banded 75mm shells which were already in widespread use and production for other 75mm weapons. This latter idea was dropped, and in October 1944 the first procurement orders were placed, for 1000 guns each with 180 rounds of HE, 90 of HEAT and 30 of smoke ammunition. Although the proposal to use standard shells was dropped, the shell bodies for the HE and smoke shells were those of the standard shells for the 75mm pack howitzer, fitted with pre-engraved bands.

The weapons and ammunition came into supply early in 1945, being standardized in June of that year, and numbers were sent to the Pacific Theater in time to be used before the war ended, although since the war ended in August, they were able to see very little action.

Variants

As with the 57mm there were large numbers of development models; the principal ones were:

T21 The original scale-up of the 57mm weapon.

T21E4 Improved T21 with a new breech mechanism. Re-designed T25.

T21E7 Designation applied to a two-piece design intended to be broken down into small loads. Development began about August 1945 and continued for some time after the war before being abandoned.

T21E13 T21E4 with the rifling twist reduced to 1 turn in 30 calibers in order to improve the hollow charge shell performance.

T25 Since the T21E4 breech components were not interchangeable with the other guns of the T21 series, its designation was changed to T25 and it was this model which was standardized for issue as the M20 in June 1945.

Aiming the US 75mm M20 recoilless gun

USA

57mm gun M1 on carriage M1A3

Caliber 57mm
Length of barrel 117.0in
Rifling 24 grooves, uniform right hand, 1 turn in 30 calibers
Breech mechanism Vertical sliding block, semi-automatic, percussion
Weight in action 2810lb
Elevation From −5 to +15 degrees
Traverse 45 degrees right or left
Projectile & weight AP Shot 6lb 4½oz
Propelling charge Smokeless powder in brass case, fixed round
Maximum range 10260yds
Muzzle velocity 2800ft/sec
Penetration 2.7in/1000yds/20 degrees

American observation of the early stages of the war soon led them to the conclusion that a heavier anti-tank gun than their 37mm would be necessary. In February 1941 the British Government placed contracts in the USA under the Lend-Lease scheme for the manufacture of 6-pounders, and the United States Ordnance Committee authorized the preparation of a set of drawings of the weapon with the dimensions, threads, gear contours and

The US 57mm anti-tank gun in action in France somewhere near St Malo

other engineering features converted to American standards. On 15 May 1941 the design was standardized as the 57mm Gun M1 and production was authorized.

The principal difference between this and the British 6-pounder Mark 2 lay in the length of the barrel; the British barrel length had been governed by the machinery available to make it at the time, but since the American manufacturers had larger machines available, the barrel was increased to 50 calibers. This change was

later adopted in Britain as production facilities for the longer barrel became available.

As with the British model a muzzle brake was later added to give the weapon more stability when fired, this changing the nomenclature to '57mm Gun M4'.

The greatest difference was that the American gun never had the range of ammunition available to the British weapon, only AP and APC projectiles ever being issued for it.

The 57mm gun being loaded in an anti-tank trap position in France during the breakout from the Normandy beachhead

Variants

As noted above, the only gun variant was the M4, which was the M1 with a muzzle brake. There is no record of any M2 or M3 design.

A number of carriage models existed:

M1 Original model with gear-operated traverse and commercial pattern wheels.

M1A1 Wheels and tires replaced by military patterns.

M1A2 Traverse gears removed and gun converted to free-swinging traverse.

M1A3 Towing hook and trail lock assembly changed to a pattern based on that used with the 75mm Gun M2A2.

M2 Addition of a caster wheel to the right trail leg, and minor changes in the positioning of toolbox, trail handles, etc. Some models had firing segments fitted to the axle.

Howitzer 105mm M3

Caliber 105mm
Length of barrel 66.0in
Rifling 34 grooves, uniform right hand, 1 turn in 20 calibers
Breech mechanism Horizontal sliding block, percussion fired
Weight in action 2500lb
Elevation From −9 to +30 degrees
Traverse 22½ degrees right and left
Projectile & weight HE 33lb
Propelling charge 5-part adjustable in brass or steel case
Maximum range 7250yds
Muzzle velocity 1020ft/sec

The 105mm Howitzer M3 represents the United States Army's first and last venture into the infantry gun field. For reasons now difficult to ascertain, some time in 1941 the idea of the 'Infantry Cannon Company' was born, and a suitable weapon was sought with which to arm them. To simplify production and provide a reasonable projectile, 105mm was selected as the desirable caliber, but the standard M2 howitzer was unacceptable on grounds of weight, as well as the fact that the entire output was earmarked for the artillery's use. As a result a cut-down weapon was produced, a short-barrelled 105mm howitzer mounted on a modified 75mm gun carriage. Weighing over a ton less than the standard 105mm M2A2 field howitzer, the M3 was much more maneuverable, but the short barrel and light construction meant that the full seven-part cartridge of the standard weapon was too powerful. Only five charges could be used, which cut the maximum range from 12,205 yards to 7250 and the muzzle velocity from 1550 to 1020ft/sec. To make the weapon more stable when fired, a jack pad suspended from the center of the axle could be

lowered and screwed down so as to lift the wheels clear of the ground and give three-point support.

The Infantry Cannon Companies were formed in 1942 and issued with the M3, and were used briefly in the North African campaign. They were not a successful innovation; it was found that the provision of men for these formations caused man-power problems, and there was nothing that the cannon companies could do that could not be done at least as well by regular artillery battalions. As a result the idea was abandoned and the cannon companies were disbanded. The M3 howitzer was then issued to airborne artillery units where its light weight was a considerable asset and its short range less of a drawback. It was more effective in this role.

Variants

Howitzer T10 Modification to reduce the barrel weight so that it could be man-carried. Used a vertical sliding breech with torsion spring semi-automatic gear. Proposed November 1943 but no results before the war ended.

Howitzer T10E1 As T10 but using a compression spring on the breech gear.

Carriage M3T M3 with tubular trail legs for lightness. Saved 11½% of weight but was too weak for service.

Carriage M3A1E2 M3 with magnesium trail legs. Project abandoned.

Carriage T10 Lighter version of M3 giving 65 degrees elevation and intended to break down for pack transport. Project began November 1943, terminated 1947.

Carriage T16 M3 carriage of aluminum and magnesium. Project began May 1944 but terminated in April 1945 as it was not showing much progress. It will be appreciated that the projects above were largely concerned with lightening the weapon for its airborne role.

45mm anti-tank gun, Model 42

Caliber 45mm
Length of barrel 117.5in
Breech mechanism Vertical sliding block, semi-automatic, percussion
Weight in action 1257lb
Elevation From −8 degrees to +25 degrees
Traverse 30 degrees right and left
Projectile & weight AP 3.15lb; HE 4.72lb; HVAP 1.88lb
Propelling charge Smokeless powder, brass cases, fixed round
Maximum range 5000m
Muzzle velocity AP 2690ft/sec; HE 1125ft/sec; HVAP 3500ft/sec
Penetration-AP 50mm/500m/30 degrees
              -HVAP 54mm/500m/30 degrees

The Soviet Army's first anti-tank gun was the 37mm PAK 37 of the German Army, numbers of which were purchased in prewar years. This was rapidly improved by substituting a 45mm barrel to make the ZIK 37 model, and this in turn was redesigned to become the Model 42.

It is a conventional design of weapon on a split trail carriage, notable for being very low-set and also easily recognizable because of its use of wire-spoked motorcycle wheels, unusual on a gun. However, few of these were issued since soon after it was superseded by the 57mm M43 (ZIS-2) anti-tank gun.

Numerous photographs of this gun were published during the war, but the vast majority of them have the appearance of posed propaganda shots—either that or the selection of anti-tank gun positions by the Soviet Army was governed by suicidal principles. It is doubtful if many were used in action since the performance was poor even by the standards of 1942. The high velocity armor piercing projectile was a tungsten cored 'Arrowhead' shot which ought to have shown considerable improvement in performance over the conventional armor-piercing steel shot, but the figures quoted above, the only performance figures available, point either to a bad design of

The sliding block breech of the Soviet 45mm anti-tank gun
Overleaf: The US 105mm M3 howitzer in the Ardennes

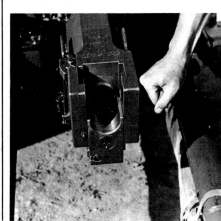

The Soviet 45mm gun backing up an infantry advance in the Caucasus

projectile or wrong figures, since an improvement of only 4mm in penetration for an increase in velocity of 1000ft/second is scarcely credible. The problem becomes more remarkable when the penetration figures for the Japanese copy of this gun are taken into account; the Japanese claimed a penetration of 70mm at 500 meters at normal impact; that is, with the shot striking the plate at exactly right-angles. Allowing for the improvement due to the more advantageous angle, the Japanese obtained better performance with steel shot at 2700ft/sec than the Russian could with tungsten shot at 3500ft/sec. And as the Duke of Wellington said, if you believe that, you will believe anything.

USSR

57mm anti-tank gun, M43 (ZIS-2)

Caliber 57mm
Length of barrel 155.53in
Breech mechanism Vertical sliding block, semi-automatic, percussion
Weight in action 2535lb
Elevation From −5 to +25 degrees
Traverse 28 degrees right and left
Projectile & weight AP 6.92lb; HE 8.27lb; HVAP 3.88lb
Propelling charge Smokeless powder, brass case, fixed round
Maximum range 9200yds
Muzzle velocity AP 3248ft/sec; HE 2295ft/sec; HVAP 4167ft/sec
Penetration–AP 86mm/500m/30 degrees
—HVAP 100m/500m/30 degrees

Once the war began in Europe in 1939, and more particularly after the Winter War against Finland, the Soviet Army realized that their 45mm anti-tank gun was already obsolete. Noting the German increase to 5cm caliber they decided to go one better and adopted a 57mm gun in 1941. By coincidence this is the same caliber as that of the British 6-pounder and American 57mm M1, but too much need not be read into this, since 57mm was a fairly common caliber of light naval and coast gun at the turn of the century, and many nations still had machinery for production of guns and ammunition of this caliber.

Practically nothing is known about the 57mm M41, except that very few were ever made, which suggests it was not particularly good. But the design was used as the basis for the M43 which was a highly successful weapon and which replaced the 45mm model and remained in Soviet service into the 1960s.

The gun itself is notable for its long and slender barrel, and the recoil system is based on the German principle of placing the recoil buffer and the recuperator in separate cylinders respectively above and below the barrel in order to lower the center of gravity of the recoiling parts and promote air-cooling of the cylinders. The carriage is a split trail type using tubular steel trail legs, and is, at first sight, excessively robust for the size of gun, but it was designed with a view to extracting more use from it, and shortly after its introduction on this gun it appeared again as the carriage for the 76mm Divisional Gun M43, thus simplifying production problems.

It is believed that the M43 did not reach the hands of troops in worthwhile numbers until late 1944. Certainly records and photographs of it in action are comparatively rare. The performance figures given above should be treated with some reserve, particularly the velocity claimed for the HVAP projectile; no details of the composition of the propelling charge are known, so that no calculations can be made, but this figure seems somewhat excessive.

Germany

2.8cm Schweres Panzerbuchse 41

Caliber 28mm at breech, 20mm at muzzle
Length of barrel 67.51in
Breech mechanism Horizontal sliding block, percussion fired
Weight in action 260lb
Elevation From −5 to +45 degrees
Traverse 90 degrees at zero elevation, 30 degrees at 45 degrees elevation
Projectile & weight APCNR 4.5oz
Propelling charge 5.35oz, in brass-coated steel case. Fixed round
Maximum range 800m
Muzzle velocity 4593ft/sec
Penetration 52mm/500m/30 degrees

This weapon, the lightest anti-tank gun used by any combatant, was the first war weapon to use the tapered bore principle. Simply put, the idea is that if the gun barrel tapers towards the muzzle, and the projectile diminishes in size as it proceeds up the bore, then, since the base area of the projectile becomes smaller in relation to the gas pressure behind it, the velocity will be increased. Certain other ballistic advantages accrue, all of which point to the advantageous use of the principle in an anti-tank weapon. It was first patented in 1903 but it took thirty years of experimenting to make it work successfully and consistently. The full military development history has never been revealed, but the 2.8cm s.PzB 41 (it was called 'heavy anti-tank rifle' as a security measure) was issued early in 1941.

Obviously the most difficult feature is the design of a projectile which will deform in the tapering barrel, and the secret lies in using a tungsten carbide core carried in a steel sheath. The sheath is provided with two skirt-like centering bands of 28mm caliber, but they are malleable and under the action of the barrel taper would swage back uniformly to the smaller caliber. Holes were drilled in the front band to allow air and gas, trapped between the two bands, to escape during the squeezing process. The use of tungsten carbide as the penetrative core was essential due to the high velocity attained. A core of steel would have worked equally well from the mechanical point of view, but at velocities in excess of 2700ft per second steel would not pierce but would merely shatter on striking a hard target due to the intense shock of impact. Only tungsten could withstand this, and for this reason tungsten carbide became more and more important in anti-tank projectile design as velocities were increased to deal with heavier armor.

As well as a cored piercing projectile, a tiny high explosive shell was also developed for this weapon, using a conventional small shell body and attaching skirt bands to it. Although it worked, it was so small as to be hardly worth the effort.

The 2.8cm was principally used in the Middle East, and, to a lesser degree, in the early days of the Russian campaign. But as

The German 28mm taper-bore gun being tested in a British experimental range

the war progressed its lightweight projectile was less and less effective against newer and heavier tanks, and finally the shortage of tungsten in Germany stopped supply of ammunition in 1942 and the weapon fell into disuse.

Variant

2.8cm S.PzB 41F A version using a light tubular steel carriage with small wheels and no shield, for use by Parachute Fallschirmjager) units. Performance etc, was as for the standard model except that the weight in action was 260lbs.

Germany

3.7cm Panzerabwehrkanone (PAK) 36

Caliber 37mm
Length of barrel 65.5in
Breech mechanism Horizontal sliding block, percussion firing
Weight in action 952lb
Elevation From −5 to +25 degrees
Traverse 30 degrees right and left
Projectile & weight AP 1.5lb; APCR 12.5oz; HE 1.33lb
Cartridge Brass-coated steel case, fixed round
Maximum range 4400yds
Muzzle velocity AP2500ft/sec; APCR 3375ft/sec
Penetration–AP 36mm/500m/30 degrees
　　　　　　–APCR 40mm/500m/30 degrees

This was the standard German anti-tank gun at the outbreak of war. It was more or less on equal terms with its contemporaries and capable of dealing with most of the tanks of its day. It had been developed in the early 1930s by the Rheinmettal Company of Dusseldorf and the first issues were made in 1936. A number were sent to Spain to be used in the Civil War and several were sold to Russia.

The design of two-wheeled split-trail carriage was efficient and highly maneuverable, and the basic layout was widely copied in other countries, notably in

The German 37mm PAK36

the USA and Japan. Its penetrative performance could have been better, but it was sufficient and it was more than compensated for by its mobility.

After 1940 it was outmatched by the improvements in armor and tank guns and it was replaced by the 5cm PAK 38. In an attempt to turn them into something useful large numbers were scrapped and their carriages used for other and newer guns. But according to one German source there were several thousands of these weapons built, and large numbers were retained in service; in the hope of providing them with a suitable anti-tank performance the 'Stick Bomb' or 'Steilgranate 41' was introduced. This was a large hollow charge bomb of 19lbs weight mounted on a stick, with a perforated tail boom carrying fins. The stick was loaded into the muzzle so that the

tail boom and fins surrounded the gun barrel. A special blank cartridge was then loaded and used to fire the stick bomb to a maximum range of 800 meters. Due to its low velocity the normal engagement range was restricted to 300 meters, and the massive hollow charge could penetrate 180mm of armor. It is believed that large numbers of these were used with good effect against Soviet tanks, and certainly some were used against British and American armor in Normandy in 1944, where the close country favored the short range of this weapon.

The normal ammunition was of two types; a steel AP shell with a small explosive charge which detonated after penetration, and a tungsten cored shot.

4.2cm Panzerjägerkanone 41

Caliber 40.6mm at breech, 29.4mm at muzzle
Length of barrel 92.52in
Breech mechanism Horizontal sliding block, percussion firing
Weight in action 1414lb
Elevation From −8 to +25 degrees
Traverse 30 degrees right and left
Projectile & weight APCNR 11¾oz
Propelling charge 15.25oz, brass case, fixed round
Maximum range 1000m
Muzzle velocity 4150ft/sec
Penetration 72mm/500m/30 degrees

The success of the 2.8cm taper bore gun led to the adoption of a second and heavier model which had been under development at the same time. The larger projectile gave a better penetrative performance and did more damage at the target than did the 2.8cm model. In order to simplify manufacture the gun was mounted on the carriage of the 3.7cm PAK 36, and the two guns are very difficult to tell apart in photographs. Production began late in 1941 but due to a shortage of manganese, used in some of the components adapting the gun to the carriage, and to the shortage of tungsten, necessary for the projectiles, production stopped in the summer of 1942 and only a small number were made. So far as is known all guns were used on the Russian Front until their ammunition supply came to an end, after which they were scrapped.

5cm Panzerabwehrkanone 38

Caliber 50mm
Length of barrel 125.5in
Breech mechanism Horizontal sliding block, semi-automatic, percussion
Weight in action 2174lb
Elevation From −8 to +27 degrees
Traverse 32½ degrees right and left
Projectile & weight AP 4.95lb; APCR 1.81lb; HE 4.3lb
Propelling charge Brass-coated steel case, fixed round
Maximum range 2890yds
Muzzle velocity AP 2700ft/sec; APCR 3930ft/sec; HE 1800ft/sec
Penetration−AP 50mm/1000m/30 degrees
　　　　　　 61mm/500m/30 degrees
　　　　　　 88mm/250m/0 degrees
　　　　 −APCR 55mm/1000m/30 degrees
　　　　　　 86mm/500m/30 degrees
　　　　　　 141mm/250m/0 degrees

The design of the 5cm PAK 38 was begun in 1938 but the gun did not reach the hands of troops until late in 1940, when it replaced the 3.7cm PAK 36. Although heavier weapons later came into service, the PAK 38 was never entirely replaced and remained in service until war's end.

It was a conventional enough gun, using a muzzle brake and mounted on a two-wheeled split-trail carriage with a double skinned shield and torsion bar suspension. The ammunition provided was basically a piercing shell, but this was supplemented by a tungsten-cored AP Composite Rigid 'Arrowhead' shot known as the Panzergranat 40. The figures above show the immense improvement in penetration resulting from the use of this projectile; at 250 meters the performance is almost doubled. But they also show the drawback; due to the light weight of the composite rigid shot, its ballistic coefficient (best visualized as its 'staying power' or 'carrying power') was poor, and at longer ranges the improvement became marginal.

As long as the Pzgr 40 shot was available, the PAK 38 was a useful weapon, but in 1942 the worsening shortage of tungsten resulted in available supplies being restricted for use in machine tools. A reserve of Pzgr 40 was allowed for the PAK 38 since nothing else available at that time had any effect on the Soviet T-34 tank, but once heavier weapons became available in numbers, the supply stopped and after that the PAK 38 was of less use. An investigation team which visited the Eastern Front in 1943 reported that, 'the armor-piercing shell is no longer sufficient. Moreover, as an infantry weapon the gun is too heavy and the tractors too high. A change of position during daylight is almost impossible'. As a short range anti-tank weapon the PAK 38 still had its uses, as the Allies discovered in Normandy in 1944, but on the wide-open steppe-lands of the Eastern Front it was of little use.

Variants
There were no variants to this gun in infantry service, but after it was superseded numbers were fitted with automatic loading gear and used in aircraft as flying tank-busters on the Russian Front during the winter of 1944–45. It was also tried as a stop-gap anti-aircraft gun under the nomenclature 'Flak 214'.

The German 5cm PAK38, from the official gun handbook

7.5cm Leichte Infanterie Geschütz 18

Caliber 75mm
Length of barrel 35.43in
Breech mechanism Shotgun, percussion firing
Weight in action 880lb
Elevation From −10 to +75 degrees
Traverse 6 degrees right and left
Projectile & weight High explosive, 13.2lb
Propelling charge Five-part; brass-coated steel case
Maximum range 3780yds
Muzzle velocity 690ft/sec

This was the first weapon to be issued to the German Army after World War I, entering service in 1927. It was a light and handy equipment and used an unusual form of construction. The gun barrel was carried in a rectangular casing which was hinged into another casing which carried the fixed breech block and firing mechanism. When the breech operating lever was moved the rear end of the barrel rose up into the air to leave the breech block and expose the chamber for loading. In this position the extractors locked and held the barrel open; as the cartridge was loaded, its rim pressed the extractors forward, released the barrel and allowed it to drop back into place under its own weight, positioning the cartridge in front of the firing pin. The whole action is reminiscent of a shotgun breech and, although unusual, it was a rapid and simple mechanism.

The carriage was a simple box trail with a shield, the wheels being either wooden-spoked iron-shod, or steel disc with pneumatic tires, depending on whether it was horse or truck drawn.

The le IG 18 was extensively used throughout the war, though its use tended

Right: Soviet soldiers inspect a collection of captured German guns; le IG 18 in the foreground, sIG 33 in the background

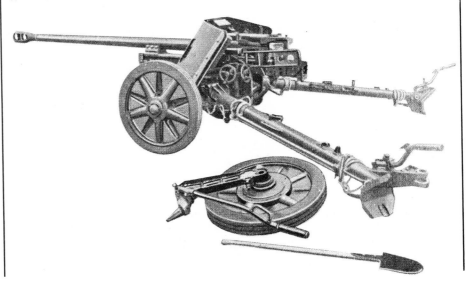

to become less towards the end when heavier weapons, and particularly tracked assault guns, were readily available for front-line support.

Variants

7.5cm le Gebirg IG 18 Introduced for mountain regiments in 1937, this was the same gun but mounted on a lightweight tubular split-rail carriage, with light-weight spoked wheels and no shield. It could be dismantled into six loads for mule transport or ten manpack loads. Its only drawback was that due to its lightness it could only fire the full propelling charge at

ranges above 2000 meters, since below this the angle of elevation meant that the recoil forces tended to make the gun jump excessively.

7.5cm le IG 18F Designed in 1939 for Parachute troops, this was little more than the mountain pattern with smaller wheels. It could be dismantled and packed into four containers for parachute dropping, each weighing about 300lbs. Six weapons were built for trials but the design was then abandoned since by that time the recoilless guns were almost in production and these promised equal performance for less weight.

7.5cm Infanterie Geschütz 37

Caliber 75mm
Length of barrel 70.75in with muzzle brake
Breech mechanism Vertical sliding block, semi-automatic, percussion
Weight in action 1124lb
Elevation From −10 to +40 degrees
Traverse 29 degrees right and left
Projectile & weight High explosive, 13.2lb
Propelling charge Six-part charge, separate loading, brass case
Maximum range 5625yds
Muzzle velocity 918ft/sec

Although numbered '37' this weapon did not enter service until 1944. It was produced in order to provide the infantry gun companies with a rather more powerful weapon than the original le IG 18, and stems not from the IG 18 but from the IG 42 design. Its nomenclature arises from the fact that the carriage is that of the 3.7cm PAK 36; when first introduced it was known as the 7.5cm PAK 37, but since this inferred that it was an anti-tank gun, which

it wasn't, the name was changed to IG 37.

The gun, based on a 1942 Krupp prototype, has a barrel almost twice as long as that of the IG 18 and was fitted with a muzzle brake which considerably reduced the recoil force. The breech mechanism was semi-automatic, a cam opening it when running back after recoil so as to eject the empty case. The block was then held open against a spring until the extractors were forced forward by the loading of the next cartridge, whereupon the breech block automatically closed.

The carriage, as mentioned above, was the tubular split-trail model originally made for the PAK 36, with disc wheels and sprung suspension. The projectiles fired were those of the IG 18, but the propelling charge had a super charge added, a separate loading of 3.5 ounces of smokeless powder which completely replaced the normal charge when maximum range was required.

Due to its late introduction, relatively few of these guns were introduced into service, and most of those appear to have gone to the Eastern Front—and stayed.

7.5cm Infanterie Geschütz 42 nA

Caliber 75mm
Length of barrel 70.75in
Breech mechanism Vertical sliding block, semi-automatic, percussion
Weight in action 1300lb
Elevation From −6 to +32 degrees
Traverse 30 degrees right and left
Projectile & weight High explosive, 13.2lb
Propelling charge Six-part, separate loading, brass case
Maximum range 5030yds
Muzzle velocity 918ft/sec

After the end of the 1940 campaign in France, the German infantry asked if they could be provided with a better weapon than the le IG 18. Their principal complaint was its short range and its ineffective anti-tank performance, and Krupp's proceeded to draw up a design which would give the soldiers what they wanted. This was provisionally called the IG 42, a very efficient looking weapon on a split-trail carriage. But by the time the designs were ready, the hollow charge anti-tank shell was in production, and this gave the le IG 18 a reasonable performance against armor; this, plus the fact that there was a shortage of production facilities which could have been used for building the new gun, meant that there was now little priority claim, and so the IG 42 project was shelved indefinitely.

In early 1944, after experience in Russia, the infantry renewed their appeal, and the project was revived. In order to avoid confusion it was now called the IG 42 nA

The German 7.5cm IG 37, a new gun on an old carriage

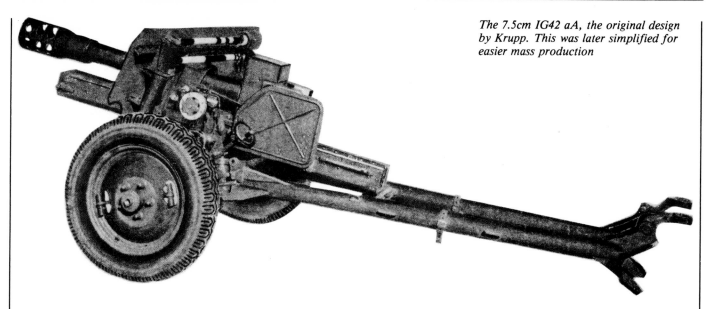

The 7.5cm IG42 aA, the original design by Krupp. This was later simplified for easier mass production

(nA = neuer Art = new pattern) and the gun, slightly modified, was assembled to the split-trail carriage which had been designed for the 8cm PAW 600 anti-tank gun. This was a very simple design which lent itself to mass-production and, being already in production, speeded up the design of the complete equipment. A shield was fitted, torsion bar suspension was used with the solid-tired wheels, and the result, while not particularly handsome, was serviceable enough. The ammunition used was the same as that of the IG 37, the shells of the IG 18 plus a new charge. Its performance in terms of maximum range was less than that of the IG 37, due to a lower maximum elevation, but the soldiers soon found that digging holes to sink the trail ends allowed them to get sufficient extra elevation on the barrel to reach 5625 yards.

It is believed that no more than a small number of these weapons were built; they were quite rare, and the majority of them were sent to the Eastern Front.

were doing. The rubber tires were also unusual; instead of being pneumatic, they were stuffed with sponge rubber and they were therefore impervious to bullets or shell splinters.

There are two minor points of interest in the nomenclature of this weapon. In the first place it is called 'Kanone' rather than 'Geschütz', the more usual term for an infantry gun. In German terminology 'Kanone' indicates a high velocity, flat trajectory weapon, and it is probably applied here because of its limited elevation and the use of a fixed round of ammunition with non-adjustable charge. The second point is that it is termed '7.5cm' although the caliber is actually 7.62cm; this again was a normal German practice, to call a weapon by a nominal caliber rather than the actual measured caliber, and is frequently found in field artillery.

Germany

7.5cm Infanterie Kanone 290(r)

Caliber 76.2mm
Length of barrel 49.5in
Breech mechanism Interrupted screw, percussion firing
Weight in action 1720lb
Elevation From —6 to +25 degrees
Traverse 3 degrees right and left
Projectile & weight High explosive, 13.75lb
Propelling charge 18oz, fixed, brass case
Maximum range 9350yds
Muzzle velocity 1270ft/sec

This weapon began life as the Soviet 76mm Regimental Gun Model 1927, which is reputed to have been the first artillery weapon designed under the Communist regime. Large numbers were captured in the initial German advances of 1942, so many in fact, that the Germans found it worthwhile to overhaul them and send them back to the front as infantry guns. Ammunition was manufactured in Germany, though the vast stocks of Russian ammunition captured kept the supply lines filled until the German production began to come through. The Germans also developed an efficient hollow charge anti-tank shell to replace the rather ineffective armor-piercing shell which the Russians used.

Not unnaturally the gun differed from standard German practice in some features; the breech mechanism, for example, was an interrupted screw block, swinging to the right on opening, instead of the almost mandatory sliding wedge used on German ordnance. The proportions of the carriage look odd, the large wheels (3ft 9in in diameter) looking far too big. But when it came to manhandling the weapon in a Russian winter, the Germans had to admit that the designers knew what they

The 7.5cm Infanterie Kanone 290(r) began life as a Russian divisional gun

7.5cm Leichte Geschütz 40

Caliber 75mm
Length of barrel 45.27in
Breech mechanism Horizontal sliding block, percussion firing
Weight in action 321lb
Elevation From −15 to +42 degrees
Traverse 360 degrees below 20 degrees Elevation, 60 degrees above
Projectile & weight High explosive, 12.85lb
Propelling charge 2.71lb; Brass-plated steel case with plastic blow-out disc in base
Maximum range 7435yds
Muzzle velocity 1150ft/sec

The German Army were the first to make effective use of recoilless guns; a primitive form of RCL had been used by the British Royal Naval Air Service in the latter days of World War I, and there are unconfirmed rumors of a Soviet design which is reputed to have been used in 1939–40.

Design work began in the early 1930s when the Rheinmettal company started work on very heavy models of large caliber for carriage beneath aircraft; stemming from this, development of a field weapon began in 1937 under a Dr. Heinrich Kleine. As with the American weapons the German system relied on discharging a stream of propellant gas to the rear at high velocity and thus producing a force which counteracted and balanced the recoil of the gun due to the projection of the shell.

The actual mechanics of the weapon were, however, quite different. The German pattern used a cartridge case with a breakable plastic base which burst under the pressure of the explosion of the cartridge to allow gas to pass through the hollow breech-block and be vented through a jet nozzle. Ignition of the charge was by a small percussion primer in the center of the plastic disc, which was actuated by a firing pin in a streamlined housing in the center of the breech-block aperture.

The gun was mounted on a tripod with two small aircraft-type wheels, and the whole equipment could be broken down into four loads for parachute dropping. Extensive use was made of light alloy in order to keep the weight of the mounting to the minimum.

The weapon was designed specifically for airborne troops, in order to give them heavy shell-power from a lightweight gun, and it was first used in action in Crete in 1941. After this affair, the importance of the German airborne force declined, and the gun was issued to mountain regiments, being used in the Carpathians and, to a lesser degree, in Italy. Production ceased early in 1944 when 450 had been made, because of a shortage of ammunition. This was due to the excessive amount of propellant consumed by recoilless guns, for in 1944 propellant supply became a critical matter in Germany.

7.5cm Panzerabwehrkanone 40

Caliber 75mm
Length of barrel 145.75in
Breech mechanism Horizontal sliding block, semi-automatic, percussion
Weight in action 3139lb
Elevation From −5 to +22 degrees
Traverse 32½ degrees right and left
Projectiles & weight AP 15lb; APCR 7.04lb; HE 12.8lb; HEAT 10.1lb
Propelling charge Steel case, lacquered. Fixed round
Maximum range 8400yds
Muzzle velocity AP 2600ft/sec; APCR 3250ft/sec; HE 1800ft/sec
Penetration–AP 89mm/1000m/30 degrees
104mm/500m/30 degrees
–APCR 96mm/1000m/30 degrees
115mm/500m/30 degrees

The 105mm Recoilless Gun LG40 fires, showing the disadvantage of the blast

The German Army foresaw the inevitable increase in tank size and strength, and in the summer of 1939 placed contracts with Krupp and Rheinmettal-Borsig for the development of a 75mm gun. At that time the 5cm PAK 38 was beginning its acceptance trials, and since this seemed likely to satisfy requirements for some time to come there was no particular urgency on the 75mm contracts. But after the invasion of Russia in 1942, the appearance of heavy Russian tanks, and particularly the T-34 with its well-angled armor, showed that the PAK 38 was being stretched, and the 75mm contracts were hurried up, so that deliveries began in November 1942.

The designs produced by the two contracting companies were quite different, and the PAK 40 was the Rheinmettal-Borsig design. To all intents it is a scale-up of the 5cm PAK 38, and indeed it is quite easy to confuse the weapons in photographs unless there is some indication of comparative size. It became the standard anti-tank gun, and remained in service throughout the war; in fact it saw service after the war too, several of the armies of Europe adopting them to form their anti-tank defense nucleus.

Its only defect in action was its bulk and the fact that its towing tractor was too conspicuous, which made movement in and

A German 7.5cm PAK 40 captured in Tunisia after the capitulation in May 1943

out of positions a hazardous affair during daylight. But once in position it was worth the effort; it could stop a T-34 at a thousand yards range.

Variant
7.5cm Feldkanone 40 This is exactly the same weapon as the PAK 40 but took on a change of name when used as a field gun by the divisional artillery regiment. This unlikely transition was made in order to give the artillery batteries a gun with a good tank-killing ability but which could also act as a field gun when wanted. The change seems to have begun late in 1944 and not all regiments were provided.

Germany

7.5cm Panzerabwehrkanone 41

Caliber 75mm at breech, 55mm at muzzle
Length of barrel 170in
Breech mechanism Horizontal sliding block, semi-automatic, percussion
Weight in action 2988lb
Elevation From −12½ to +16¾ degrees
Traverse 30 degrees right and left
Projectile & weight APCNR 5.72lb
Propelling charge 5.71lb, steel case, fixed round
Maximum range Not known
Muzzle velocity 3700ft/sec
Penetration 171mm/500m/30 degrees; 145mm/1000m/30 degrees; 102mm/2000m/30 degrees

The PAK 41 was the Krupp 75mm design developed in response to the Army's 1939 request. It was completely unorthodox and a brilliant technical feat which unfortunately foundered on a rock unsuspected by the designers.

The first feature to claim distinction is the tapering barrel. This was another adaptation of the Gerlich system used in the 28mm and 42mm models, but instead of the barrel tapering evenly throughout its length, it was a normally-rifled, parallel barrel for 116 inches with a 37-inch squeeze-bore section screwed on the end. As the shot entered this section it went through a portion tapered at 1/20 for ten inches, then into a section more steeply tapered at 1/12 for seven inches, and finally into a parallel-sided 5.5cm caliber section for the rest of its travel. All this squeeze unit was smoothbore, and a muzzle brake was attached to the front.

The effect of this was discernible in its performance. Firing at right-angles to its target, it could pierce 177mm (6.96in) of homogeneous armor at 100 meters range, an impressive performance for 1942. But, of course, it demanded tungsten-cored ammunition to do this, and after 150 guns had been built the tungsten shortage put paid to the ammunition supply and the production of guns was stopped. After all the ammunition stock had been fired, the guns were withdrawn and most of them scrapped.

The carriage was equally brilliant. Instead of using the axletree as a foundation

for everything, which was (and still is) the usual system, the designers used the shield as the basic piece, making it a structural member instead of the more common sheet of iron hung on as an afterthought. The trail legs were hinged to the shield, and the torsion bar suspension for the wheels was built into its double-skin thickness. The gun itself was mounted in a ball-like gimbal unit in the middle of the shield, leaving no gaps for small arms fire to get around the barrel.

The PAK 41's action was confined to the Russian Front, due to its short life-span, but while there it was the ruler of the battlefield. Quite literally, any tank which could be seen could be killed with this weapon, and reports of combat effectiveness were glowing in their commendations.

Germany

8cm Panzerabwehrwerfer 600 (also known as PAW 8H63)

Caliber 81.4mm
Length of barrel 116.2in
Breech mechanism Vertical sliding block, electric firing
Weight in action 1322lb
Elevation From −6 to +32 degrees
Traverse 27½ degrees right and left
Projectile & weight HEAT 5.94lb; HE 9.59lb
Propelling charge Steel spirally wrapped case with venturi plate
Maximum range HE 6780yds; HEAT 850yds
Muzzle velocity HEAT 1700ft/sec; HE 1375ft/sec
Penetration 140mm at 0 degrees, all ranges

This unusual weapon was one of the few really new innovations in ballistics to appear during the war, and its design was

The Krupp mock-up of the 7.5cm PAK 41, showing the barrel's ball-mounting

more or less forced on the Army by the gradual worsening of the propellant supply situation in the latter part of the war.

The basic problem was that the infantry required a lightweight anti-tank gun. The 88mm PAK 43 was a splendid weapon, but it weighed almost four tons. What they wanted was a return to the sort of mobility the 3.7cm had given them, something which could be pushed around by a handful of men. By this time there were a number of shoulder-fired weapons in use, and the recoilless guns were also available, but none of these gave the complete answer. The shoulder weapons had no range worth speaking of and the RCL guns were insufficiently accurate (due to their short barrels) and had their backblast problems. Most vital, both these solutions were wasteful of propellant. The Army asked for a gun which would be as light as possible, use as little propellant as possible, yet be capable of penetrating contemporary armor and capable of putting all its shots into a one-meter-square target at 750 meters range.

As it happened, Rheinmettal-Borsig had been developing an idea of their own for some time, and this looked like the opportunity to try it out. Called the 'High and Low Pressure System', the idea was to confine the explosion of the charge in a strong chamber but allow the gas to leak at low pressure into a lightweight barrel to propel the projectile. The system gave the advantages of ballistic regularity and efficiency which came from exploding the charge in a confined space to develop high pressure, but the gun barrel could be light in weight since it had to resist low pressure.

A captured 8cm PAW 8H63 at Aberdeen

In order not to complicate matters the barrel was smoothbored and the projectile fin-stabilized; in fact, it was a somewhat modified 81mm mortar bomb. The cartridge case was a normal 105mm field howitzer case with a heavy steel plate in the mouth, pierced with a number of venturi nozzles and with a central spigot holding the projectile. On firing, the propellant burned in the case at about seven tons per square inch, and the gas bled through the venturi holes to fill the space behind the projectile. When the pressure in the barrel reached $3\frac{1}{4}$ tons per square inch, the spigot broke and allowed the bomb to be projected from the barrel.

The carriage as originally designed was so light that it was too weak to stand the travelling stresses and had to be rapidly re-designed. The issue model was a tubular steel split-trail pattern with two wheels and a small shield. About 260 of these guns were built between December 1944 and the end of March 1945. They were effective weapons and aroused a great deal of interest in Allied ordnance engineering circles after the war. However, except for a Swiss tank gun, no artillery piece using this principle has since been made.

Variant

None. The weapon was later renamed the 8cm PAW or PWK 8H63, in accordance with a revised nomenclature system authorized late in 1944, and this caused a certain amount of confusion in Allied intelligence agencies. But in spite of the new name it was the same weapon. The term 'PWK' stands for 'PANZER-WERFKANONE' and is believed to have been applied because of the fact that it was a smoothbore.

8.8cm PAK 43

Caliber 88mm
Length of barrel 260.225in
Breech mechanism Vertical sliding block, semi-automatic, electric firing
Weight in action 8150lb
Elevation From −8 to +40 degrees
Traverse 360 degrees
Projectile & weight AP 22.9lb; APCR 16lb; HE 20.3lb
Propelling charge Lacquered steel case, fixed round
Maximum range 19,100yds
Muzzle velocity AP 3282ft/sec; APCR 3710ft/sec; HE 2640ft/sec
Penetration-AP 167mm/1000m/30 degrees
139mm/2000m/30 degrees
-APCR 192mm/1000m/30 degrees
136mm/2000m/30 degrees

In 1940 Krupp and Rheinmettal were given contracts to develop an improved model of the 8.8cm anti-aircraft gun. The Rheinmettal model eventually entered service as such, but the Krupp project was abandoned for various reasons and the de-velopment turned into an anti-tank gun and tank gun design which became the PAK 43 and its tank equivalent the Kampfwagenkanone 42.

By any standards this was an outstanding design. The gun was long, generating a high velocity and giving ample penetrating power with great accuracy. The carriage was a four-legged platform carried on two two-wheeled trailers, bearing close resemblance to anti-aircraft gun practice. As an anti-tank gun its maximum elevation was half that of an anti-aircraft gun and as a result it could be set closer to the ground to make concealment easier. This form of construction gave all-round traverse, and although it was a trifle slow to bring into action, this mattered little; most of the time, anti-tank guns were in prepared defensive positions and a few extra minutes spent in preparation were of no consequence. For the rare occasion when a target appeared while the gun was on the move, the designers allowed sufficient strength in the suspension to allow it to be fired off its wheels, simply swinging the side outriggers out and placing firing pedestals under the jack feet to stabilize the gun for flank firing.

The firing mechanism was electric, an unusual feature for a field weapon, and safety switches were built in to ensure that the gun would not fire if it happened to be at such a bearing and elevation that the breech might strike one of the platform legs when recoiling.

The PAK 43 was a highly successful weapon wherever it appeared, and it was the master of the Eastern Front in the fight against the Soviet. Reports spoke of knocking out tanks at ranges up to 3500 meters—over two miles. One report reads, 'penetrative performance of the Panzergranat 39 [the standard armor-piercing shell] is satisfactory at all ranges, so that all enemy tanks appearing in this sector—T-34, KV1, JS2—could be engaged with destroying effect. On being hit the tanks showed a darting flame 3 meters high and were burned out. Turrets were mostly knocked off and torn away. A T-34 was hit from the rear at a range of 400 meters and the engine block was flung out a distance of 5 meters and the turret cupola for 15 meters.'

A captured 78mm PAK 43/41 at the Bovingdon Tank Museum, England

The PAK 43/41 incurred the penalty of excess bulk & weight

Variant
8.8cm PAK 43/41 Due to delays in the manufacture of the PAK 43's cruciform carriage, a number of barrels were mounted on two-wheeled split-trail carriages of conventional pattern, made up from various components already in production or store for other weapons and which could be suitably married together. The result was a somewhat cumbersome equipment but its performance was exactly the same as that of the PAK 43 and it was well-received by the users. Its only defect was a vibration period in the long barrel at high rates of fire—above 15 rounds per minute—which led to inaccuracy, but provided the rate of fire was kept below this figure the vibrations did not occur and the gun was as accurate as it was in the proper carriage.

The gun was exactly as for the PAK 43 except that it used a horizontal sliding breech block and a different semi-automatic gear. Elevation was from —5 to +38 degrees, traverse 28 degrees right and left and the weight in action 9656lbs.

Germany

10.5cm Leicht Geschütz 42

Caliber 105mm
Length of barrel 72.28in
Breech mechanism Horizontal sliding block, percussion firing
Weight in action 1191lb
Elevation From —15 to +42½ degrees
Traverse 360 degrees below 20 degrees elevation, 71¼ degrees above
Projectile & weight HE 32.6lb
Propelling charge Two-charge system. Brass case with side primer and blow-out plastic base
Maximum range 8695yds
Muzzle velocity 1099ft/sec

After the 75mm recoilless gun had been in use for some time, certain defects became apparent. One serious matter was that the rush of gas from the rear of the cartridge case severely eroded the firing mechanism housing in the center of the breech-block and led to fouling and damage to the firing mechanism within. Another problem was that after three or four hundred rounds had been fired the mounting began to break up, due principally to the twisting moment placed on the barrel by the shell passing up the rifling.

A 105mm version was in the design stage at this time and the opportunity was taken to make some changes to try and cure these ills. The firing mechanism was repositioned on top of the chamber, with the firing pin operating downwards, which meant relocating the percussion primer in the cartridge in the side instead of the base. The primer was screwed into a raised seating which was shaped to fit into a recess in the chamber wall. This left the base of the case a plain plastic blow-out disc and removed

Breech end of the 105mm LG 42

obstruction from the rear jet, but it meant that loading the cartridge was made slightly more difficult, particularly at night.

The twisting of the gun was countered by welding curved vanes into the jet nozzle at the rear; thus the flow of gas was given a twisting motion to oppose the torque due to the rifling.

The remainder of the design was more or less a scale-up of the 75mm model, a light tubular tripod fitted with wheels. It could be broken into four parachute loads, and to ensure stability in action the elevating

and traversing gears were linked so that if the jet nozzle pointed outside the arc of the rear tripod legs the gun could not be elevated above 20 degrees.

Like other recoilless guns the LG42 had a sizeable danger area in the rear of the jet; this was due not only to the jet gas itself but also the stones and other debris kicked up by the blast, which could easily injure the unwary. As with the 75mm model, it was originally used by Airborne units but was then issued to Mountain regiments.

Variants

LG40-1 and 40-2 This was a similar weapon but developed by Krupp, the LG42 being the Rheinmetall design. It differed principally in having an interrupted-lug breech-block and in having a box-trail carriage with two large wheels. Very few were made, the LG42 being the preferred design.

LG 42-1 and 42-2 Both the LG40 and the LG42 were originally made with a number of light alloy components in their carriages. These were the —1 models. When alloys became restricted, the carriages were made in steel; these were the —2 models and were some 36lbs heavier.

reduced by 330lbs, which wasn't very much of an improvement. In any case few of these light alloy weapons were made since the design was not cleared for production until 1939 and shortly thereafter a revision of priorities decreed that most of the available light alloys were to be reserved for aircraft production.

The s.I.G.33 was widely used wherever the German Army fought. Its standard ammunition was either a high explosive shell or a screening smoke shell, which sufficed to deal with most tactical requirements. An anti-tank shell using the hollow charge principle was issued in 1941, but the most remarkable projectile was the '15cm Steilgranate 42', a 200lb stick bomb used for short range demolition work. This had a high explosive warhead mounted on a 'driving rod' and carrying three fins on off-set arms. It was muzzle-loaded, the rod entered into the barrel and the fins lying alongside the muzzle. A special blank cartridge was used to launch the bomb. About 150 yards from the muzzle the driving rod fell away and left the finned warhead to go to the target, a maximum range of about 1000 meters. The warhead was filled with 60lbs of explosive, a formidable missile for use against strongpoints and wire obstacles. It was, apparently, extensively used in Russia but there are few reports of its appearance in the West.

15cm Schwere Infanterie Geschütz 33

Caliber 150mm
Length of barrel 68.8in
Breech mechanism Horizontal sliding block, percussion firing
Weight in action 3722lb
Elevation From zero to +73 degrees
Traverse 5¾ degrees right and left
Projectile & weight High explosive, 83.6lb
Propelling charge Six-part charge, brass-coated steel case, separate loading
Maximum range 5140yds
Muzzle velocity 790ft/sec

In spite of the nomenclature '33' this weapon was originally issued in 1927. It was built by the Rheinmetall Company and formed part of the equipment of the Heavy Gun Company of the Infantry Regiment.

It was an entirely conventional gun, notable only in that it was the heaviest weapon ever issued as an infantry gun by any nation. It was reliable and robust, but the weight led to complaints from the users and in the late 1930s the whole weapon was re-designed so as to incorporate as much light alloy as possible. Due to strength problems, this turned out to be rather less than was hoped and the weight was only

37mm Anti-tank gun, Model 94

Caliber 37mm
Length of barrel 72in
Breech mechanism Horizontal sliding block, semi-automatic, percussion
Weight in action 815lb
Elevation From —10 to +27 degrees
Traverse 30 degrees right and left
Projectile & weight AP 1.42lb; HE 1.54lb
Propelling charge Brass case, fixed round
Maximum range 5450yds
Muzzle velocity 2300ft/sec
Penetration 32mm/500m/30 degrees

Although classified by the Allies as an anti-tank gun, the Model 94 was known by the Japanese Army simply as a 'Rapid Fire Gun' and was used for infantry support with high explosive ammunition. As an anti-tank gun it illustrates the tendency of designers to match their guns against their own knowledge of their own tanks. The performance of this weapon was far below that of its European contemporaries and it would have been marginal against a British or German tank. But the Japanese tanks were less well protected, and using these as a yardstick the gun is serviceable. It was rarely used against US tanks with effect, most of them being too well armored unless

The 15cm sIG33 infantry support gun, a cumbersome but effective weapon

Ammunition for the Japanese 37mm anti-tank gun

the gun crew were willing to let the tank get within a few yards before firing.

The weapon itself was quite conventional and was mounted on a simple two-wheeled split-trail carriage with a small shield. It was reputed to be accurate, but, based on examination, I would assert that the ammunition was poor stuff.

Variation

37mm Anti-Tank Gun Model 37 This gun, used by the Japanese in very small numbers, was the German 3.7cm PAK 36, sold to them in 1938. Details will be found under that heading in the German section. It was found occasionally in the South Pacific area.

47mm Anti-tank gun, Model 01

Caliber 47mm
Length of barrel 99.48in
Breech mechanism Horizontal sliding block, semi-automatic, percussion
Weight in action 1660lb
Elevation −11 to +19 degrees
Traverse 30 degrees right and left
Projectile & weight AP 3.1lb; HE 3.37lb
Propelling charge Brass case, fixed round
Maximum range 8400yds
Muzzle velocity 2700ft/sec
Penetration 70mm/500m/0 degrees

The history of this weapon is somewhat cloudy, but it appears to be a Japanese copy of a Russian adaptation of a German original. The Russians bought a number of 3.7cm PAK 36 from Germany and later improved them by putting 45mm barrels on the carriages. Apparently one or two of these were captured by the Japanese Army in one of those little-known border skirmishes between the Siberian Army Corps and the Japanese Army in 1938–39. Using these guns as their model, the Japanese then developed a 47mm weapon, probably selecting this caliber because it was already standard in the Japanese Navy and their machinery was available for barrel boring and rifling and the manufacture of ammunition.

The general design was modern and the gun had a heavily reinforced muzzle section, suggesting rather high stressing of the barrel. The carriage was a split-trail four two-wheeled type with shield, and the track of the wheels is unusually wide, giving a very stable weapon in action.

Although named '01', which relates to the Japanese calendar and signifies 1941 in the Christian calendar as the year of adoption, manufacture at Osaka Arsenal did not begin until early in 1942, and only then on a relatively small scale. The weapon was occasionally used against US forces in the Southwest Pacific area.

The 47mm Type 1 anti-tank gun

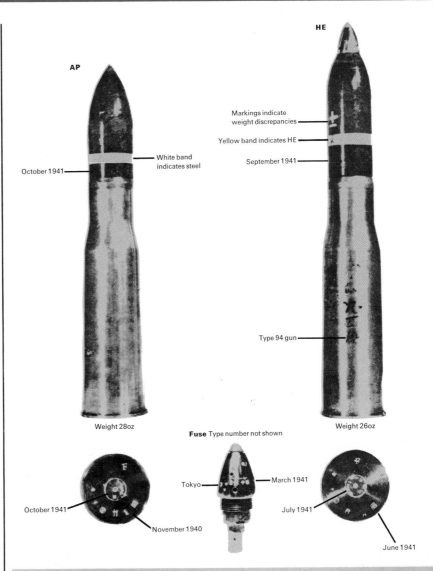

AP

HE

October 1941 — White band indicates steel

Markings indicate weight discrepancies
Yellow band indicates HE
September 1941
Type 94 gun

Weight 28oz

Weight 26oz

Fuse Type number not shown

October 1941
November 1940
Tokyo — March 1941
July 1941
June 1941

70mm Infantry howitzer, Model 92

Caliber 70mm
Length of barrel 28.5in
Breech mechanism Interrupted screw, percussion firing
Weight in action 468lb
Elevation From −4 to +75 degrees
Traverse 22½ degrees right and left
Projectile & weight High explosive, 8.3lb
Propelling charge Four charges; semi-fixed round
Maximum range 3050yds
Muzzle velocity 650ft/sec

This was most common of all the Japanese infantry support weapons, being issued on a scale of two howitzers per infantry battalion. Light and versatile, it functioned principally in the role of a long range mortar, but it was capable of direct fire and was provided with a hollow charge anti-tank shell of moderate efficiency.

Numerous Allied intelligence reports during the war claimed that it was unreliable and inefficient and, 'viewed somewhat unfavorably by the Japanese', but it appears likely that the Japanese hadn't heard the news. In any event it was in common use and after the war it was used by the Chinese Communist Army for many years, they having captured large numbers in Manchuria.

The design was robust and simple. The short-barrelled gun was held in a cradle containing a hydro-spring recoil system, which in turn was mounted in a saddle pivoting on a cross-beam holding the trail legs and stub axles for the wheels. These stub axles were cranked so that the gun could be low-set for direct shooting or high-set for howitzer firing. A shield was fitted, which had a sliding section elevating with the gun.

Ammunition for the 70mm Batallion howitzer

75mm regimental gun, Model 41

Caliber 75mm
Length of barrel 86in
Breech mechanism Interrupted screw, percussion firing
Weight in action 2158lb
Elevation −8 to +16½ degrees
Traverse 3 degrees right and left
Projectile & weight High explosive 12.5lb
Propelling charge Brass or brass-plated steel case. Fixed round
Maximum range 11,990yds
Muzzle velocity 1672ft/sec

This gun was originally issued to the Field Artillery in 1908 and later, when they received better weapons, it became the standard equipment of Mountain Artillery batteries. In 1935 a new and improved mountain gun was provided, and the Type 41 was withdrawn and issued to Infantry and Cavalry regiments on a scale of four

Red band ⅛in wide

Yellow band ½in wide

4.8

White band ½in wide

Copper driving band ⅝in wide

Base of case
Diameter 3 7/32 in

Brass case
Diameter 2¾in (70mm)

guns per regiment. Intended for use as heavy support weapons, they were placed under the Regimental Commander rather than being allotted to Battalions.

The gun is well representative of its era, with large wooden-spoked wheels and shield; with its history as a mountain gun it is rather remarkable that it is not capable of being dismantled into pack-loads. The trail is an unusual form of box pattern made of tubular steel, joined by a transom and terminating in a single tube carrying the spade. The design appears to have been loosely copied from a Krupp model of about 1906. The limited elevation and traverse are also indicative of its age, a maximum elevation of $16\frac{1}{2}$ degrees being almost an international standard in the early days of this century.

The Model 41 was widely used and it was usually employed as a single gun to assist the infantry by direct shooting over open sights. It was the first Japanese weapon with a hollow-charge anti-tank shell, the design being based on information provided by Germany.

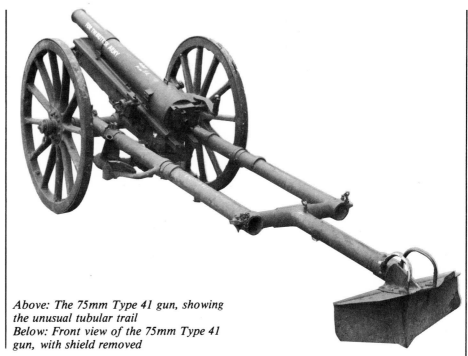

Above: The 75mm Type 41 gun, showing the unusual tubular trail
Below: Front view of the 75mm Type 41 gun, with shield removed

ANTI-TANK RIFLES AND LAUNCHERS

When the tank appeared on the battlefield in 1916, numerous antidotes were thought up by the German Army, and one of them was a high-powered rifle developed by the Mauser company. It was nothing more than the usual Mauser bolt action and barrel, but in massive size to fire a 13mm bullet at 3000 feet per second, a performance quite sufficient to punch holes in the tanks of the day. The result of this was

to attract a number of designers to this sort of weapon as an answer to the anti-tank defense problem in the postwar years. As is well known there was a good deal of acrimonious discussion in those years as to the proper employment of the tank; what is less well known is that there was almost as much argument about how to stop the tank. The first thoughts on the subject were that the natural enemy of the tank was

another tank and that the whole thing would resolve itself into a stately minuet as two tanks circled round each other like British heavyweights. Eventually the flaw in this argument was seen to be the possibility that an attacking tank might be lucky enough to evade a defender, after which he could cruise around the areas behind the lines raising all sorts of havoc unless he was attended to by somebody

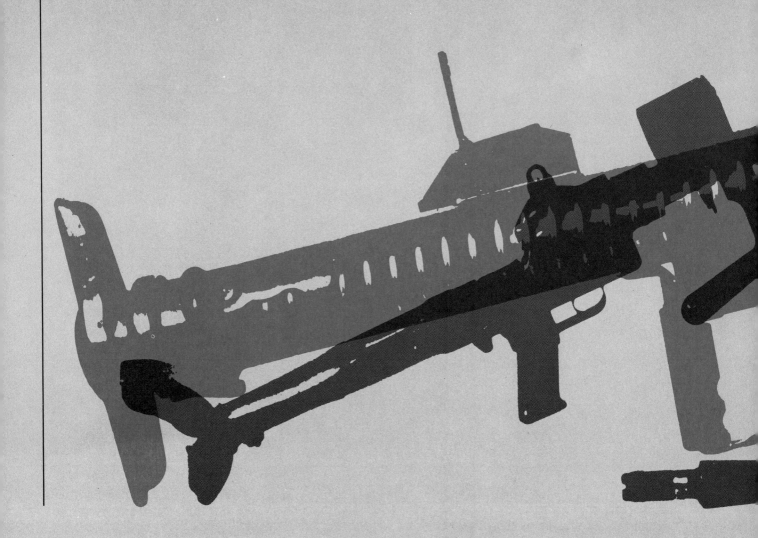

else; and, of course, that somebody else had to be the infantry.

This thought was followed by a period in which a variety of ordnance were proposed, tried, and turned down because they were too heavy, too weak, too big, demanded too many men or cost too much. One much-touted weapon was one of the numerous 20mm cannon which were appearing on the market, notably the Oerlikon and Solothurn models from Switzerland; many countries bought these and more tried them out. Britain had a particularly ingenious model of Oerlikon on tracked trailer on trial in the late 1920s. But many countries were not keen to buy abroad what they thought they could make at home, and eventually most nations turned to the anti-tank rifle as being likely to give the best balance between portability, power and price.

But no sooner had the anti-tank rifles been issued and mastered than they were obsolescent, for the simple reason that tanks were more concerned with the weapons which the other tanks might be carrying, and these, being heavier than anti-tank rifles, called for thicker armor. And once the armor got thicker the anti-tank rifle was out of the running. It stayed in service though, for the simple enough reason that there was no other way of putting an anti-tank weapon into the infantry's hands; and even if it wasn't very good, it was better than nothing at all; if nothing else, the feeling went, it gave the troops a feeling of protection. In fact, of course, it did nothing of the sort, for the troops were the first to realize that the anti-tank rifle was useless, long before it was officially admitted. On the other hand, it must be recalled that in 1938, when these weapons were at the height of their popularity and production, everybody knew a man who had a friend whose second cousin twice removed had been in Germany on holiday last year and just happened to be near some German Army maneuvers; and he saw a street accident where a small car collided with a German tank, and, do you know, it wasn't a real tank at all, it was just a lorry chassis covered in plywood and cardboard?

But the soldiers of the world's armies knew full well that the tanks they might be called on to meet wouldn't be made of cardboard, and they were frantically searching for something to replace the anti-tank rifle.

The solution came in the form of the hollow charge explosive warhead. In this device the shell or other missile is made with the head end formed into a cone of explosive lined with metal in such a fashion that when the explosive is detonated the cone acts to focus the blast. A stream of molten metal and explosive gas is propelled at something like 20,000 feet per second to strike the armor and punch a hole in it. Once this system was perfected, the replacement for the anti-tank rifle was at hand. The only problem now lay in how to put the device into a weapon which, like the rifle, could be carried by one man and manipulated by not more than two. Britain adopted the spigot discharger as her solution, while the Americans adopted the rocket; the Germans copied the Americans and then went on to invent some ideas of their own, while the Russians, for reasons best known to themselves, took no notice and carried on with their anti-tank rifles—which, it must be admitted, were rather better than most—until the end of the war. They've made up for it since.

UK

Rifle, Boys, Mark 1

Caliber 0.55in
Length 63.5in
Weight 36lb
Barrel 36in long, 7 grooves, right hand twist
Feed system 5-round, top-mounted, detachable box magazine
System of operation Bolt action
Muzzle velocity 3250ft/sec
Penetration 20mm/500m/0 degrees
Manufacturer Royal Small Arms Factory, Enfield Lock

After its brief flirtation with the Oerlikon 20mm cannon, the British Army tried to promote the development of a native weapon, the 0.8-inch Elswick machine gun, but this failed to come up to expectations and work began on developing a high-velocity anti-tank rifle.

Work was completed in 1936 and the weapon, code-named 'Stanchion', was about to enter production when Captain Boys, a member of the Small Arms Committee and one of the principal designers of the weapon, unfortunately died. As a tribute to his labors, the Small Arms Committee decided that the new rifle should be named in his memory, and so it entered service as the 'Boys Rifle', being officially approved on 24 November 1937.

It was probably the best of its class at the time. Firing a steel-cored bullet at 3250ft/sec it could penetrate any current tank at 250 yards. It is fashionable today to ridicule the anti-tank rifle, but it must be remembered that in 1937 the average tank armor was 15mm thick, so that the Boys Rifle stood a good chance of making its presence felt. The recoil of the heavy cartridge was considerable, and the gun was fitted with a muzzle brake and allowed to recoil in a cradle mounting against a powerful buffer spring. A monopod acted as front support, and the butt was thickly padded with rubber. But for all that, some hair-raising tales were told to recruits about men who had dug their feet into the ground or braced themselves against a wall or tree before firing, suffering, as a result, from everything from athlete's foot to a broken spine—the punchline depended on the recruit's credulousness.

The Boys saw action in France, Norway and the Far East, but it was rarely entirely successful. The trouble lay less with the rifle than with the tactical theories behind it. To be used from a trench, behind cover, against a tank coming in an expected direction, it was marginally effective. But to be used against wide-ranging blitzkrieg tactics, with tanks appearing suddenly, was alien to its philosophy. It was rarely seen after 1941, being replaced by less conventional but more effective weapons.

Variant
Rifle, Boys, Mark 2 Approved on 4 July 1942 this version had a barrel 4.5in shorter than the Mark 1, with certain unstressed components of aluminum and the butt pad stuffed with feathers, all in an endeavor to produce a lighter model for use by Airborne troops. Although approved, it was never taken into action; shortening the barrel had reduced the velocity and penetration, and by the time the Airborne troops went into action they had been provided with something better.

USSR

Anti-tank rifle, PTRD 1941

Caliber 14.5mm
Length 79in
Weight 38lb
Barrel 48.3in long, 8 grooves, right hand twist
Feed system Single shot
System of operation Bolt action
Muzzle velocity 3300ft/sec
Penetration 25mm/500m/0 degrees
Manufacturer State Arsenals

During the years between the wars the Soviets had developed a 12.7mm bolt-action anti-tank rifle copied from the Mauser of 1918, using a cartridge originally developed as a heavy machine gun round. The performance was relatively poor, and being a highly tank-conscious nation, a fresh design was begun in 1932. For this, a completely new cartridge of 14.5mm caliber, one of the heaviest ever developed, was produced.

The weapon, designed by Degtyarev, looks extremely simple, even agricultural, but it conceals one or two refinements beneath its rough exterior. The barrel recoils within a slide so that the recoil carries the bolt handle against a cam and lifts it to unlock the breech; the bolt is then held while the barrel moves back to its firing position, during which movement the empty case is extracted and ejected. The firer then inserts a fresh cartridge and closes the bolt by hand. Such operation is a little difficult to classify; the opening action belongs to the class known as 'long recoil', but completing the operation by hand makes it quite unique.

The bullet fired by the PTRD was originally a steel-cored streamlined type carrying a small charge of incendiary composition in the nose which gave a flash on impact to indicate the point of strike. But streamlined bullets are only of value in long-range weapons, and in 1941 a new design of square-based bullet with a tungsten carbide core was introduced. This improved velocity and penetration at the short ranges. The rifle appears to have remained in service throughout the war.

'Stanchion', prototype of the Boys rifle

Anti-tank rifle, PTRS 1941

Caliber 14.5mm
Length 84in
Weight 46lb
Barrel 48in long, 8 grooves, right hand twist
Feed system 5-round box magazine
System of operation Gas; semi-automatic; tipping bolt
Muzzle velocity 3320ft/sec
Penetration 25mm/500m/0 degrees
Manufacturer State Arsenals

The PTRS rifle was developed at the same time as the PTRD by the well-known designer Simonov, and the mechanism exhibits many similarities with his better known automatic rifle designs. It was a very advanced weapon, using a top-mounted gas cylinder and piston to operate a bolt carrier. This cammed the bolt down to unlock it, then moved it back to extract and eject in the usual loading cycle. The magazine, front-hinged for cleaning like other Simonov designs, took 5 rounds loaded with a special clip which could only be loaded one way—not the best system for use in battle.

Although a more advanced design than the PTRD, the PTRS was much less robust in use as well as being heavier and larger. Although retained in service until the late 1940s it is believed that relatively few were manufactured, the PTRD having the same performance (since it used the same ammunition) and being easier to use and produce. There is reason to believe that both models were accepted for service as an insurance policy in case either should turn out to be unsuccessful, and that once the PTRD had demonstrated its reliability, production of the PTRS was either closed down or converted to the PTRD.

Soviet anti-tank rifle PTRD-41, protected by a sub-machine gunner

Panzerbuchse 38

The German Panzerbuchse 38 anti-tank rifle

Caliber 7.92mm
Length 51in
Weight 35lb
Barrel 43in long, 4 grooves, right hand twist
Feed system Single shot
System of operation Vertical sliding block, semi-automatic
Muzzle velocity 3975ft/sec
Penetration 25mm/300m/30 degrees
Manufacturer Rheinmettal-Borsig AG, Dusseldorf

The German PzB 38 anti-tank rifle was an elegant design with a very good performance obtained by using a 7.92mm bullet allied to a 13mm cartridge so as to give an extremely powerful propelling charge. The mechanism was unusual in that the breech closure was by a vertical sliding block on the lines of an artillery weapon. To operate the weapon the breech was opened by swinging the pistol grip forward and down, whereupon the block was held open by the extractors and the pistol grip could be returned to its normal place. A cartridge was then loaded by hand, releasing the extractors and allowing the breech block to close by spring pressure. On firing, the weapon recoiled in its stock and a cam opened the block to eject the empty case on the return movement of the barrel, coming to rest with the block held open ready for the next round to be loaded.

The ammunition was unusual in that the bullet contained a steel core and a small capsule of lachrymatory (tear) gas, the intention being to penetrate the tank and there liberate the gas to contaminate the atmosphere inside and force the crew to evacuate the vehicle. In this it seems to have been quite unsuccessful. The chemical agent was only 0.4 grains in weight, and since it was next to the tracer element it seems probable that the chemical had been destroyed by the heat of the tracer before it ever reached the target. In any event no one ever appears to have noticed the lachrymatory effect and it was not known by the Allies until specimens of ammunition were captured and examined. The legality of such a cartridge seems to sail rather close to the Geneva Convention on gas, though it probably escapes the letter of the law by being primarily a piercing projectile and not a chemical projectile.

So far as is known the PzB 38 seems to have been little used in combat. The only likely theater for its use would have been the Polish campaign, since it was largely replaced in service by the PzB 39 before the 1940 campaign in France. Moreover the rapid movements of the German Army did not invite the use of anti-tank rifles.

Germany

Panzerbuchse 39

Caliber 7.92mm
Length 62.25in
Weight 27.25lb
Barrel 42.75in long, 4 grooves, right hand twist
Feed system Single shot
System of operation Vertical sliding block, hand operated
Muzzle velocity 3975ft/sec
Penetration 25mm/300m/30 degrees
Manufacturers Rheinmettal-Borsig, Dusseldorf
Steyr-Daimler-Puch AG, Vienna

The PzB 38 was a satisfactory weapon, but like much of the German Army's early equipment it was too luxurious a solution and ill-suited to manufacture in quantity. It was therefore decided to develop a simplified version, and the PzB 39 was the result. The vertical sliding breech-block was retained but the semi-automatic feature was discarded, the block being entirely hand operated by swinging the pistol grip back and forth. The recoiling barrel was also dropped, but by way of recompense it was now fitted with a muzzle brake, so that the recoil felt by the firer was

The PzB39 rifle, showing the method of opening the breech and the 'ready-use' ammunition holder on the side

A German outpost in the desert, with the PzB 39 anti-tank rifle at the ready

about the same as before. A minor addition was the fitting of two 'ready-use magazines', small boxes each containing ten rounds clipped to brackets at each side of the breech where they could be reached easily by the firer. This was an interesting reversion to the 'quick-loader' which was common on Continental single-shot military rifles in the 1880s.

Since the barrel was almost the same length and the ammunition was the same, the performance of the PzB 39 was equal to that of the PzB 38. But apart from very limited use in the 1940 campaign in France, the PzB saw practically no action.

An interesting comment was made in a British report on the examination of a captured specimen in October 1941: 'This weapon appears to be as cheap as a Sten gun; it would be difficult to better it.'

Variant
Granatbuchse 39 Once the anti-tank rifle's usefulness was put to an end by the increasing armor of tanks, the German Army very ingeniously converted numbers of the PzB 39 rifles into grenade dischargers. The barrel was cut down to 24in length and fitted with the usual 3cm rifled discharger cup, and a special discharger cartridge, using the 13mm case with a special propelling charge and wooden bullet, was provided to launch the grenades. Its effective range in this role was 500 meters.

Italy/Germany

2cm Panzerbuchse S 18-1000

Caliber 20mm
Length 85in
Weight 120lb
Barrel 57in long, 8 grooves, right hand twist
Feed system 5 or 10-round detachable box magazine
System of operation Recoil, semi-automatic, rotating bolt
Muzzle velocity 3000ft/sec
Penetration 35mm/300m/0 degrees
Manufacturer Rheinmettal-Borsig/Solothurn AG

As already mentioned, during the 1920s the Rheinmettal company obtained control of a Swiss firm, Solothurn AG, and through them a controlling interest in the Austrian Steyr company, enabling them to produce and sell weapons which they could not deal with in Germany due to the Versailles Treaty. One of the weapons so developed was a 20mm anti-tank rifle known as the S 18-100, which was sold to a number of countries either for trials (as, for example, Britain) or for adoption into service (as, for example, Hungary). It was later improved by lengthening the barrel and providing a more powerful cartridge, and this model was known as the S 18-1000, and was adopted by Switzerland, Holland, Italy and Germany.

It would appear that the number bought by Germany was relatively small and that the weapon was adopted largely on an extended trial basis; it never achieved the distinction of a model number or a vocabulary identification number and it was rarely seen in action. While the 20mm armor-piercing shell, with explosive filling

The Swiss Solothurn S18-1000 anti-tank rifle, as used by German forces

and base fuse, was efficient, the weapon itself was too heavy and cumbersome to show much advantage over the PzB 38 and 39 rifles.

Operation was semi-automatic; the barrel recoiled within a support sleeve and the rotating bolt then unlocked, moved rearwards to extract and eject the fired case, and then returned to chamber a fresh cartridge. The magazine was mounted on the left side of the gun and the weapon was supported by a bipod and butt monopod. As well as the usual type of open sight, a telescope sight was issued with some models, and there was also a two-wheeled mounting provided for movement, pulled by the two-man team.

Japan

20mm Anti-tank rifle, Type 97

Caliber 20mm
Length 82.25in
Weight 115lb
Barrel 41.875in long, 8 grooves, right hand twist
Feed system 7-round detachable box magazine
System of operation Gas & blowback, tipping bolt, selective fire
Muzzle velocity 2640ft/sec
Penetration 12mm/200m/0 degrees
Manufacturer State Arsenals

This weapon appears to be based on an amalgam of ideas from other weapons, its system of operation being very close to the Swiss Hispano-Suiza 20mm cannon. The Japanese Army bought a number of Oerlikon, Solothurn and Hispano weapons for evaluation in the early 1930s, and from a study of these came the Type 97, introduced in 1937. It was a heavy and complicated design, but it was undoubtedly

capable of dealing with the lighter type of tank which the Japanese anticipated meeting in their Chinese and Manchurian campaigns.

The Type 97 operates on a combination of gas and blowback action; the bolt is unlocked by a gas piston but thereafter is driven back by the blowback of the spent cartridge case. As an additional complication, the entire barrel and receiver are allowed to recoil in a cradle mounting which carries the bipod, pistol grip, monopod and butt. An oil buffer recoil and recuperator mechanism was fitted, and probably all this complication was added in an effort to cut the recoil blow down to a level which the average Japanese soldier could withstand.

In order to transport the weapon it was provided with attachments beneath the butt and under the cradle to which carrying handles could be fitted to allow it to be carried by four men. A shield was also provided, and with handles and shield in place the whole affair weighed 150lbs. An unusual feature of this weapon is its ability to fire in the automatic mode as a cannon or heavy machine gun; the rate of fire is not known but it is estimated to have been about 350–400rpm.

There are very few reports of this weapon's appearance during World War II; it appears to have been used once or twice in the actions in Malaya and Singapore and to have made a brief appearance in the Southwest Pacific area, but its performance was relatively poor and it was soon outclassed by tank development. There are some reports of it having been used as a beach defense weapon on some of the islands of the Pacific, used to shoot at incoming landing craft; but specimens were rarely captured and there are very few in existence today.

Poland

Karabin WZ/35 'Marosczek'

Caliber 7.92mm
Length 70.0in
Weight 19.5lb
Barrel 47.25in long, 4 grooves, right hand twist
Feed system 10-round detachable box magazine
System of operation Bolt action
Muzzle velocity 4200ft/sec
Penetration 20mm/300m/0 degrees
Manufacturer Fabryca Brony Radomu (State Arsenal)

With two untrustworthy neighbors, both of whom had a deep interest in tanks, it is hardly surprising that the Poles began development of an anti-tank rifle in the early 1930s, taking the Mauser of 1918 as their starting point. In order to get the highest velocity possible, they pioneered the use of a standard rifle-caliber bullet backed by an oversize cartridge, a technique later copied by the Germans. The most notable feature of the Marosczek rifle was its light weight, little more than half the weight of its contemporaries, making it a very handy weapon but giving it a somewhat fierce recoil, in spite of using an efficient muzzle brake.

In order to achieve the desired high velocity a very energetic and hot propellant was employed, and this led to rapid erosion of the barrel. After 200 rounds had been fired the velocity had fallen to about 3800ft/sec and the penetration performance had deteriorated in proportion. Penetration was helped by adopting a bullet with a tungsten carbide core, and their effective use during the short Polish campaign in 1939 led to the development of similar bullets in Germany and Russia.

Japanese 20mm Type 97 anti-tank rifle

The Polish 'Marosczek' anti-tank rifle, used both against and by the Germans

Although known as the Model 35, it is believed that general issue did not commence until early in 1937 and that less than a thousand rifles had been manufactured before the outbreak of war. Such weapons as were serviceable after the defeat were taken into use by the German Army for a short time, until the general use of anti-tank rifles was abandoned.

Variant

There was no actual variant of the Model 35, but it is worth recording that in 1939 design work began on a new rifle using a barrel tapering from 11mm to 7.92mm, to fire a suitable cored bullet. When Poland was invaded the design drawings and prototype model were removed to France, where development was carried on by a small team of Polish designers. The design was brought to a successful conclusion and the perfected model was undergoing its final tests with a view to commencing production, when the German Army overran France in 1940. In the subsequent confusion the rifle and the drawings were lost and have never been seen since. From statements by other Polish weapons designers who escaped to Britain it appears that the velocity of this weapon was about 5000ft/sec and the penetrative performance approximately double that of the Model 35.

UK

Projector, infantry, anti-tank

Caliber Not applicable
Length 39in
Weight 32lb
Barrel None
Feed system Single shot
System of operation Spigot discharger
Muzzle velocity ca 350ft/sec
Penetration ca 75mm
Projectile & weight Hollow charge, 3lb

The Projector, Infantry, Anti-Tank (or PIAT, by which name it inevitably became known) was the result of several years of trial and experiment by Lt-Col Blacker, RA. This officer had long been attracted by the idea of a spigot discharger; such a device dispenses with the usual barrel and replaces it with a hollow tail unit on the projectile. A percussion cartridge within this tail unit is struck by a firing spigot, a heavy steel rod which is driven into the tail while the projectile is supported on a simple tray. The explosion of the cartridge blows the projectile from the spigot, the length of its travel along the spigot being sufficient to impart direction.

Blacker's first patent for this type of weapon appeared in the early 1930s and by

1937 he had produced a weapon called the 'Arbalest', specimens of which were made by the Parnell Aircraft Company for trials by the Army in 1939. It was rejected in May of that year since it appeared that the 2in Mortar was a better proposition as a bomb-thrower.

In 1940 Lt-Col. Blacker became involved with MD1 (Ministry of Defence 1) a military establishment concerned with the development of unorthodox weapons, particularly for use by clandestine organizations, and after redesigning the Arbalest he put it forward again as a combined anti-tank and bombardment weapon which had, it was claimed, the anti-tank effect of the 2-pounder gun and almost the same range as the 3in mortar. MD1 put this design forward in late 1940 and although it was regarded askance by most of the approving authorities, it eventually entered service as the 29mm Spigot Mortar or 'Blacker Bombard' in 1941 and was used extensively by Home Guard and Airfield Defense units.

Blacker now developed a smaller, man-portable, version which he called the 'Baby Bombard', but before he could do much with it he left MD1 for another post which left him with less time for experimenting. The prototype Baby Bombard was left with

The British PIAT with its hollow charge bomb loaded into the firing trough and the sights raised

A PIAT cut open to reveal its workings.
The monopod is non-standard

MD1 where it was worked on by a Major Jefferis (later Major-General M. R. Jefferis, CBE, MC) and in June 1941 the 'Bombard, Baby, 0.625 inch No. 1' (the measurement being the diameter of the spigot) was given its first trials before the Ordnance Board. They were not impressed, reporting that, 'the Baby Bombard would prove ineffective as an anti-tank weapon under any conceivable conditions of employment'. This view was concurred in by such eminent figures as the Director of Artillery and the Assistant to the CIGS, and on 11 August 1941 it was officially dropped. Among other things it was the ineffective light bomb which led to this decision, and in the following months Jefferis developed an effective hollow charge bomb which he explained to various interested parties in February 1942. This seems to have turned the scales, and by mid-March pilot models of the PIAT were being made and the possibility of

producing high explosive, smoke, flare and signal projectiles was being explored. Trials of the new bomb were successful and the weapon went into production, final approval being given on 31 August 1942.

The mechanism of the PIAT was very simple; an enormous spring was compressed by unlatching the shoulder pad, standing on it, and lifting the weapon so that the spring and spigot were withdrawn into the body and held by a simple sear mechanism. The body was then returned to the shoulder pad and the weapon was ready to fire. A bomb was placed in guideways at the front and on pressing the trigger the spigot was released, entering the tail unit of the bomb and exploding the propelling cartridge therein. This explosion blew the bomb off, and at the same time blew the spigot back into the body of the weapon, recocking it ready for the next shot. The maximum engagement range

was about 100 yards, although the bomb could reach to 750 yards. The proposed anti-personnel and signal bombs never materialized.

Within its limitations the PIAT was a startlingly effective weapon, but it would be fulsome to say it was popular. It was heavy and cumbersome to carry, awkward and strenuous to cock, and violent to fire, but in spite of all that it was grudgingly respected as a weapon which did what it set out to do and could effectively stop a tank when used by a resolute man. Undoubtedly the most famous incident involving the PIAT was the action in Italy in which Fusilier Jefferson dashed into the open and fired it from the hip, stopping two Tiger tanks at close range. He was awarded the Victoria Cross for this remarkable feat, and the general opinion in the ranks was that he deserved it for firing the thing from the hip, let alone killing two tanks with it.

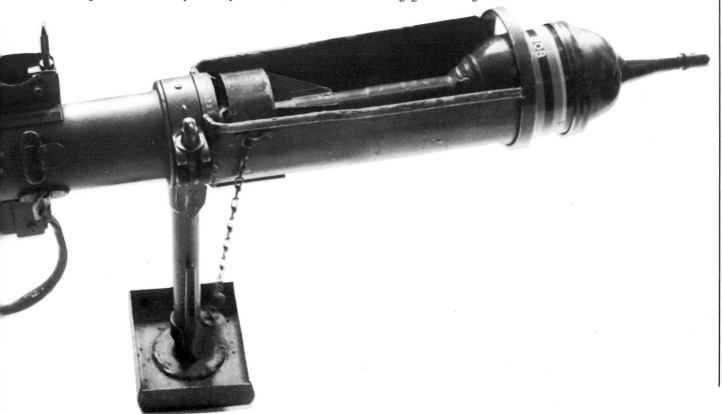

USA

Launcher, rocket, 2.36 inch anti-tank, M1

Caliber 2.36in
Length 54in
Weight 13.25lb
Barrel Smoothbore
Firing system Electric; 2 dry batteries in pistol grip
Projectile & weight HEAT 3.4lb Rocket
Maximum range 400yds
Muzzle velocity 300ft/sec
Penetration ca 80mm

In 1918 the American scientist and experimenter Goddard developed a small rocket launcher from which a lightweight projectile could be fired. The idea was offered to the United States and British governments, but as the end of the war came at about the same time there was a shortage of interest. Moreover, there seemed little point in it; a trench mortar could deliver a bigger payload and at less cost in propellant, and was an indirect fire weapon into the bargain, one which did not require its operator to be in sight of his target.

There the matter rested until 1941 when it was taken out and reconsidered. In the intervening years two factors had entered the scene; the tank and the hollow charge warhead. Unlike European armies the US Army had not adopted an anti-tank rifle or other lightweight anti-tank weapon, while the perfection of the hollow charge promised a method of defeating tanks with low velocity missiles.

As a result, the 2.36in launcher came into service in 1942 in time to be used by the US troops in North Africa. At that time one of America's favorite comedians was a Mr. Bob Burns, and one of his props was a complex and fearful wind instrument of his own invention which he called his 'Bazooka'. The similarity between this and the long pipe of the 2.36in launcher caught the fancy of some unsung GI, and ever since, shoulder-fired rocket launchers have been called 'Bazookas', though strictly speaking only this one is entitled to the name.

A larger version, of 3.45in caliber, was developed towards the end of the war, but since the 2.36in appeared to be capable of doing all that was needed, the 'Super-

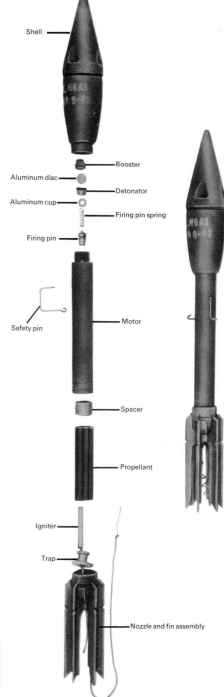

Top left: The 2.36 inch rocket launcher M9A1 being demonstrated
Above: M6A1 hollow charge rocket and its component parts
Right: An American ambush party in Normandy wait with their Bazooka for the Panzers to arrive

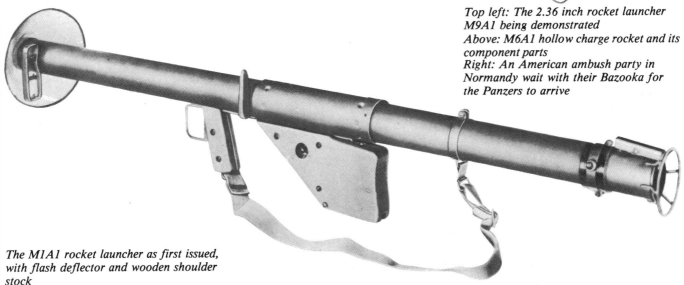

The M1A1 rocket launcher as first issued, with flash deflector and wooden shoulder stock

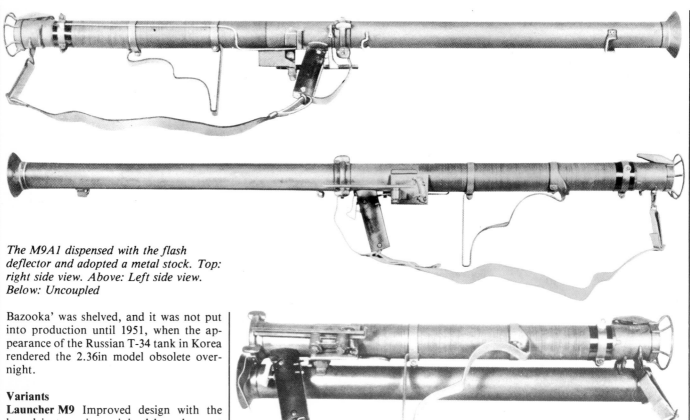

The M9A1 dispensed with the flash deflector and adopted a metal stock. Top: right side view. Above: Left side view. Below: Uncoupled

Bazooka' was shelved, and it was not put into production until 1951, when the appearance of the Russian T-34 tank in Korea rendered the 2.36in model obsolete overnight.

Variants
Launcher M9 Improved design with the barrel in two pieces, joined by a bayonet catch, so that it could be dismantled and carried more easily. The firing gear was changed to an impulse magneto in the pistol grip. The shoulder stock and other fittings were improved, and the weight became 16.0lbs.

Rockets M6, M6A1,2,3, etc. A number of differing models of rocket were issued, changes being made in such details as electrical contacts, fin assembly and so forth, as use and trials indicated areas capable of improvement. Early models had a pointed nose; the M6A3 and subsequent models had a hemispherical nose.

Rocket M10 This rocket carried a warhead loaded with white phosphorus for producing smoke screens and also for anti-personnel use.

Germany

The Panzerfaust

	30K	30	60	100	150
Length—Tube	31.5in	31.5in	31.5in	31.5in	31.5in
—Bomb	14.25in	19.5in	19.5in	19.25in	21.85in
Diameter, bomb	3.95in	5.9in	5.9in	5.95in	4.13in
Velocity ft/sec	98	98	148	200	270
Penetration at 30°	140mm	200mm	200mm	200mm	200mm
Weight complete	7.5lb	11.5lb	15lb	15lb	14.75lb

The appearance of heavy Russian tanks in 1942 led to a demand for a light but potent anti-tank weapon for infantry use, and a Dr. Langweiler of the Hugo Schneider Aktien Gesellschaft (HASAG) was given the task of developing a suitable weapon during the summer of that year.

Langweiler produced a simple recoil-less device called the 'Faustpatrone', which consisted of a 14-in tube carrying a small gunpowder charge in its center and with a hollow charge bomb in one end. This device was grasped and held at arms length, and a trigger fired the gunpowder charge. This launched the bomb forward, while the rearward blast from the other end of the tube balanced the recoil. Mechanically it was successful, but as a weapon it was of little use since it had no sights nor indeed any provision for aiming it.

Since the addition of sights meant that it had to be brought closer to the firer, the tube was extended in length so that the flash was directed behind the holder. The bomb was given thin sheet steel fins which wrapped around the tail shaft while the bomb lay in the tube; the warhead was of much greater diameter than the tube. A simple sight was fitted and this device was named Panzerfaust 30, the figure indicating the fighting range in meters. After a variety of tests it was put into production in October 1943 at a rate of 200,000 per month. Another version, the Panzerfaust 30 Klein, using a small diameter bomb, was also put into production, its target figure being 100,000 per month.

Since the penetration of the Panzerfaust 30 seemed adequate (140mm at 30°), experiment was now directed to improving the weapon's range. The propellant charge was increased (which also meant using thicker discharge tubes) raising the velocity and increasing the range. The design was completed early in 1944 and during the summer production was switched from the Panzerfaust 30 to the Panzerfaust 60.

Further development to increase range led to the Panzerfaust 100, in which the propelling charge was designed in two units separated by an air gap in order to achieve staggered ignition and a more sustained thrust. This went into production in November 1944 in addition to the 60.

All the Panzerfaust models so far had been one-shot weapons, the firing tube being thrown away after use. In an attempt to economise, as well as improve performance, the Panzerfaust 150 was now developed, in which the propellant charge

Opposite top: A dubious Volkssturm soldier is introduced to the Panzerfaust. Whole Volkssturm units were armed solely with the Panzerfaust
Right: 'Grossdeutschland' division soldier preparing to fire a Panzerfaust. Note also the egg grenade hanging from his belt

was attached to the tail of the bomb and the firing mechanism used a strip of ignition camps. In this way it was hoped the tube could be rapidly re-loaded by the user up to ten times before it became unserviceable. The bomb was also redesigned to economize in explosive while still retaining the same penetrative performance and, as an anti-personnel device, a fragmentation sleeve of notched cast iron could be slipped over the warhead when desired. Production of this model began in January 1945 and continued until April, during which time about 100,000 were made, but very few of them reached the hands of troops owing to the difficult transport situation at that time.

Finally a Panzerfaust 250 was in the process of development when the war ended. This was to use a bomb with a longer tail shaft and an improved propelling charge electrically ignited. The general arrangement had been designed and experiments with the propellant system were taking place, but that was as far as it got.

A general description of the Panzerfaust 60 will suffice to describe all the other models which saw service. The basic portion was a mild steel tube with a slight restriction in the rear end to serve as a venturi nozzle, and a simple trigger mechanism and rear sight unit on top. The bomb was of thin sheet metal on a wooden tail rod which carried the flexible fins. The propelling charge was in a paper tube behind the bomb and beneath the trigger unit. The foresight was a pin on the edge of the bomb warhead. To fire, the safety pin locking the trigger was withdrawn and the rear sight leaf erected; this had three aper-

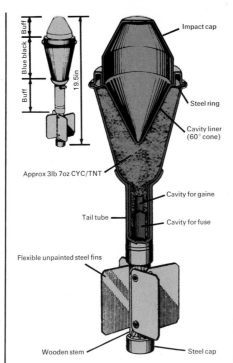

The Panzerfaust bomb, showing the hollow charge head and flexible fins

tures for 30, 60 and 80 meters. Lifting the sight leaf also freed the trigger. The user now tucked the tube beneath his arm and took aim at the target, squeezing the trigger downward to fire. This lifted and released a leaf spring carrying a small firing pin, allowing it to snap down on to a percussion cap which ignited the charge and expelled the bomb.

It seems to be customary in recent war

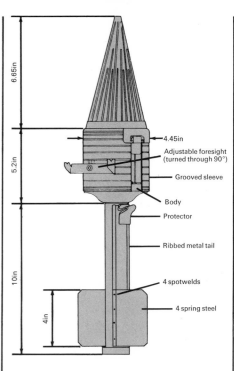

Bomb for the more modern, improved Panzerfaust 150

novels to write off the Panzerfaust as a primitive and ineffective piece of rubbish issued to Volkssturm units in the last days of the war. This was far from the truth; it was a highly effective anti-tank weapon and it was widely used by the Army both on the Eastern and Western Fronts. In the hands of a determined man it could stop any tank in existence in those days. It could still make an impression today.

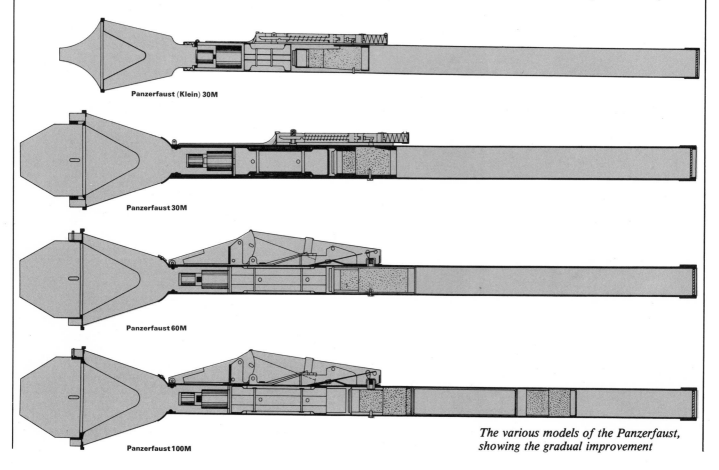

Panzerfaust (Klein) 30M

Panzerfaust 30M

Panzerfaust 60M

Panzerfaust 100M

The various models of the Panzerfaust, showing the gradual improvement

Germany

8.8cm Raketen Panzer-buchse 54 ('Ofenrohr' or 'Panzerschreck')

Caliber 88.9mm
Length 64.5in
Weight 20.25lb
Barrel 62.5in long, smoothbore
System of operation Single shot rocket launcher
Projectile & weight Hollow charge, 7.25lb
Effective range 150m
Penetration ca 100mm at 0 degrees

Ofenrohr (Stovepipe) or Panzerschreck (Tank Terror) was a shoulder fired rocket launcher inspired by the US Army's 2.36in Bazooka after specimens had been captured by the Germans. At that time the German Army were casting about for a suitable weapon to use against Soviet

Soldiers of the 'Grossdeutschland' division with their 'Panzerschreck' in the remains of a Russian farmhouse

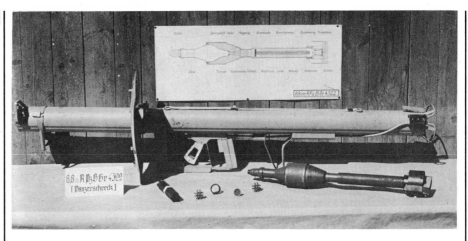

tanks, and after trials of the Bazooka it was decided to produce a German equivalent as quickly as possible.

The opportunity was taken of making a few improvements in the original American design which, it is interesting to see, were later incorporated by the Americans in later models of their weapon. The caliber was increased to 88mm in order to provide a better and more effective warhead; a

Original German photograph of the first production 'Ofenrohr'

drum tail was used, and the electric firing current was derived from an impulse magneto driven by squeezing the firing gap. As with most of the first-generation launchers, the rocket motor was still burning when it left the launcher and therefore a shield, which incorporated the rear sight,

was provided. The weapon became notorious for the flame and smoke which came from the rear end when it was fired, a circumstance which gave rise to the nickname 'Ofenrohr'.

The Panzerschreck was widely used, being first issued in 1943 to units on the Eastern Front and remaining on issue throughout the war. As the propellant situation became more critical, other weapons were developed to replace it, but few reached the hands of troops, so in spite of this logistic drawback it stayed in use. It was highly effective against the tanks of the time, and appears to have been well liked by the soldiers.

Right: 88mm Panzerschreck with bomb
Below: The Panzerschreck in action

Below: Details of the Panzerschreck bomb hollow charge warhead

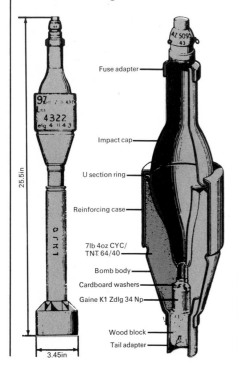

8.8cm Racketenwerfer 43 (Püppchen)

Caliber 8.8cm
Length of barrel 63in
Weight 315lb
Barrel Smoothbore
Feed system Single shot
System of operation Closed breech rocket launcher
Elevation From −14 to +23 degrees
Maximum range 750m
Muzzle velocity 460ft/sec
Penetration ca 100mm/0 degrees
Manufacturer Westfalische Anhaltische Sprengstoff AG, Reinsdorf

In 1944 the German Army requested designs of a light anti-tank gun for infantry use. One of the designs put forward was this weapon, developed by Dr. Erich von Holt of the Westfalische Anhaltische Sprengstoff AG of Reinsdorf (known as WASAG). In effect it is the 8.8cm Panzerschreck rocket launcher mounted on the carriage of the 2.8cm schweres Panzer-

buchse 41 taper-bore gun (which by that time was obsolete), and with the rear end of the launcher closed by a breech mechanism of simple sliding block pattern. This did away with the back blast which was always an objectionable feature of open tube launchers and, by confining the rocket blast within a closed tube, improved the velocity and hence the range. On the other hand, of course, closing the rear end introduced a certain amount of recoil but this was easily controlled by the existing system as designed for the 28mm gun.

The projectile was the same rocket propelled hollow charge bomb as used with the Panzerschreck, but with the addition of an obturating (sealing) unit on the tail drum which resembled a short cartridge case. This formed the necessary seal at the rear end of the tube when the breech was closed and prevented the leakage of gas from the rear. Ignition was now by a percussion arrangement, a firing pin in the breech-block struck an extension pin held by the obturating unit and this transferred the blow to a percussion cap in the middle of the rocket motor venturi. Explosion of this cap ignited a powder charge which lit the sticks of propellant forming the rocket motor.

The exact number of RW43 which saw use is in some doubt; some reports speak of 'several', others refer to it as a prototype. Obviously it did not meet the requirements of the Army in one respect in that it still used a rocket, and the demand was for a weapon using less propellant than a rocket solution. But it seems likely that upwards of a hundred were actually in the hands of troops when the war ended, and what few accounts there are seem to indicate that the design was successful.

Right: The 8.8cm Puppchen rocket
Below: US soldier examines a captured 'Puppchen'

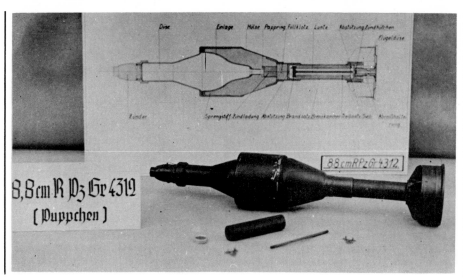

GRENADES

The hand grenade is a weapon of long standing, but it had more or less died out during the latter part of the 19th century, to be revived during the Russo-Japanese War and then brought to its full estate by the peculiar conditions of trench warfare during the 1914–18 period. At the termination of that war there were something like 150 different types of grenade in use on the Western Front, good, bad and indifferent, and one of the first postwar tasks was to throw most of them out and start afresh with a clean sheet of paper. Strangely enough, every country who did this failed dismally and eventually had to fall back on one of its World War I designs, suitably cleaned up and standardized for production. The British Army spent from 1916 to 1935 trying to perfect a new grenade, the No. 54, which was to be the grenade to end all grenades and solve all problems, but in fact the 54 was thrown out in 1935 and the Army fell back on the well-tried No. 36M Mills Grenade, which indeed is still serving today, almost sixty years after the original patents were taken out.

The reason for this state of affairs lay in the stringent requirements laid down for the ideal grenade; most countries produced such a specification, and the British example, as laid down in the *Textbook of Ammunition 1926* is quite representative of them; to anyone who thinks a grenade is a simple proposition, this will come as a surprise:

1. The mechanism had to be capable of detonating the grenade whatever the angle of impact with the ground;
2. It had to be of a pattern to allow hand or rifle projection without the need for changes, adjustments or addition of any other components;
3. It had to be free from external fittings which might catch in the user's clothes;
4. It had to be watertight;
5. It had to be safe if the thrower fell—as, for example, by being shot or wounded—after he had prepared the grenade for throwing;
6. It has to give an all-round killing effect over a ten-yard radius;
7. It had to have the longest possible range which could be achieved without damaging the rifle;
8. It had to have good keeping qualities in store.

Needless to say, no grenade yet made fits all these requirements; and the long pursuit of the unattainable was just one more example of 'the best being the enemy of the good'.

One of the greatest drawbacks to efficient grenade design was the demand, implicit in the above specification, that it should be all things at once; it had to be highly lethal but not hurt the man who threw it; it had to be heavy enough to have a good lethal effect with a lot of fragments and blast, but light enough to be launched from a rifle without damaging the rifle; it had to be simple but it had to be foolproof; and above all it had to be cheap and easy to manufacture, for World War I had shown that grenade expenditure ran into millions.

Eventually, of course, the facts had to be faced and the truth recognized that if you want grenades to do five different jobs, then you are better off with five specialized grenades. In this way came the first major sub-division in the grenade world, into 'Offensive' and 'Defensive'

grenades; this classification was adopted by the French in about 1916 and has remained standard ever since. The offensive grenade is used in the attack, by a man who is running forward; he wants to throw the grenade ahead and not have to seek cover, therefore it needs to have a localized effect and not fling chunks of metal back to the man who threw it. Therefore it needs a lightweight casing which breaks into tiny fragments, so light and small as not to carry for long distances and deriving much of the effect from the blast of the explosive. The defensive grenade, on the other hand, is for use by the man holding a position where he has cover available to him once he has thrown; in which case the maximum possible lethal fragmentation is required and the grenade can have a large lethal area.

One of the most recognizable points about a defensive grenade is, therefore, the traditional serrated cast iron body, fondly imagined to be in the cause of promoting fragmentation. If a grenade is detonated under controlled conditions and the fragments collected and examined, it will be seen that the serrations have about as much effect on the fragmentation as has the state of the tide at London Bridge. There is some evidence to suggest that when Mr. Mills patented his archetypal grenade with serrations he was more concerned with making sure that the thrower got a good grip with a muddy hand; certainly, as experiments during World War II proved conclusively, external serrations have no effect whatever on controlling fragmentation. On the other hand serrations on the inside surface of the grenade have considerable bearing on the shape and size of fragments, but unfortunately serrating the inside is not so easy. And, as we have already said, cheapness and ease of manufacture are paramount considerations in grenade design.

With a standard hand grenade design settled in the various armies, that, it was felt, was that. But the progress of World War II brought more and more specialized grenades into play until, as before, the war's end saw hundreds of different types in the inventories of the world's armies. Obviously, some were produced only in small numbers, failed to be as good as was hoped, and thus are relatively unimportant, and because of limitations of space it has proved impossible to list every grenade of the war in these pages; only the most common patterns are described. Grenades for anti-tank offence were required, both hand thrown and rifle discharged; grenades giving smoke for both screening and signalling purposes; grenades giving light for night attacks; more and improved offensive and defensive grenades; grenades of new materials either because they were thought to be an improvement on older patterns or because they were forced on the makers by shortages of material. In this context one should note that the German Army, in the last days of the war, were using grenades made of wood or concrete and, according to one official statement, their grenade manufacturing policy in 1944–45 was determined not so much by what was wanted as by what materials were available to make them from.

On the whole, grenade design was not particularly inventive when it came to mechanisms; the standard fuses and igniters were usually carried over from one design to another; if nothing else it at least made life more simple for the soldier who didn't have to learn something totally new. But some of the most unusual designs never got into service at all; one might cite the American 'Beano' grenade, the same shape and size as a baseball, so designed in order to capitalize on the ball-playing ability of all right-thinking American youths and thus remove one item from the training schedule—if he could throw a baseball he could throw a grenade. Another, and probably the most odd of all, was the British Grenade No. 67; a hundred-watt electric light bulb filled with tear gas and sealed with plaster-of-paris; no fuse, no pins to pull; just a label which read, 'Instructions for Use. Throw bulb about 30 feet into the air so as to fall and break upwind of target.' Simpler than that, they do not come.

Grenade, hand or rifle, No. 36M

Length 3.75in
Weight 1lb 11½oz
Filling 2.5oz Baratol
Fusing 4 or 7-second delay

British grenade 36, sectioned and whole

The 36M grenade, popularly known as the 'Mills Bomb', has a long and involved history. It began in 1915 as the No. 5 Grenade; it was then fitted with a tail rod to allow it to be fired from a rifle and re-Christened the No. 23 grenade. Then in 1918 it was given a 2½in detachable base plate to allow it to be fired from a rifle discharger cup and it was renumbered the 36. Shortly afterwards numbers were specially waterproofed and prepared for issue in Mesopotamia, and were numbered 36M. The 5 and 23 were discarded in 1918, the 36 declared obsolete in 1932, and the 36M has remained as the standard grenade.

The mechanism has changed little since Mills took out his original patent in May 1915. A central channel holds, at the top, a striker, retained against the pressure of a spring by a curved lever, which in turn is held securely by a split pin. Beneath the striker is an 'igniter set' comprising a .22 rimfire cartridge, a short length of safety fuse and a detonator. This igniter set is U-shaped so that while the .22 cap enters the central channel, the detonator enters a pocket alongside, and the set can be inserted or removed by grasping the curved section of fuse. Once the set is inserted, the grenade is said to be 'primed' and a base plug is screwed in place to hold the set in

place. The fuse originally burned to give a 7-second delay, this length of time being necessary when launching the grenade from a rifle cup discharger. But in 1940 the British Expeditionary Force complained that the delay was too long for hand throwing, the Germans being adept at picking them up and throwing them back, and a four-second igniter set was quickly developed and issued, which led to a number of surprised German soldiers before the word got round. Subsequently the 4-second set was retained for hand use while the 7-second set was available for rifle launching.

The 36M was extensively used by British troops in every theater of war. It was a 'defensive' pattern grenade, and the fragmentation could be erratic, large pieces often being flung up to a hundred yards or more from the explosion point; consequently it was vital for the thrower to take cover as soon as he had got rid of the grenade. From time to time various authorities would point this out, along with other theoretical defects, and attempt to design grenades which would show an improvement. None of them ever did, and the 36M has continued to give stalwart service up to the present day.

Internal arrangements of the Grenade 36

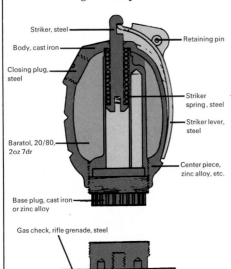

Striker, steel
Body, cast iron
Closing plug, steel
Baratol, 20/80, 2oz 7dr
Base plug, cast iron or zinc alloy
Gas check, rifle grenade, steel
Retaining pin
Striker spring, steel
Striker lever, steel
Center piece, zinc alloy, etc.

Grenade, rifle, No. 68

Length 6.5in
Weight 1lb 15.5oz
Filling 5.5oz Lyddite, Pentolite, or RDX/Beeswax
Range ca 100yds
Penetration 50mm/100m/0 degrees
Fusing Impact

The No. 68 grenade has the distinction of being the first hollow-charge weapon ever to enter service in any army. Its development began before the war; In January 1939 two Swiss demonstrated what they claimed to be a, 'new and powerful explosive' for penetrating armor. The explosive was contained in a grenade fitted to a rod and fired from a rifle, and the effect was to blow a hole in a steel plate target. British observers attending the demonstration were struck with the resemblance between the effect obtained by this Swiss grenade and that obtained by the 'Monroe'

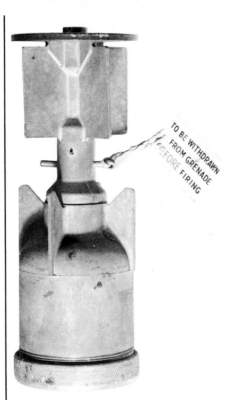

Original model of the 68 grenade, with body fins and gas-check in place

or 'Neumann' effect of placing a hollowed-out explosive charge in contact with a steel-plate target. This effect had been known for many years and although several experimenters had proposed putting it to use as a weapon, no one had ever done so. The Research Department of Woolwich Arsenal had done some experiments on this effect, and after the Swiss demonstration they were spurred on to develop a similar grenade.

Work began by using a 2in mortar bomb body and making various types of conical, hemispherical and other shapes of liner for the cavity in the explosive, and by August 1939 sufficient knowledge had been gained to allow work to begin on a rifle grenade to be fired from a discharger cup. The work was completed and the Grenade No. 68 placed in production in May 1940. Although intended for equipment of the infantry section, it is not believed to have seen wide use. A small number were sent to France in 1940 and to the Western Desert, but by the time of the Normandy invasion other and better weapons were available and the 68 Grenade took a back seat. It was widely issued to Home Guard units in Britain in 1941-42 who, in addition to firing it from the discharger cup, also fired it from the 'Northover Projector', a primitive smoothbore gun. A slightly off-beat suggestion was put up in 1941 to fire the grenade from a crossbow, so as to have a silent and flashless discharger, and the Ordnance Board were asked to comment on this idea. After assessing the requirements they concluded, 'A catapult giving ballistics equivalent to those given by explosive means could scarcely be produced as a load portable by one man. The bow portion alone, for example, would have to be something resembling the road spring of a lorry. . . . The Board are convinced that catapult projection has nothing to offer and recommend no further action.'

Variants

Mark 1 Has small vanes on the body. In the original models a circular gascheck plate was held at the rear of the fins by a bakelite screw and discarded in flight. Later models used a steel screw and retained the gascheck in flight.
Mark 2 No body vanes, longer fins. Gascheck held by brass screw or rivet.
Mark 3 Hollow-charge cavity cylindro-conoidal instead of hemispherical.
Mark 4 Similar to Mark 3 but with improvements to the detonator holder.
Mark 5 As Mark 4 but with gascheck secured by a steel rivet.
Mark 6 As Mark 5 but manufactured in the USA under contract.

UK

Grenade, hand, No. 69

Length 4.5in
Weight 13.5oz
Filling 3.25oz Lyddite, Baratol or Amatol
Fusing Impact

The 69 grenade was one of the type known as 'Offensive' grenades, in that its bark was worse than its bite. It was simply a barrel-shaped casing of black plastic material filled with an explosive and with an 'all-ways' fuse on one end. Consequently its effect was primarily blast and shock, and there were very few lethal fragments. Its principal purpose was in assault or house-to-house fighting, where it could be thrown so as to shake up the recipients and leave them shocked while the thrower followed up the grenade with a sub-machine gun.

Unfortunately, when it was first issued it was publicized as a 'non-lethal' grenade, which led to its unauthorized use as a training grenade, and it took one or two serious accidents to convince people that there was, after all, a certain amount of danger attached to it.

The 69 Grenade (center) and examples of the fragmentation sleeves

The fuse was operated by a lead ball; this was retained safely by a pin attached to a short length of tape having a weight at its free end. The tape and weight were wrapped round the fuse and held by a safety cap. To throw the grenade, this cap was unscrewed and removed, and when the grenade left the thrower's hand its movement through the air caused the tape to unwind, so that the pull of the weight removed the safety pin. The grenade was then armed; on landing, at any angle, the lead ball's momentum would cause it to move, and one way or another, drive a needle into a detonator and detonate the grenade filling. Hence the term 'all-ways'.

The Grenade No. 69 was quite widely used, particularly in Northwest Europe, as an adjunct to house clearing. No variant entered service, but in 1944 cast iron jackets, which could be fitted around the grenade so as to give lethal fragments, were tried. They proved to be inferior in effect to a properly designed defensive grenade such as the 36M, and also made an awkward handful for throwing. The trials were abandoned in July 1944.

UK

Grenade, hand, No. 70

Length 3.85in
Weight 1lb
Filling Baratol
Fusing Impact

In discussing the 36M grenade, we noted that from time to time a new design could be put forward to supplant the old faithful, and the Grenade No. 70 was one of these young hopefuls. Three particular objections raised to the 36M were firstly its weight, secondly the fact that since the detonator was off to one side the propagation of detonation through the explosive filling was theoretically faulty, and thirdly that if a man dropped the grenade in the act of throwing, either by accident or by becoming a casualty, the lever flew off and the fuse began to burn, and unless he could pick it up and get rid of it he was liable to be hoist with his own petard. And in the case of a man wounded in the act of

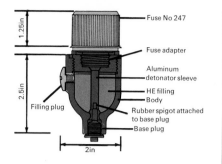

The Grenade No. 70

throwing, the chances of his being capable of disposing of the live grenade were slender indeed.

The No. 70 grenade set out to remedy these faults. In fact it was very little more than an up-to-date version of the Grenade No. 54, a 1920s design which had attempted to solve the same problems. The weight was reduced to 1lb, enabling the soldier to carry more and throw it farther; the detonator was fitted centrally to give better initiation, and thus produce fragmentation as good as, if not better than, the 36M; and the grenade was fitted with the No. 247 'all-ways' fuse as used on the No. 69 grenade. Design work began in 1944 and numerous types of explosive were tried before settling on the tried and true Baratol. A good deal of trouble arose over the sensitivity of the fuse but eventually, early in 1945, a quantity of grenades were sent to the 14th Army in Burma for extended trials in combat. They appear to have performed reasonably well, though from all accounts the troops preferred the 36M. In any case there was still trouble with the fuse and since there seemed to be some doubt about its safety, the remaining grenades were withdrawn and destroyed in bulk. Although experimentation continued for some time after the war, the design was finally abandoned and the grenade declared obsolete.

Variants

Mark 1 Experimental Model, never issued; fused No. 247 Mk 1.
Mark 2 Issue model; fused No. 247 Mk 2.
Mark 3 Slight changes in construction; never issued.

UK

Grenade, hand, No. 74 (The sticky bomb)

Length 9.5in
Weight 2lb 4oz
Filling 1lb 4oz Nitro-Glycerin
Fusing 5-second delay

The Grenade No. 74, known always as the 'Sticky Bomb', was developed privately (i.e. not in a Government establishment) in the summer of 1940 as an anti-tank grenade. It was offered for trial but turned down on the grounds of safety; the device was a spherical glass flask filled with nitro-glycerin; the neck of the flask was formed into a screw-thread and a handle

The No. 74 'Sticky' grenade

was attached by a connecting ring. This handle contained a spring-driven striker, fuse and detonator, operated by a lever, similar to that used in the 36M grenade. The outer surface of the flask was covered in stockinette material and coated with a tenacious adhesive bearing some resemblance to bird-lime. Two thin metal hemispheres, spring-loaded to fly apart when a pin was released, were closed over the flask and secured to the handle so that the grenade could be carried and stored without sticking to everything it touched.

After its refusal by the more conventional authorities, it was offered to MD1, the department responsible for developing and producing less orthodox weapons for clandestine organizations, and through them it entered service, eventually being issued to the army and the Home Guard, as well as being supplied to partisan units in Occupied Europe.

The first design was not entirely satisfactory, the striker giving misfires and the glass flask being prone to leaks and breakage, and it came before the Ordnance Board in September 1940 with a request that they improve the design. Since they were the people who had refused it in the first place, they were less than pleased to find themselves burdened with the problem of turning it into a workable proposition, and their first report contained the phrase, 'The whole article is most objectionable', which was fair comment. Their redesign improved the striker, used plastic for the flask instead of glass, and connected handle and flask directly instead of through an intermediate ring.

The operation of this grenade called for some courage; while it could be thrown, it was preferable to place it in position. The operator first released the pin holding the hemispheres, allowing them to fall away and expose the adhesive flask. He then ran to the tank, jabbed the bomb into the selected spot, released the handle and then had five seconds in which to take cover. The breaking of the flask against the tank released the nitro-glycerin, but the stockinette bag kept it in place until the detonation. When properly used it was an effective weapon, but beyond being used by partisans for demolitions in Europe, there is no record of it ever having been used in combat. Although not officially obsolete until 1951, it was rarely seen after 1944.

UK

Grenade, Anti-tank, No. 75 (The Hawkins grenade)

Length 6.5in
Weight 2.25lb
Filling 1.74lb Ammonal, Burrowite or Nobel's 704B
Fusing Crush igniter

The 75 grenade was always known as the 'Hawkins' after its inventor, a practice relatively common in the grenades of World War I. Although called a grenade it was actually an anti-tank mine, small but effective against early tanks; it was normally placed, though with some skill it could be thrown so as to land in front of a tank. It was necessary for the tank to drive

Hawkins grenade with chemical igniter

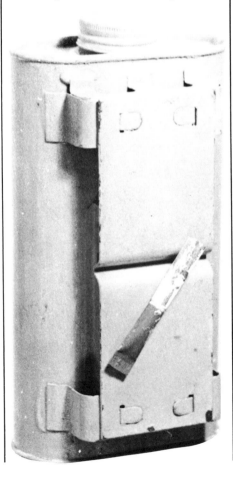

over it since detonation was by two 'crush igniters' beneath the cover of the mine. These contained a chemical compound and a glass capsule of acid; when the top plate of the mine was crushed by the tank, the capsule broke and the acid ran into the compound to generate flame and thus initiate the explosive train which finished in detonation of the charge.

Generally the Hawkins was buried in some suitable place, but one recommended practice was to tie a number together at intervals on a long string and place them at the roadside, suitably concealed by grass or straw. The end of the string led across the road to an operator hidden in a slit trench. On the approach of the tank, he waited until it was so close that both he and the mines would be below the tank crew's line of vision, and then rapidly pulled on the string to drag the line of grenades across the tank's path. He then ducked into his trench to await the bang.

It was also of a convenient size for cutting railway track, since it would fit snugly into the web of the rail between head and foot, though when so used it was necessary to remove the crush igniters and replace them with conventional detonators fired either electrically or by a length of burning safety fuse.

The Hawkins was widely used in the Middle East, where it was found to be quite sufficient to break the track of the Panzer III, and although it saw little employment during the latter stages of the war it remained officially in service until 1955.

Variants
There were three marks of the Hawkins, but the indifferences were largely in matters of filling arrangements. The only recognizable difference between them was that in the Mark 1 the igniters fitted in pockets parallel to the body of the mine, while in the Marks 2 and 3 the pockets ran obliquely across the mine.

UK

Grenade, hand or projector, No. 76

Length 6in
Weight 1lb 3oz
Filling A mixture of phosphorus, benzine, etc.
Fusing None

This grenade is more commonly remembered as the 'S.I.P.' or 'Self Igniting Phosphorus' grenade. In its early days, it was also called the 'A.W. Bomb' after Messrs Albright & Wilson of Oldbury who were the principal producers of white phosphorus at that time and who devised the grenade. It appears to have been first demonstrated on 29 July 1940; a contemporary report noted, 'Glass bottles filled with the incendiary mixture were thrown at pieces of wood and into a hut. In every case a fierce fire was started.' Originally, it seems, the idea was to use the

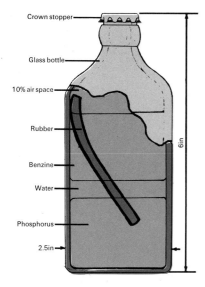

No. 76 Self-igniting Phosphorus grenade, a dangerous weapon to both sides

mixture as an incendiary bomb filling for RAF use, the throwing of glass bottles being merely a convenient way of demonstrating its self-igniting property. But the RAF, while admitting it was highly effective, turned the proposal down on the (quite reasonable) grounds that, 'the carriage of spontaneously inflammable liquids in aircraft is not considered to be desirable.'

However, the germ of the idea took root, and some time later in the year the No. 76 Grenade was born. The grenade body was simply a half-pint glass bottle, and the filling was a mixture of phosphorus, benzine, water and other chemicals, together with a strip of crude rubber. The rubber softened and partly dissolved during storage to give an adhesive quality to the mixture. When thrown, the bottle broke and the contents ignited spontaneously, and the grenade was primarily issued as an anti-tank weapon.

Sometime in 1941 somebody had the idea of firing this grenade from the Home Guard's Northover Projector. The original bottles were rather weak and frequently shattered under the force of the propelling charge, so a stronger bottle was provided. In order to distinguish these, they were sealed with a green Crown Cap, the hand-thrown versions having a red one. When fired from the projector a cardboard ring was slipped over the bottle neck; this was a tight fit in the weapon's barrel and prevented the bottle from sliding down or even out of the barrel when fired at angles of depression.

The No. 76 Grenade was issued to army units in Britain during 1940–41, but was largely an issue to Home Guard. It was officially declared obsolete in February 1944, but vast numbers had been issued in 1940–41 without very strict accounting. Many were buried in caches against a possible invasion and later forgotten; today they are often unearthed during building operations, and even after over thirty years of burial they are still highly dangerous devices.

Grenade, hand, No. 80 WP

Length 5.5in
Weight 1lb 3½oz
Filling 11¼oz White Phosphorus
Fusing 2½ to 4-second delay

During the course of the war numerous smoke grenades were developed and issued, and of these the 80 has been selected as a representative model. It was first issued early in 1943 and is still in military use today in an improved form.

The construction is quite simple; a tin-plate cylindrical body with the top end threaded to accept a striker mechanism and filled with white phosphorus. The striker mechanism is a variant of the 'Bouchon Igniter' first developed in France during World War I and later improved by the US Army during the 1930s. A fly-off lever, held by the usual safety pin, holds a spring-loaded arm away from a percussion cap. Withdrawing the pin and releasing the lever allows it to be flung off by the striker arm's spring-loading, allowing the arm to swing through an arc of about 200° and drive a small striker into the cap; the action of the arm leads to the class of mechanism

No. 80 white phosphorus smoke grenade

called the 'Mouse-trap igniter'.

When the cap has been struck, the subsequent flame ignites a short length of fuse which in turn ignites a detonator. This is sufficiently powerful to burst open the grenade body and fling the white phosphorus over a radius of about ten yards. The phosphorus, self-igniting in the presence of air, provides an immediate smoke cloud and also has some value as an incendiary and anti-personnel agent.

Like the 36M, the 80 saw service in all theaters of war. For airborne use the carriage of white phosphorus was considered hazardous; see the entry for the No. 76 grenade for the RAF's views on carriage of WP in aircraft. As a result, the Grenade No. 79 was offered as an alternative; this used an 'all-ways' fuse and was filled with a burning composition, giving a dense smoke cloud but taking several seconds to build up instead of being instantaneous.

Grenade, hand, No. 82 (The Gammon grenade)

Dimensions Variable--see text
Fusing Impact, all-ways

The Gammon Grenade goes down in military history as the only officially issued 'Do-it-yourself' grenade. The design appears to have originated with the Airborne forces, and their object was to try and relieve the airborne soldier of some of the weight with which he was being threatened as the list of desirable accessories grew longer and longer. Among the many things he was expected to carry was a supply of plastic explosive in sticks; when demolitions were needed, a quick levy around the men in the area would thus be sure of producing the necessary explosive, since in the environment in which airborne troops expected to fight it would not always be convenient to go looking for an engineer specialist.

Another desirable item was, of course, a supply of grenades, and it must have occurred to someone that a grenade was little more than a fuse with a quantity of explosive underneath; and since the soldiers were already carrying explosives, why not just give them the fuse and they could bring the two together as and when required.

Thus the No. 82 grenade was born; as issued it consisted of no more than an all-ways fuse attached to a cloth bag which was open at the bottom and gathered by a strong elastic band. Quite a number of these could be crushed together and carried in the soldier's pockets or pouches, and they added little weight to his burden. When a grenade was wanted, a quantity of plastic explosive was pushed into the bag, around the base of the fuse, the cap removed and the assembly thrown. The amount of plastic used depended on the user's requirement; a half-stick for blowing in a house door or clearing a dugout, two sticks to attack a tank, or any suitable amount in between.

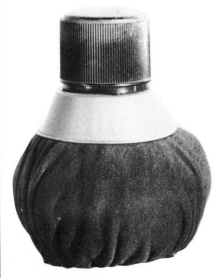

The Gammon grenade, filled and empty

The fuse originally issued had a 4in tape, which removed the pin and armed the fuse almost as soon as it left the thrower's hand; but this, apparently, was a little too dangerous, and most production used the normal 11.5in tape. The name 'Gammon' is said to have been given due to the filled grenade's resemblance to a wrapped gammon. Beauty is in the eye of the beholder.

The Gammon seems to have been used

on most airborne operations from North Africa onwards down to the end of the war; its principal applications were either as an anti-tank bomb or for house-to-house work, where it was particularly useful for 'mouse-holing', i.e. blowing holes in connecting walls to allow clearing parties to move from house to house in a street without having to go outside the house to do it.

Grenade, rifle, No. 85

Length 10.5in
Weight 1lb 4¼oz
Filling 4¼oz RDX/TNT
Fusing Impact

This, as its appearance might suggest, is the British Army's copy of the American M9A1 grenade. The Grenade No. 68, while effective at the target, was a poor ballistic shape and demanded a cup discharger fitted to the rifle. The M9A1, while slightly less effective, was a better ballistic shape, leading to more accuracy and greater range, and used a different design of spigot launcher which was less cumbersome on the rifle. As a result, designs of a similar grenade were begun.

The grenade consisted of a hollow charge head on the end of a tail tube which carried three tail vanes surrounded by a circular drum. A simple impact fuse in the forepart of the tail unit had a safety pin which was withdrawn before firing. The hollow tail unit slipped over the rifle discharger, and a special ballistite cartridge was loaded into the rifle breech. When fired, the gas propelled the grenade from the spigot and at the same time acted on a diaphragm in the fuse to arm the mechanism so that it would detonate the grenade on impact.

The No. 85 grenade was introduced in April 1945 and was only supplied for the final stages of the Far East campaign. It was intended to supplement it with a fragmentation grenade, the 86, which resembled a 36 M grenade on the same tail unit, and a signal and illuminating grenade, the 89. Before the design of the 86 was completed, a Mark 3 model of the 85 was developed (see below) and, since this appeared likely to serve both anti-tank and anti-personnel roles, the 86 was abandoned. However, in 1946 the entire line of rifle grenades was reviewed and a policy decision taken to abandon them entirely. As a result the 89 was abandoned and the 85 declared obsolete in 1947.

Variants
Mark 1 Service grenade described above.
Mark 2 Fitted with a different model of fuse. The drawings of this mark were 'sealed for record only' which is an indication that few, if any, were made.
Mark 3 Had the body wrapped with hardened steel wire so as to give fragments for anti-personnel effect as well as an anti-tank effect. Based on the Mark 2, it was never introduced into service.

US M9A1 grenade, from which the British No. 85 was developed; only markings differ

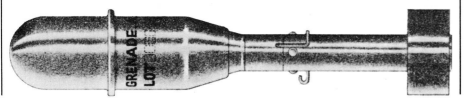

Fragmentation grenade, Mark 11A1

Length 4.5in
Weight 1.31lb
Filling ½oz E. C. Blank Fire Powder (smokeless powder flakes)
Fusing 4.5-second delay

This grenade is, as its appearance might suggest, a contemporary of the British 36M 'Mills' grenade, having originally appeared during World War I. It began as the French Army's standard defensive grenade which was adopted by the US Army in 1917. After the war they retained it as their standard hand grenade but the ignition system was somewhat improved from the original French pattern. It is of the type known as the 'Bouchon Igniter' or, more commonly, 'Mouse-trap' igniter, and the system is explained in the section on the British No. 80 grenade. Some minor

The American MkIIA1 fragmentation grenade, a relic of World War I

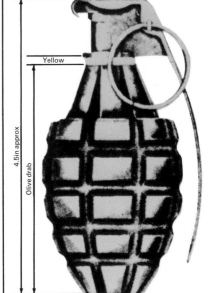

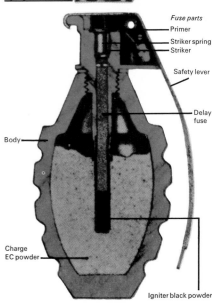

Fuse parts
Primer
Striker spring
Striker
Safety lever
Delay fuse
Body
Charge EC powder
Igniter black powder

changes in design took place during the 1920s and 1930s which culminated in the Mark IIAI pattern which remained standard throughout World War II and was phased out in the postwar period.

The body is of cast iron, serrated externally in the usual fashion. The filling is most unusual; flakes of smokeless powder. The original version (Mk II) had a filling of TNT but it was found that the violence of TNT over-fragmented the grenade, and the less violent filling of smokeless powder was sufficient to produce an adequate number of lethal fragments. Moreover, it simplified the fusing, since there was no need to fit a detonator; a length of safety fuse was terminated by a small igniter of gunpowder which delivered sufficient flash to explode the smokeless powder.

As well as being hand thrown, the Mark IIAI could also be rifle launched by means of a 'Grenade Projector Adapter M1', a tail tube with fin assembly which, by means of four spring claws, gripped the Mark IIAI grenade. One claw had an arming clip

into which fitted the lever of the grenade. When the assembled grenade and adapter was placed on the rifle discharger, the safety pin of the grenade was withdrawn; the arming clip prevented the grenade lever from moving. On firing, the set-back force of acceleration caused the arming clip to move rearward and release the grenade lever, allowing the igniter to function.

Both in its hand and rifle roles the Mark IIAI saw widespread use throughout the war years. As with the British 36M, numerous attempts were made to produce a more up-to-date grenade, without much success, and it was not until the war had ended that a replacement was finally introduced.

Variant

Grenade, Rifle, Impact, M17 This was developed to replace the combination of Mark IIAI and Rifle Adapter, and it consisted of the tail unit of the M9A1 anti-tank grenade screwed into the fuse cavity of the Mark IIAI grenade body.

US grenades fitted to projection adapters for firing from rifles

Offensive hand grenade, Mark 111A2

Length 5.35in
Weight 14oz
Filling 6½oz TNT
Fusing 4½-second delay

This is one of the more unusual grenades, in that it is made almost entirely of fiberboard and relies on blast for its effect. It is simply a fiber-board cylinder filled with TNT and having an axial well at one end to accept the usual fly-off lever igniter set. The casing is actually in two parts, the junction between being concealed by a wrapping of waterproof tape and an identifying label.

The official texts stated that 'the principal use of this grenade is for demolition, and though no protection is needed from fragments of the grenade, care should be exercised to have cover available against fragments of the structure demolished.' In spite of this it appears to have had considerable use as a pure offensive grenade in house-clearing and bunker clearing in the South Pacific Theater.

Earlier versions were the Mark IIIA1, which differed in having the ends of the body formed of pressed sheet metal crimped to the fiber-board, and the Mark III which was of similar compound construction but had thicker walls to the body and thus contained less TNT.

US 'offensive' hand grenades, relying on blast for their effect

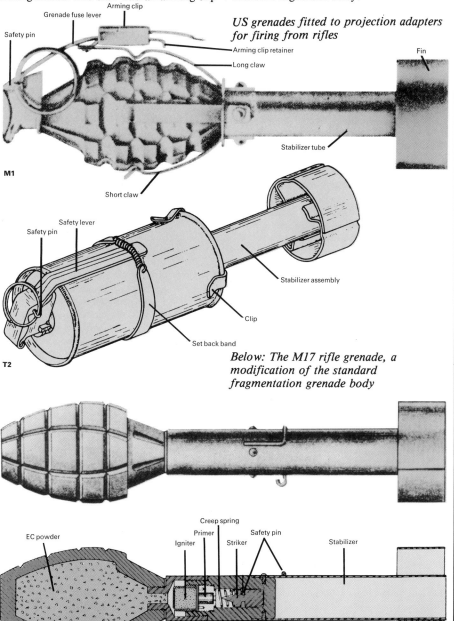

Below: The M17 rifle grenade, a modification of the standard fragmentation grenade body

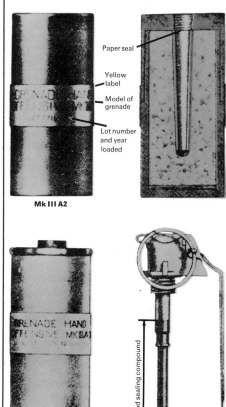

Mk III A2

Mk III A1   M6 A3 fuse

Anti-tank grenade, M9

Length 11.15in
Weight 1.23lb
Filling 4oz TNT
Fusing Impact

When the war began, the US Army was completely without any form of lightweight anti-tank weapon. The development of an anti-tank rifle had not been pursued particularly strenuously, since the .50 Browning machine gun was considered a capable anti-tank weapon; unfortunately there were few .50 Brownings, and none available for infantry to cart about as anti-tank guns. As a result the war led to a hurried search for a suitable weapon, and a spigot launched grenade was considered to be the best solution.

According to some reports Dr. Mohaupt of Switzerland, who had done some early research into hollow charge, was retained as a design consultant for the US Government. This has never been officially confirmed, but in any event, hollow charge was the only possible solution and two designs were developed, the M9 for use with the .30 rifle and the M10 for use with the 0.50 machine gun. The latter design was abandoned—there was still the question of providing sufficient machine guns—and was eventually taken as the starting point for the 2.36in rocket design. The M9 grenade was perfected and issued in 1941 but was soon superseded by the

The M9 anti-tank grenade, also the UK No. 85

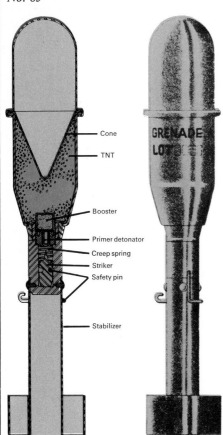

- Cone
- TNT
- Booster
- Primer detonator
- Creep spring
- Striker
- Safety pin
- Stabilizer

M9A1. The M9, indeed, was so quickly in and out of service that none of the wartime manuals has a picture of it; it is described as having an 'Acorn-shaped' head and being fitted with a nose fuse. But initiation of a hollow charge explosive must be done from the base, and although it is possible with a nose fuse—the British PIAT is one example—it is a complicated method, and the M9A1 used a base fuse, and consequently had a hemispherical nose.

Like any other wartime anti-tank device it was officially described as, 'capable of penetrating any known tank', which was a fine-sounding and reassuring phrase beloved of text-book writers, who conveniently overlooked the fact that it was the unknown tanks which always caused the trouble. In fact the penetration of the M9 was little better than 40mm due to the nose fuse interfering with the penetrative action of the hollow charge jet, but the M9A1 improved on this and could defeat about 60mm of plate. Like all rifle grenades it was virtually useless if fired against a frontal plate or turret face, but if the firer could get a shot at the rear plates or engine compartment, he stood a fair chance of stopping the tank and setting fire to it into the bargain.

The M9A1 remained standard issue throughout the war, but it was rarely used.

Smoke grenade (WP) M15

Length 5.0in
Weight
Filling White Phosphorus
Fusing 4½-second delay

This grenade was very similar to the British No. 80 and carried white phosphorus inside a sealed canister with a 'mouse-trap' igniter screwed into one end. It was easily recognized by being painted yellow and having rounded edges. The fuse unit terminated in a detonator which was powerful enough to break open the grenade and scatter the contents over an area about 25 yards in diameter. It was widely used as an anti-personnel grenade, particularly in the Pacific theaters.

Variants
Of similar appearance, though with angular edges, were:
Grenade, smoke, white, (HC) AN-M8
Grenade, incendiary, AN-M14
Grenade, smoke colored, M16
Grenade, smoke colored, M18

These were all types using smoke compositions which burned and emitted a smoke cloud only, and thus were of no anti-personnel application. The M8 used a hexachloroethane mixture to produce white smoke; the M16 and M18 were available in Red, Orange, Blue, Green, Black, Violet and Yellow colors. The principal difference between the M16 and the M18 was in the duration of smoke emission; the M16 delivered smoke for 2¼

The US M15 smoke grenade

minutes, while the M18 delivered it for only one minute. The M8 emitted smoke for three minutes.

The Incendiary M14 was filled with Thermite, an aluminum/iron mixture which produced sufficient local heat to melt steel. As well as being used in an offensive role to burn out strongpoints, the M14 was also the recommended method of destroying equipment to prevent it falling into enemy hands in serviceable condition. An incendiary grenade inside the breech of an artillery piece can make a mess of the chamber and breech mechanism.

The terminology AN-M used with the M8 and M14 models indicated joint standardization between the US Army and Navy.

Grenade, Model 1914/30

Length 9.3in
Weight 1lb 5oz
Filling TNT
Fusing 4 to 5-second delay

As the nomenclature implies, this grenade was a product of World War I which was somewhat improved in 1930. It was a stick grenade using a fly-off handle type of igniter, the handle lying flush with the stick and retained by a wire loop until ready to

Opposite: US troops at Cherbourg used the M9 anti-tank grenade to flush snipers out of buildings

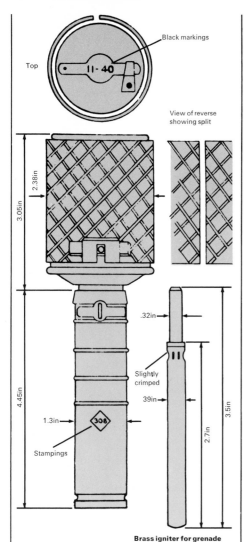

Top

Black markings

View of reverse showing split

3.05in

2.38in

4.45in

.32in

Slightly crimped

39in

2.7in

3.5in

1.3in

308

Stampings

Brass igniter for grenade

The Soviet 1914/30 stick grenade

throw. In standard form the grenade was of the 'offensive' pattern, being no more than a thin sheet steel container on the end of the stick handle, but a segmented fragmentation sleeve was available to convert it into a more lethal 'defensive' type.

These grenades were widely used during the early days of the war, notably in the fighting around Moscow, but as the stocks dwindled they were replaced by models which were easier and quicker to manufacture.

Variant
Model 1933 This was developed as a potential replacement for the 1914/30, and was also a stick grenade with optional fragmentation sleeve. Its distinction lay in one of the most complex and ridiculous firing systems ever inflicted on a grenade. The fuse mechanism was buried inside the head; to operate, the head and handle were grasped, the handle pulled away from the head against a spring and given a half-turn to the right; a safety slide on the head was then pushed across to the left, and the grenade thrown, when an inertia mechanism armed the impact fuse. Needless to say, this contraption had a short service career.

USSR

Fragmentation grenade, F-1

Length 4in
Weight 1lb 4oz
Filling 1.6oz TNT
Fusing 4 to 5-second delay

This was a conventional 'defensive' grenade with the typical serrated body of the breed. An external handle and safety pin resemble the Mills pattern but the action is entirely different. When the grenade is grasped and the handle held, the pin is removed. When the grenade is thrown, the handle is flung off axially, not radially; a compressed spring in the cap attached to the handle pushes the cap off and releases a striker to initiate the delay fuse. It follows that, since the handle moves longitudinally, it needs a good firm grip, and if the hands or the grenade are at all wet or slippery, the handle can very easily slip from under the fingers.

Variant
RTD 1942 An economy version, consisting of a tin canister with a fragmentation sleeve inside and a TNT filling, using the same igniter and lever system as the F-1. It completely replaced the F-1 during the war and remained a standard issue grenade for many years afterwards.

The Soviet F-1 fragmentation grenade, showing the peculiar striker mechanism which flied off axially

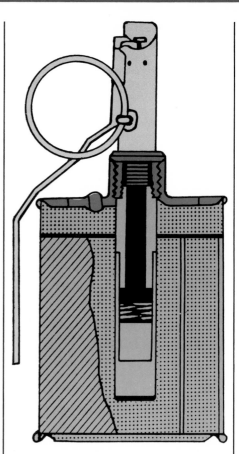

Sectioned drawing of the Soviet RTD-1942 economy grenade

USSR

Anti-tank grenade, RPG–43

Length 8in
Weight 2lb 12oz
Filling TNT
Fusing Impact

The first Russian anti-tank grenade, the RPG–40, was little more than an overgrown stick grenade, relying entirely on blast for its effect. It was far from satisfactory, and as soon as specimens of German hollow charge weapons were captured, the Soviets began work on a more scientific grenade.

The basis was a stick grenade with fly-off lever, attached to a cylindrical head containing the hollow charge assembly. A conical sleeve fitted over the handle, close against the head, and concealed two fabric strips. When thrown, the lever flew off and armed the impact fuse, and at the same time it released the conical sleeve, which slipped from the handle and dragged behind the grenade at the end of the cloth strips, stabilizing the grenade so that it arrived at the target head first. On striking, a firing pin was thrown forward to strike a detonator and initiate the explosive charge.

It was claimed that the grenade could pierce three inches of homogeneous plate; the charge diameter was 3.75in and one would be entitled to expect a better performance than that from it, though prob-

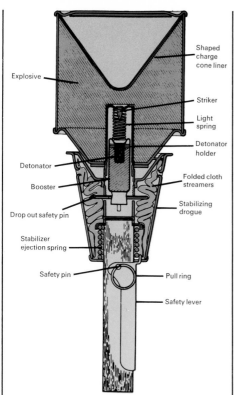

Soviet RPG-1943 anti-tank grenade, showing details of the stabilizing system

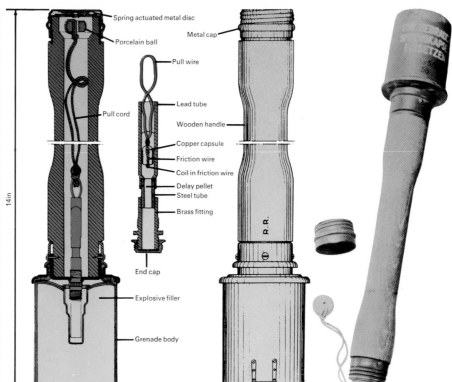

Above left: German stick grenade
Above: Details of the German stick grenade

ably the absence of any arrangement to 'stand off' the charge to allow the penetrative jet to form more efficiently was responsible for this relatively poor performance. Nevertheless, it was sufficient to deal with most German tanks, provided the thrower picked his point of aim, and it was extensively and effectively used throughout the war.

Germany

Steilhandgranate 39

Length 16in
Weight 1lb 6oz
Filling 7oz TNT
Fusing 4½-second delay

This grenade was the standard German hand grenade, and was little changed from the StG24 introduced during World War I. It consisted of a thin metal cylindrical head with a high explosive filling, screwed to a hollow wooden handle. The igniter consisted of a friction pull igniter connected by a short length of lead-covered safety fuse to a detonator. The pull wire of the friction igniter was attached to a length of cord ending in a porcelain ball. To prepare the grenade for use the handle was unscrewed from the head, and a metal cap removed from the bottom of the handle. The igniter unit was then passed through the hollow handle and the detonator screwed into a socket in the head unit. Head and handle were then screwed together again, and the end of the cord, with its porcelain ball, tucked into the hollow handle where it was retained by a spring washer. The cap was then screwed back on

to the end of the handle. The grenade could then be carried quite safely, usually in the belt or in the boot-top.

To use the grenade the screw cap was removed from the handle, allowing the ball and cord to fall out. On taking the grenade in the hand to throw, the other hand grasped the string and, as the thrower swung his arm back, so he pulled the cord, drawing the pin of the friction igniter through the composition and generating a flame which lit the safety fuse. The grenade was then thrown overarm, the average range being thirty yards or so.

Universally employed as a hand grenade, it could also be used as a form of booby-trap by hanging it head down from a barbed wire obstacle by the pull-cord. In this employment, any movement of the wire obstacle would cause the weight of the grenade to drag the cord free and function the igniter.

It was also used as an anti-tank and anti-emplacement charge by lashing six grenade heads around a complete grenade, using the central grenade to act as the detonator for all, producing considerable blast effect.

Variants

In order to improve fragmentation effect, a steel fragmentation sleeve was supplied and could be clipped round the head of the grenade.

StG 24 This was an older model, but basically the same as the StG 39; it was two inches shorter and slightly lighter in weight.

Nebelhandgranat 39 This was identical in appearance with the StG 39 but had the head filled with smoke composition, and was the standard German smoke grenade.

StG 43 Similar to the StG 39 but the head was permanently fixed to the handle and a

pull igniter was screwed into the flat top of the grenade head.

Behelfs-Handgranate Holz An emergency grenade produced late in the war, this resembled the StG 39 but was entirely of wood. It used the same igniter system but relied entirely on blast for its effect.

Behelfs Handgranate Beton This appeared in North Africa and is believed to have been a local expedient. It resembled the StG 39 in shape and size, but the head consisted of a 100-gram explosive charge contained in a casing of half-an-inch thick concrete.

German tank fighter with Tellermine and bundle charge awaits the arrival of Soviets

Eihandgranate 39

Length 3.0in
Weight 10oz
Filling 6oz TNT
Fusing 4 to 5-second delay

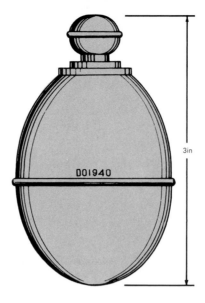

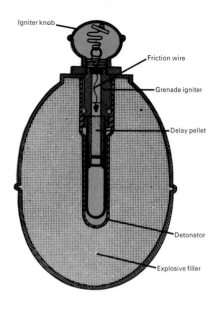

The Eihandgranate 39 was an offensive grenade, using a thin metal body with a high proportion of high explosive. Ignition was by the Brennzunder fur Eihandgranate (BZE) igniter screwed into the center. To use this igniter, the head cap was unscrewed and pulled sharply away from the grenade; the cap was connected by a length of string to a friction igniter which ignited the usual delay fuse and detonator assembly.

The design of this igniter set lent itself to some adaptations. One official variation had a one-second delay fuse, which turned the grenade into an effective booby-trap; in order to distinguish these, the cap of the igniter was painted red instead of the usual light blue of the normal model. To use it, it could be placed in position and the cap unscrewed and tied to a trip wire, or it could simply be left lying around in the hope that the finder would try and use it in the normal way. When this trick became too well known to Soviet troops, a more subtle and unofficial variation was invented; the igniter set was removed and, with two pairs of pliers, dismantled so as to remove the safety fuse section. The friction igniter was then screwed directly into the detonator housing and the igniter set replaced in the grenade. This was then left in a conspicuous place when retreating. The effect, of course, was to detonate the grenade as soon as the cap was pulled off.

In order to adapt the grenade to defensive situations a fragmentation sleeve was produced. This was made in two identical half-egg shapes, and two could be clamped around a grenade and locked by a quarter turn. The sleeves were serrated, of 3/32nd inch cast iron, and under ideal conditions would disintegrate into 96 fragments each $\frac{1}{2} \times \frac{3}{8}$ of an inch.

Variants

There were numerous minor modifications in manufacture from time to time, but none was identified by special nomenclature. Perhaps the most significant variant was that in which the friction igniter was replaced by a spring-loaded striker. This version was identified by having a royal blue cap on the igniter set, and was operated by simply unscrewing and removing the cap; this released the striker which initiated the delay system.

Another, less common variant, was distinguished by a prominent screwed joint around the center of the body. This was to allow the explosive charge to be preformed into a shaped block, dropped into the bottom half of the grenade, and then the top half could be screwed on, a system evolved during the war to speed up production.

Above: Details of the German 'Egg' grenade, which replaced the stick type

Below: German soldiers preparing bundle charges, with egg and stick grenades

Germany

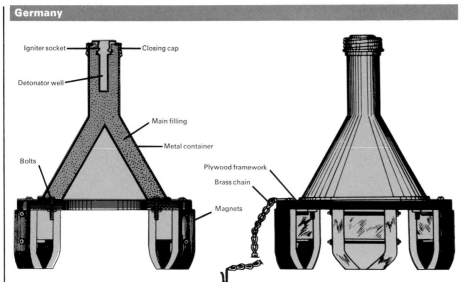

Igniter socket
Closing cap
Detonator well
Main filling
Metal container
Bolts
Plywood framework
Brass chain
Magnets

Heft Hohladung granate 3 KG

Length
Weight 7lb 11oz
Filling 3lb 5oz TNT
Fusing 4½ or 7-second delay
Penetration 110mm

This is one of a series of magnetic grenades, all of similar design, ranging from two to ten kilograms in weight. This, the three kilogram (nominally) was probably the most common, since it was the most convenient size.

The grenade resembled a funnel, into the wide part of which fitted a conical hollow charge liner, and around the circumference of which were fixed three Alnico permanent magnets. The body behind the conical liner was filled with explosive and the handle terminated in a screwed closing cap, beneath which was a friction igniter. Two different igniter sets were available, the 4½-second, with a blue cap, for use when the grenade was thrown, and a 7-second, with yellow cap, for when the grenade was placed by hand, so as to give the placer time to get clear before the detonation.

These grenades were exceptionally effective, and could defeat the armor of any tank. They were also highly effective against strongpoints, being able to pierce twenty in of reinforced concrete. In this application, obviously, the magnets were useless and a brass hook and chain were attached to the rim of the grenade, by which it could be hung from a nail on a wall, or it could be stood upright on a flat surface.

The magnetic grenades were used to good effect against Russian tanks and later against British and US tanks in Normandy, though in the latter part of the war the supply of magnets became difficult and the grenade was largely superseded by other types. It is noteworthy that the Germans had enough respect for this type of weapon to go to the trouble of developing a special antimagnetic coating, known as Zimmerit-Paste, for painting on their tanks. This substance, which consisted of Poly-

German 3Kg magnetic anti-tank grenade

vinyl, wood fiber, barium sulphate and zinc sulphate was suitably colored and applied thickly to all German armored vehicles and formed an effective method of preventing the adhesion of magnetic grenades; it derived its name from the Chemische Werk Zimmer AG of Berlin who developed it. It was a clever development but entirely wasted, since no Allied army developed a magnetic grenade.

Germany

Nipolit grenades

One of the many outstanding technical innovations of the war was the development in Germany of a new explosive substance called Nipolit. It was developed by the Westfalische Anhaltische Sprengstoff AG (WASAG), a prominent chemical and explosives concern, in an endeavor to put to some use large quantities of old gun propellant which was no longer ballistically suitable for its original purpose. Moreover, the process made considerable savings in the consumption of nitric acid; whereas 1000 tons of TNT required the use of 1100 tons of acid, 1000 tons of Nipolit could be produced for the consumption of only 430 tons of acid.

The most remarkable (and apparently unexpected) property of Nipolit was its high mechanical strength; it could be cut,

shaped, milled, threaded or bored rather like a plastic material. The first result of this discovery seems to have been a proposal to produce pre-formed fillings for grenades and mines, but doubtless somebody pointed out that the metal portion of an offensive grenade or a mine does little more than hold everything together and protect the explosive. There seemed little point in putting a casing round Nipolit since it was waterproof and strong enough to hold all the necessary components of fuses or igniters. And so the Nipolit grenade was born; a lump of Nipolit, cast or cut to the desired shape, drilled and tapped for the igniter, and that was that.

The first model seems to have been a plain disc of Nipolit 85mm in diameter and 13mm thick, with a threaded hole in the circumference into which the egg grenade pull igniter was screwed. Then came two egg grenades, a large (95mm long) and a small (65mm long), again simply turned pieces of Nipolit with a central hole for the igniter. Next came a cylinder of Nipolit wrapped with a steel fragmentation sleeve, then a new head for the stick grenade, followed inevitably by a complete stick grenade in which the entire unit, stick and head, was of one piece of Nipolit. An egg grenade pull igniter was screwed into the bottom of the handle; it was no longer necessary to put the igniter in the head, since the entire grenade was now explosive.

It is difficult to say how many of these types of grenade were manufactured or went into service, since much of the development took place towards the latter end of 1944, but the egg and disc patterns were certainly encountered in the field by Allied troops in Germany. Other types, together with mine fillings and demolition charges, were found in Germany after the war.

It is perhaps surprising that no further work seems to have been done on this type of material; this is probably due to the problems of storage and fire prevention. A normally cased grenade is (comparatively speaking) a low fire risk, but a naked lump of explosive, even when in a crate, poses problems in transit and storage, and in most countries would be quite outside the pale of existing explosives legislation and regulations.

A German 'Nipolit' stick grenade

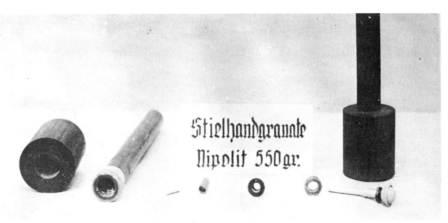

Stielhandgranate
Nipolit 550gr.

Gewehr Sprenggranaten – rifle grenades

The standard system of firing rifle grenades in the German Army was by the use of a rifled discharger cup—the Schiessbecker—of 3cm caliber, which was attached to the rifle muzzle by a quick clamping system. Special propelling cartridges were provided; each grenade was packed separately in a carton and the appropriate cartridge attached by a paper strip. The grenades had either a grooved body or a grooved driving band which engaged in the rifling of the discharger cup when loaded and which spun the grenade on launch to stabilize it in flight and thus improve both range and accuracy. Early designs were of 3cm caliber throughout, almost the whole grenade entering the cup, but when hollow charge grenades were introduced it was found necessary to make the warheads of greater diameter in order to achieve a worthwhile effect, a 3cm caliber stem behind the warhead entering the discharger cup.

The number of different rifle grenades developed and issued was so great that to devote a whole page to each would take more space than can be afforded.

Below: Type 2 rifle grenade launcher
Below right: Section of grenade launcher for the Mauser rifle

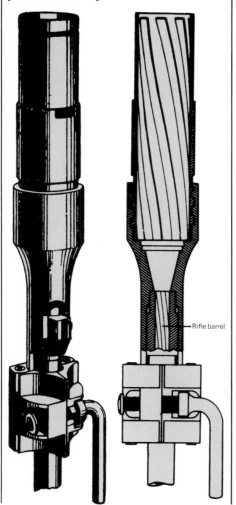

Rifle barrel

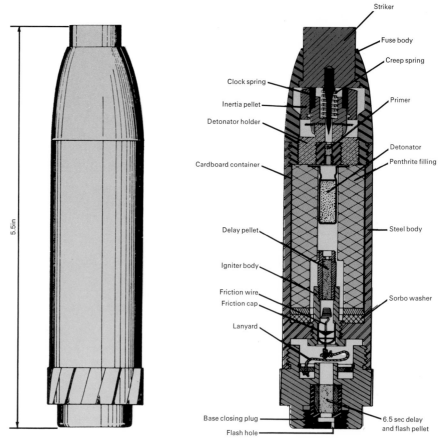

Striker
Fuse body
Creep spring
Clock spring
Inertia pellet
Detonator holder
Primer
Cardboard container
Detonator
Penthrite filling
Delay pellet
Steel body
Igniter body
Friction wire
Friction cap
Sorbo washer
Lanyard
Base closing plug
6.5 sec delay and flash pellet
Flash hole

Above: German rifle grenade Gew Spr Gr 30/1, showing internal details

5.5in

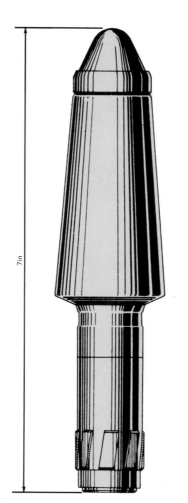

7in

Below: German rifle grenade Gross Gew. Pz. Gr. for anti-tank shooting

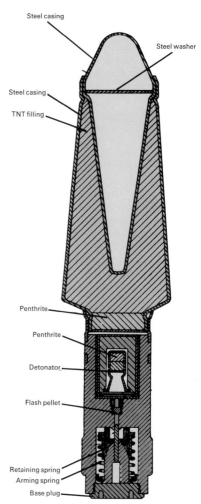

Steel casing
Steel washer
Steel casing
TNT filling
Penthrite
Penthrite
Detonator
Flash pellet
Retaining spring
Arming spring
Base plug

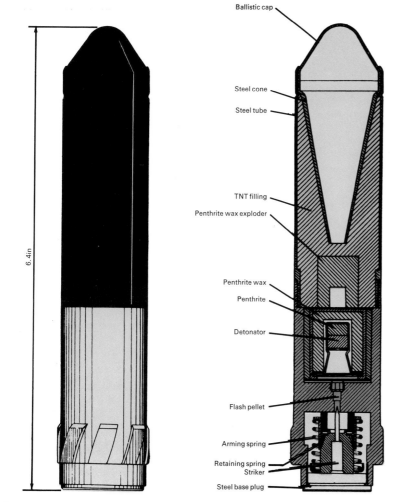

Ballistic cap

Steel cone

Steel tube

TNT filling

Penthrite wax exploder

Penthrite wax

Penthrite

Detonator

Flash pellet

Arming spring

Retaining spring
Striker

Steel base plug

6.4in

Above: Aiming with a grenade launcher
Below left: The Klein Gew. Pz. Gr.
hollow charge rifle grenade
Below: Loading the Type 30/1 rifle
grenade into the launching attachment

German rifle grenades

Grenade	Type	Description	Launcher cartridge
Gew Sprgr 30/1	HE	Yellow body, black nose, brown plastic pre-rifled base. Impact or all-ways fuse, with 11-second delay to self-destruction. Range normally 275m. Could be hand-thrown by removing fuse and fitting friction igniter.	1. Crimped mouth, yellow cap. 2. Long neck with wood plug, yellow cap. 3. Normal case with blue wood bullet.
Gew Sprgr 30/2	HE	As 30/1 but with impact fuse only. Could be hand thrown.	As for 30/1.
Gew Sprgr 30/3	HE	As for 30/2 but not capable of hand-throwing.	As for 30/1
Gew Sprgr 30/4	HE	As for 30/3 but for long range to 500m. Stenciled 'Weitschuss'.	As for 30/1 plus a special long range cartridge with yellow wooden bullet.
Gew Sprgr 30/5	HE	As for 30/4 but a different fuse.	As for 30/4.
Gew Sprgr 30/6	HE	As 30/4 but with an all-ways fuse.	As for 30/4.
Gew Sprgr 30 Ub	Practice	Similar to 30/1 but with a small spotting charge.	As for 30/1.
Gross Gew Panzergr	Anti-tank	Enlarged head on shank with pre-rifled band. Penetration 40mm; range 100m.	Normal case, black wood bullet.
Klein Gew Panzergr	Anti-tank	Constant 3cm diameter. Pre-rifled band. Penetration 40mm; range 100m.	Case with crimped mouth and black cap annulus.
Gew Panzergr 46mm	Anti-tank	Enlarged head of 46mm diameter. 3cm tail with pre-rifling formed on it. Penetration 90mm; range 100m.	Case with crimped mouth and brass percussion cap.
SS Gew Panzergr 61	Anti-tank	Enlarged head of 61mm diameter, tail as for 46mm model. Penetration 125mm; range 200m.	Long, necked, cartridge closed by wooden plug. Zinc percussion cap.
Gew Blendgranat 42	Smoke	Large grooved skirt which lay outside the discharger cup when loaded and which stabilized the grenade in flight. A pre-rifled stem entered the cup in the usual way.	Case with crimped mouth and yellow percussion cap.
Gew Fallschirm Leuchtgr	Parachute illuminating	Similar to HE 30/1 but painted brown with a white nose. 32,000 candlepower flare which burned 25 seconds and illuminated targets up to 700 meters away.	Case with yellow wooden bullet and uncolored percussion cap.
Gew Propagandagr	Leaflets	Cylindrical body with loose fitting nosecap and a small charge to expel the leaflets. Range 500m with 2oz of leaflets.	Long, necked, cartridge case with brownish-yellow bullet of wood.

Germany

The Kampfpistole
(Battle Pistol)

The Leuchtpistole
(Signal Pistol)

Like every other army the Germans used a smooth-bore 27mm caliber signal pistol for firing a wide (much wider than anyone else's) variety of signaling cartridge, emitting colored stars, smoke puffs and even sound signals. However, they took the idea a stage further by producing small grenades which could also be launched from the Leuchtpistole. These proved to be quite effective within their limits, and so, to try and extend these limits, the Kampfpistole was introduced. This was based on the signal pistol but adopted the same pattern of rifling as was used with the rifle discharger cup, in the interest of longer range and better accuracy.

There were two basic models of Kampfpistole. The first to be issued was simply

Firing the original Kampfpistole Opposite: A German infantry squad, grenades and rifles at the ready, prepare for the final assault on their objective

Demonstrating the second model of battle

the standard Walther Leuchtpistole with the barrel bored out and rifled with eight lands and grooves. A small bubble-type clinometer sight was attached to the left rear of the pistol, above the butt. Four types of grenade were developed for use with this pistol, but in addition, the standard smooth-bore Leuchtpistole ammunition could also be fired from it, though with some risk of bulged cartridge cases and some slight loss of range.

The improved model was again a modification of the Leuchtpistole, but in this version the barrel was bored out and a rifled steel liner inserted. This liner was formed with a collar at the base end which prevented loading any of the normal breech-loading Leuchtpistole or Kampf-pistole ammunition. A removable sight was fitted to the barrel and a folding butt was provided. By removing the liner (quickly done with the aid of a screwdriver) and replacing it with a smooth-bore liner, any ammunition for the smooth-bore Leucht-pistole could be fired. But none of the rounds for the original Kampfpistole could be fired from this second model.

The Kampfpistolen were widely used, probably more on the Eastern Front than anywhere else, but they were principally employed for anti-personnel work.

Grenades for the Leuchtpistole

Wurfkorper 361 LP An Egg Grenade 39 screwed to a stem. Before firing, a brass reinforcing tube had to be fitted into the barrel of the pistol from the breech end. At the base of the grenade stem was a percussion cap and small propelling charge. This also lit a delay of $4\frac{1}{2}$ seconds to detonate the grenade. Range 75 to 100m.

Wurfgranat Patrone 326 LP A small finned bomb in a signal-type cartridge case. On firing, a safety pin slid from the tail and armed the impact fuse. Range 300m with short-barrelled pistol, 500m with long.

Sprenggranat Pat. LP Cylindrical projectile with rounded nose held in a signal-type cartridge case. Only for close-quarter fighting from tanks or cover, since the range was only about 5m, less than the danger area. Delay fuse of 1 second.

Panzerwurfkorper 42LP Pear-shaped hollow charge head on pre-rifled stem. Only used with a specially modified pistol having a 23mm rifled liner, fore-end grip, butt and special sights. Range 80m, penetration 80mm.

Nebelgranate 42/11 The Egg Smoke grenade 42 on a stem, similar to the WKp 361 LP.

Grenades for the original Kampfpistole

Sprengpatrone fur KP High explosive pre-rifled projectile with nose fuse, fitted into a short aluminium cartridge case. Range 100m.

Nebelparone f. KP A smoke round of similar size and appearance to the HE round.

Deutpatrone f. KP A target-indicating round, similar to the previous models but with a rounded nose instead of a fuse. The propelling charge lit a pyrotechnic delay which ignited the composition in the projectile, which them emitted red-brown smoke.

Fallschirm Leuchtpatr. f. KP A parachute illuminating round. Similar to the Deut-patrone except that the nose was of black plastic. Fired into the air it ejected a white star on a parachute.

Fallschirm Signalpatr. f. KP Similar to the illuminating round but with a green star.

Nachrichtenpatrone f. KP A message-carrying projectile. The hollow body had a black plastic nose and was issued with a message form and pencil inside. The nose was unscrewed, the message written and placed inside, the nose replaced, and the round fired.

Grenades for the improved Kampfpistole

Wurfkorper 361 KP Similar to the 361 LP (above) but with a special stem having a pre-rifled band to suit the insert.

Nebelpatrone 42/11 KP An egg smoke grenade on a special pre-rifled stem.

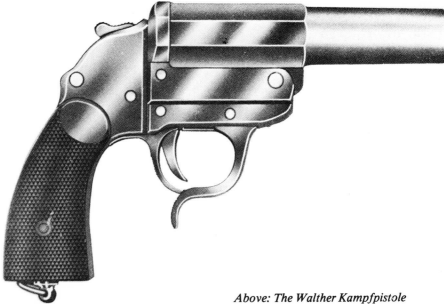

Above: The Walther Kampfpistole

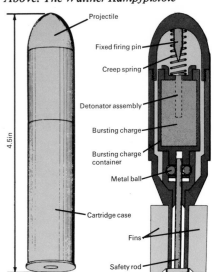

Projectile
Fixed firing pin
Creep spring
Detonator assembly
Bursting charge
Bursting charge container
Metal ball
4.5in
Cartridge case
Fins
Safety rod

Above: Battle pistol grenade 326LP

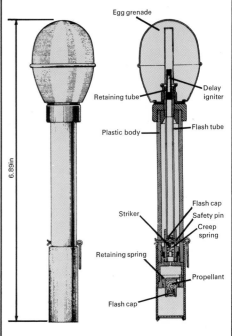

Egg grenade
Retaining tube
Plastic body
Delay igniter
Flash tube
6.89in
Flash cap
Striker
Safety pin
Creep spring
Retaining spring
Propellant
Flash cap

Battle pistol grenade 361 LP, made by fitting an egg grenade to a stem with fuse

Red Devil hand grenades

The Italian Army used three grenades, all very similar in appearance and all painted pillar-box red. They were known as the 'Red Devil Grenades' to allied troops in the Western Desert.

Breda Model 35

(Bomba a Mano Breda Modello 35)

Length 3.8in
Weight 7oz
Filling 2oz TNT
Fusing All-ways impact

This grenade had a light metal, ribbed body with rounded ends. A black safety cap on top was retained by a U-shaped safety strip which passed through the head of the grenade, separating the firing pin from the detonator. On the end of the safety strip was a cloth tab. Pulling the tab released the cap and, on throwing, the cap came off, pulling with it a brass strip and a second safety pin. On striking the ground the all-ways fuse detonated the grenade—sometimes. Sometimes it did not, but disturbing the grenade later could well cause the fuse to function, and this led to the 'Devil' part of the nickname.

Below: Italian Breda 35 hand grenade, or 'Red Devil'

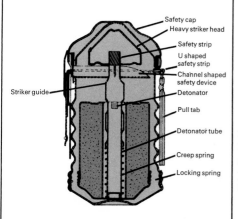

Safety cap
Heavy striker head
Safety strip
U shaped safety strip
Channel shaped safety device
Detonator
Pull tab
Detonator tube
Creep spring
Locking spring
Striker guide

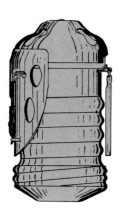

OTO Model 35

Length 3.4in
Weight 7.4oz
Filling 2½oz TNT
Fusing All-ways impact

This was shorter and fatter than the Breda, but otherwise of the same general appearance and with a similar fuse mechanism having the same defect.

Right: The OTO Model 35 grenade, showing the pull tab and safety cover
Below: The pull tab has been withdrawn and the safety cover removed so that the grenade is now armed

SRCM Model 35

Length 3.1in
Weight 7oz
Filling 1.5oz TNT
Fusing All-ways impact

Similar to the others in general appearance, this was in the form of two concentric containers, an inner holding a charge of explosive and the outer serving to protect the inner and carry the fuse mechanism. The inner container was surrounded by a steel sleeve and wrapped with wire in order to produce a better fragmentation effect than either the Breda or OTO grenades.

Italian SRCM Model 35 grenade, another of the 'Red Devil' tribe

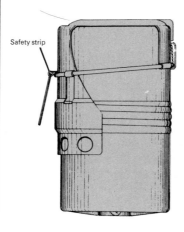

Safety strip

Variants

Breda Model 40 This was a stick grenade constructed by attaching a Breda 35 grenade to a wooden handle by means of an adapter. A spring lying along the handle gave the safety cap an assist in flying off, after which the all-ways fuse was armed. Due to the stabilizing effect of the handle, which ensured that the grenade landed in a favorable attitude, this version was much more reliable than the original Model 35.

Breda Model 42 This was the Model 40 stick grenade with the addition of a spherical explosive container screwed on to the head of the Model 35 Grenade Unit. This increased the explosive content to about 1.5lbs of TNT, and it was intended for use as an anti-tank grenade. Instructions issued with the weapon stressed that it should

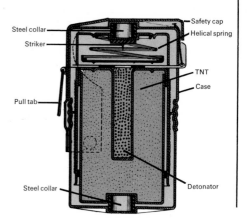

Steel collar
Striker
Pull tab
Safety cap
Helical spring
TNT
Case
Steel collar
Detonator

Grenades

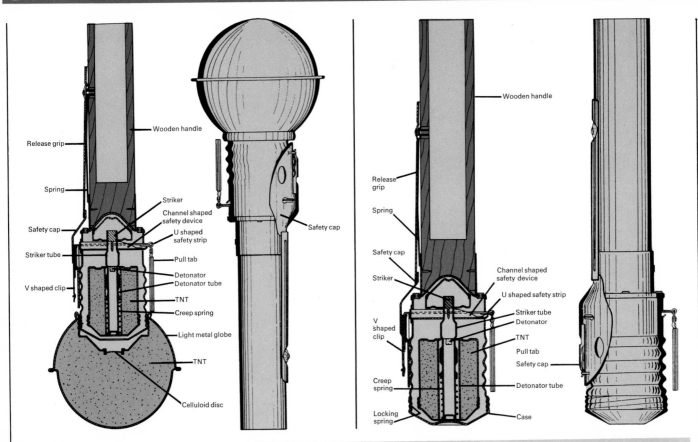

Release grip

Wooden handle

Spring

Safety cap

Striker tube

V shaped clip

Striker

Channel shaped
safety device

U shaped
safety strip

Pull tab

Detonator

Detonator tube

TNT

Creep spring

Light metal globe

TNT

Celluloid disc

Safety cap

Wooden handle

Release
grip

Spring

Safety cap

Striker

V
shaped
clip

Creep
spring

Locking
spring

Channel shaped
safety device

U shaped safety strip

Striker tube

Detonator

TNT

Pull tab

Safety cap

Detonator tube

Case

*The Breda Model 40, a conversion of the
Model 35 to a stick grenade
The Breda Model 42 anti-tank grenade*

never be used against targets less than 15
meters away, for the sake of the thrower's
safety.

Hand grenades, types 91 and 97

Length 4in
Weight 1lb
Filling 2oz TNT
Fusing 4½-second delay (97); 7½-second delay (91)

These two grenades are considered together
since they were similar in size, shape and
appearance. Both were cylindrical with an
igniter assembly protruding from the top.
The Type 91 had a recessed conical base to
which could be screwed a finned tail unit to
allow it to be discharged from a rifle, or a
propellant container and percussion cap
which turned it into a projectile for the
Type 89 Grenade Launcher. For this reason
the fuse delay was a nominal 7½ seconds.
The Type 97, on the other hand, was only
for hand throwing and had a solid base and
a 4½-second fuse.

Both had the body segmented in the
usual attempt to influence fragmentation;
the igniter sets were held safe by a two-
pronged safety pin which was withdrawn
when ready to throw. The grenade was then
grasped and the head of the striker banged
against any convenient solid object—the
boot heel if nothing better offered—which
drove a firing pin into the cap and lit the
fuse.

The Types 91 and 97 were not among the
better grenade designs. While they made a
loud noise their fragmentation was poor
and the fuses were notoriously unreliable
after a period of storage. It was extremely
hazardous to hold the grenade after striking the igniter, as, for example, to cut
down the burning time for a short throw to
insure it didn't come back; once lit, it had
to be got rid of instantly.

Variants

The Kiska Grenade This was an improved
Type 97; the official Japanese terminology
was 'Type 00' but it was always known to
the Allies as the 'Kiska' model, since the

first specimens were found in the Aleutian
Islands campaign. The general design was
much the same as that of the 97, but the
body was smooth and the base flat. The
fuse was of a slightly different internal construction but it functioned in the same way
and seems to have been little more reliable
than that on the other models.

The 'Pull Type' Grenade The Allied Intelligence staffs never found the correct name
of this model and it went into the records as

*The Type 91 grenade, showing it in hand-
thrown and rifle-launched configuration,
and with a propellant chamber for firing
from the 5cm grenade launcher*

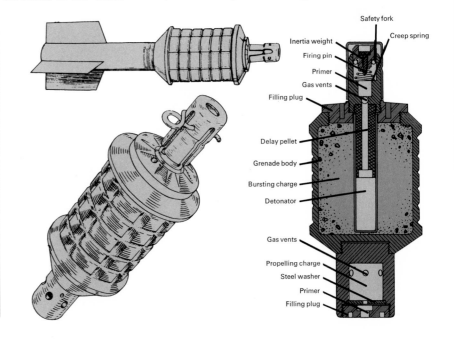

Safety fork

Creep spring

Inertia weight

Firing pin

Primer

Gas vents

Filling plug

Delay pellet

Grenade body

Bursting charge

Detonator

Gas vents

Propelling charge

Steel washer

Primer

Filling plug

Right: Japanese 'Pull type' showing friction igniter
Below: Japanese '00' Type grenade details

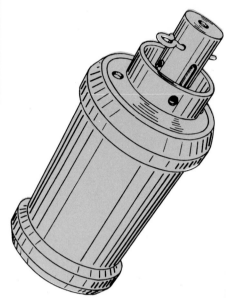

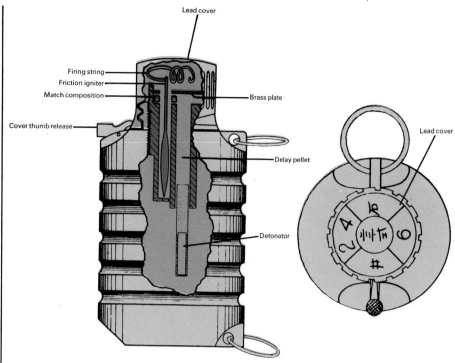

Lead cover
Firing string
Friction igniter
Match composition
Cover thumb release
Brass plate
Delay pellet
Detonator
Lead cover

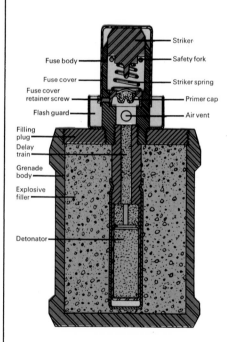

Striker
Fuse body
Safety fork
Fuse cover
Striker spring
Fuse cover retainer screw
Primer cap
Flash guard
Air vent
Filling plug
Delay train
Grenade body
Explosive filler
Detonator

the 'Pull Type' since it was the only small hand grenade to be operated in that way. Much the same general size as the 91 or 97, which it seemed to be destined to replace, the body had five circumferential grooves and, at top and bottom, a lug with a metal split-ring for linking grenades together, carrying them or anchoring them in booby-trap applications.

The fuse was concealed beneath a lead cap, retained in place by a spring-loaded catch. Pressing the catch allowed the cap to be removed by giving it one-and-a-half turns, when the pull-string of the friction igniter was revealed.

Little is known of the relative efficiency of this grenade, since few appear to have been captured for testing. They were certainly rarely encountered, and they do not appear to have been issued before mid-1943.

Japan

Stick grenade

Length 7.75in
Weight 1lb 3oz
Filling 3oz cast Picric Acid
Fusing 4½-second delay

Although smaller and more crudely made than the German stick grenade, this Japanese model was rather more dangerous, giving much more fragmentation from its cast iron head.

The construction was much simpler than the German model; the hollow wooden handle had the smooth cast-iron head secured to it by four wood-screws. Inside the head was a friction igniter, fuse and detonator similar to the German pattern, with a string running down inside the handle and attached to a screwed end-cap. To throw, the cap was removed and the string pulled to initiate the friction igniter. As with other Japanese grenades, the fuse was erratic in its behavior, particularly after storage in a humid atmosphere. Cases are on record where, when tested (under precautions) by Allied experimental stations, the detonation was almost immediate when the string was pulled.

Apparently the grenade was considered obsolete when the war broke out, and the stocks in use were elderly, which may account for the erratic fuse. In spite of this, it was in use throughout the war and it was encountered by the author in 1952 in Korea, being used by the Chinese Communist Army who had presumably inherited stocks from the Japanese in Manchuria in 1945 by way of the departing Russians. Needless to say its behavior was even more unpredictable by that time as I know to my cost!

The Japanese stick grenade, a very simply constructed device

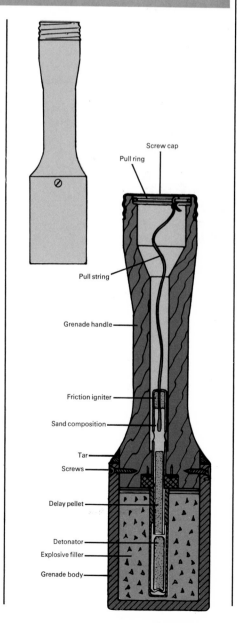

Screw cap
Pull ring
Pull string
Grenade handle
Friction igniter
Sand composition
Tar
Screws
Delay pellet
Detonator
Explosive filler
Grenade body

SMALL ARMS AMMUNITION

UK

.303in for rifles and machine guns

Rimmed, bottle-necked case,
brass, 2.211in long.
Complete round length 3.05in

Ctg SA ball .303in Mk 7 Pointed, square base bullet with cupro-nickel envelope. Cap annulus dark purple.
Ctg SA ball .303in Mk 7Z As Mk 7 but using a nitro-cellulose propellant instead of cordite.
Ctg SA ball .303in Mk 8Z For machine guns only. Pointed, streamlined bullet nitro-cellulose propellant, dark purple annulus.
Ctg SA .303in tracer G Mk 2 Red tracer. Cap annulus red.
Ctg SA .303in tracer G Mk 7 Dark ignition tracer (i.e. lit some distance from the muzzle to avoid dazzling the firer). Cap annulus red.
Ctg SA .303in tracer G Mk 8 Improved design of dark ignition. Cap annulus red.
Ctg SA .303in incendiary B Mk 7 Cap annulus and bullet tip blue.
Ctg SA .303in observing O Mk 1 Gave smoke puff on impact. Annulus and tip black.
Ctg SA .303in AP type W Mk 1 Hard steel piercing core. Cap annulus green.
Ctg SA rifle grenade H Mk 1Z For grenades; case blackened for half its length.
Ctg SA rifle grenade H Mk 4 For Grenade No. 85 only; blacked at mouth and base.

.38in for revolvers

Rimmed straight case,
brass, 0.770in long.
Complete round length 1.245in

Ctg SA ball Mk 1 Lead alloy bullet with two cannelures.
Ctg SA ball Mk 2 Jacketed bullet, cupro-nickel or gunmetal.

9mm for pistols and sub-machine guns

Rimless straight case,
brass, 0.760in long.
Complete round length 1.153in

Ctg SA ball Mk 1Z Dark purple cap annulus.
Ctg SA ball Mk 2Z No marking; used a different propelling charge.

.55in Boys anti-tank rifles

Belted rimless, bottle-necked case,
brass, 3.95in long.
Complete round length 5.31in

Ctg SA ball Mk 1 Lead/antimony core, cupro-nickel envelope. Purple annulus.
Ctg SA ball Mk 2 Mild steel core. Purple annulus.
Ctg SA ball Mk 3 Shorter bullet, more powerful charge. Purple annulus.
Ctg SA AP W Mk 1 Steel piercing core. Green annulus.
Ctg SA AP W Mk 2 Lighter bullet, more powerful charge. Green annulus.
Ctg SA AP W Mk 3 Tungsten core and light alloy/plastic envelope.
Ctg SA tracer G Mk 1 Ball with tracer added. Red annulus.
Ctg SA ball practice P Mk 1 Lead-antimony bullet core. Blue band around base of cartridge case.
Ctg SA ball practice P Mk 2 Aluminum bullet core. Blue band around case.

USA

.30 carbines

Rimless straight case,
brass, 1.275in long.
Complete round length 1.68in

Ctg carbine cal .30 M1 Gilding metal envelope. Bullets manufactured before 12.2.42 have hollow bases.
Ctg carbine tracer M16 Similar to ball. Bullet has $\frac{1}{8}$-inch red tip.
Ctg grenade carbine M6 Case with crimped mouth.

.30 machine guns and rifles

Rimless bottle-necked case,
brass, 2.494in long.
Complete round length 3.135in

Ctg ball cal .30 M1 Bullet with streamlined base. Headstamp dates 25 to 41 only.
Ctg ball cal .30 M2 Bullet has flat base. Headstamp dates 38 onward. From 38 to September 40 bullets were tin-plated.
Ctg AP cal .30 M1 One cannelure. Headstamp dates 25 to 41 only.
Ctg AP cal .30 M2 One cannelure and groove for case mouth. Headstamp dates from 41 onwards. 5/16th inch black tip.
Ctg tracer cal .30 M1 5/16th inch red tip. Red trace from 125 to 800 yds.
Ctg incendiary cal .30 M1 5/16th inch blue tip.
Ctg rifle grenade cal .30 M3 Cannelure in case $\frac{1}{4}$-inch from mouth. Mouth crimped.

.45in pistols, revolvers and sub-machine guns

Case rimless, straight,
brass or lacquered steel, 0.898in long.
Complete round length 1.263in

Ctg ball cal .45 M1911 Gilding metal jacketed bullet.
Ctg tracer cal .45 M1 0.18in red tip to bullet. Case always brass.

USSR

7.62mm automatic pistols and sub-machine guns

Rimless bottle-necked case,
brass, 0.97in long.
Complete round length 1.36in

Ctg ball type P Lead/Antimony core, gilding metal envelope.
Ctg AP incendiary type P-41 Hard steel core with incendiary in nose. Black tip with red ring beneath.

7.62mm revolvers

Rimmed case, 1.51in long,
with bullet enclosed inside case.

Ctg revolver type R Flat-nosed bullet with steel jacket.

7.62mm rifles and machine guns

Rimmed, tapered, bottle-necked case,
brass or steel, 2.11in long.
Complete round length 3.02in

Ctg light ball M1908 type L Lead/antimony core, gilding metal envelope, flat base bullet.
Ctg heavy ball M1930 type D Lead core, gilding metal envelope, streamlined base bullet. Yellow bullet tip.
Ctg AP M1930 (B-30) Steel core. Bullet has black tip.
Ctg incendiary/observing type ZP Incendiary pellet and explosive primer. Bullet has red tip. Prone to burst at the muzzle.
Ctg AP/tracer Steel core. Flat base bullet with purple tip.
Ctg AP/incendiary M1940 Tungsten core, flat base, incendiary pellet. Bullet has surface painted red with black tip. Base of case black.
Ctg AP/incendiary M1932 Steel core with incendiary pellet in base. Black tip with red ring beneath.
Ctg AP/incendiary/tracer Steel core, incendiary in nose, tracer in base. Bullet has purple tip with red ring beneath.
Ctg ball tracer M1930 type T Lead/antimony core. Green tip.

183

Small arms ammunition

Heavy calibers

.5 Vickers machine gun   .55 Boys anti-tank rifle   .50 Browning machine gun

Short rifle rounds

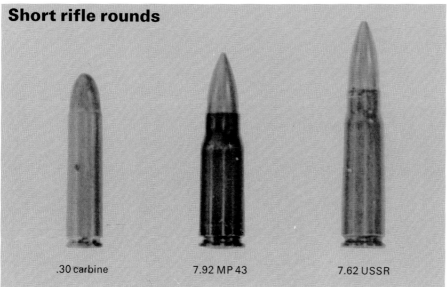

.30 carbine   7.92 MP 43   7.62 USSR

Service rifles and machine gun rounds

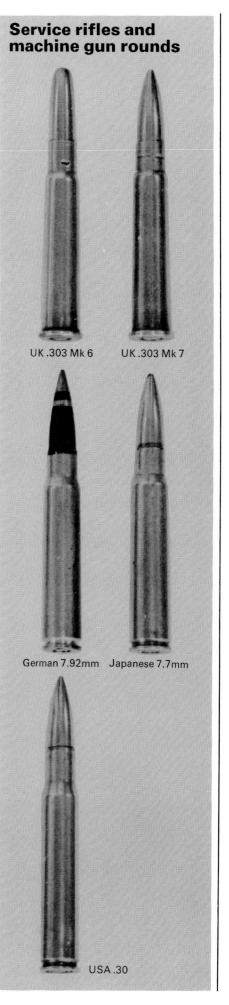

UK .303 Mk 6   UK .303 Mk 7

German 7.92mm   Japanese 7.7mm

USA .30

9mm cartridges

British service

US commercial

British commercial

German sintered iron bullet

German cored bullet

9mm Stegr

9mm Mauser export

Service pistol cartridges

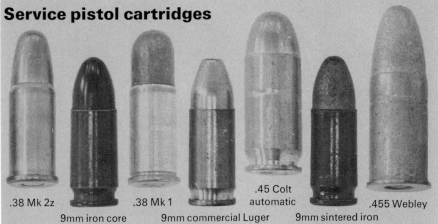

.38 Mk 2z

9mm iron core

.38 Mk 1

9mm commercial Luger

.45 Colt automatic

9mm sintered iron

.455 Webley

Heavy caliber

.5 Vickers   .50 Browning   15mm BESA   12.7mm Soviet   14.5mm Soviet

12.7mm machine guns

Rimless bottle-necked brass case,
4.25in long.
Complete round length 5.76in

Ctg AP/incendiary/tracer Steel core. Bullet has purple tip and red band.
Ctg AP/incendiary M1932 Steel core; black tip and red band beneath.
Ctg AP/incendiary Steel core, black tip with yellow ring beneath.
Ctg AP/incendiary M1941 Tungsten core. Red bullet with black tip, black percussion cap to cartridge case.
Ctg AP M1930 Steel core. Black tip.
Ctg high explosive/incendiary Steel bullet, copper-coated, fused.

14.5mm anti-tank rifles

Ctg AP/incendiary M1932 Steel core. Bullet 2.61in long with streamlined base, black tip with red ring beneath.
Ctg AP/incendiary M1941 Tungsten core. Bullet 1.93in long, flat-based. Red bullet with black tip and black cap to case.

9mm pistols and sub-machine guns

Rimless straight case,
brass or lacquered steel, 0.74in long.
Complete round length 1.09 in

Ball (pist patr 08) Lead core, gilding metal envelope. Black cap annulus.
Ball, mild steel core Magnetic steel core. Annulus originally black, later plain. Bullet originally black, later plain.
Ball, sintered iron bullet Bullet of pressed powdered iron, grey with lacquer coating. Cap annulus black.
Low velocity For silenced weapons. Case lacquered bright green.

7.92mm rifles and machine guns

Rimless bottle-necked case,
brass, brass-coated steel, copper-coated steel or lacquered steel,
Complete round length 3.165in

Heavy pointed ball Green cap annulus.
Zinc coated ball For use in machine guns only; gave longer barrel life. Grey bullet, light blue cap annulus.
Cored long bullet Bullet lengthened to compensate for lighter weight due to less lead content. Bullet set deeper into case so overall length is normal. Zinc cap with colorless varnish painted over.
Sniper's cored bullet Similar to heavy ball but to tighter specification for improved accuracy. Blue cap annulus.

Semi-armor-piercing Mild steel core. Deep green cap annulus.

Incendiary observing Contains detonator and white phosphorus. Cap annulus black, bullet black with chromed tip or gilding metal tip. Reputedly for training and ballistic trials only.

Practice tracer Aluminium core. 5mm green lacquer band across base. Black tip to bullet.

AP/incendiary Black cap annulus, 10mm green tip to bullet or 1.5mm wide green band beneath bullet tip.

AP Tungsten core. Red cap annulus or red cap. Bullet, post-1940, black; pre-1940 gilding metal coated.

AP/incendiary, cored Steel core, contains white phosphorus. Black or red cap annulus or red band across base of case.

AP/tracer Steel core. Red cap annulus, red ring around case-bullet junction. 10mm black tip to bullet.

7.92/13mm for anti-tank rifles

Rimless, sharply bottle-necked brass case, 3.75in long.
Complete round length 4.64in

AP/trace tear gas Tungsten core in lead sleeve. Red cap annulus, 10mm black tip to bullet.

Practice Lead cored bullet. Green cap annulus.

Italy

9mm pistols

Rimless, straight, brass case
0.675in long. Complete round length 1.10in

Known commercially as 9mm Short or .380 automatic pistol.

Ball for pist mod 34 Lead/Antimony core in cupro-nickel envelope. Bullet has hemispherical nose.

9mm pistols and sub-machine guns

Rimless, straight, brass case 0.76in long.
Complete round length 1.09in

Known also as 9mm Glisenti, the dimensions are the same as 9mm Parabellum but the propelling charge is less powerful.

Ball for pist auto M1910 & sub-machine guns Bullet of truncated cone shape.

Ball for sub-machine guns M38A Round-nosed bullet. Case headstamp includes '38A' and the primer annulus or case-bullet junction are lacquered bright green.

6.5mm rifles, carbines and machine guns

Cartucci per armi mod 91 e per mitragliatrici
Rimless bottle-necked brass case, 2.05in long. Complete round length 3.02in

Ball model 91–95 Round nosed bullet.
Machine gun ball Unusual over-long bullet composed of 10 semi-cylindrical segments of lead in a cupro-nickel sleeve, the tip closed by a hemispherical lead slug.
Frangible ball Lead tip merging into a cupro-nickel sleeve which contains fine lead shot.

7.35mm rifles and machine guns

Cartucci per armi portatil Mod 38
Rimless bottle-necked brass case, 2.01in long. Complete round length 2.98in

Ball Model 38 Pointed bullet, lead/antimony core with aluminium nose plug. Cupro-nickel or 'Tombak' envelope.
Machine-gun ball Similar to the 6.5mm model, having 12 semi-cylindrical lead pieces in a cupro-nickel envelope.

8mm Schwarzlose machine guns

Cartucci a Pollotolla per armi Mannlicher e per Mitriagliatrice Schwarzlose.
Rimmed, bottle-necked brass case, 1.98in long. Complete round length 3.00 in

This is the Austrian service round retained for use in Mannlicher rifles and Schwarzlose machine guns taken in 1919.
Ball Round-nosed bullet.

8mm FIAT and Breda machine guns

Cartucci a pallotola cal .8 mod 35 per Mitragliatrice.
Rebated rimless, bottle-necked case, brass, 2.32in long.
Complete round length 3.11in

Ball Pointed and streamlined bullet.
Armor piercing Mod 37 Steel core, lead jacket, 'Tombak' alloy envelope. Bullet has white tip.

Japan

8mm pistols and sub-machine guns

Rimless necked brass case, 0.84in long.
Complete round length 1.24in

Ball Lead core, cupro-nickel jacket.

9mm revolver

Rimmed, straight taper, brass case, 0.85in long. Complete round length 0.19in

Ball Lead alloy unjacketed bullet. No markings.

6.5mm rifles and machine guns

Semi-rimmed bottle-necked brass case, 1.99in long. Complete round length 2.99in

Ball Pointed bullet. Case-bullet junction crimped, with pink band painted around. Note that the reduced charge machine gun round had no distinguishing marks, the identification being on the package.
Training ball Lead alloy bullet in gilding metal jacket. No paint markings.

7.7mm rifles and machine guns

Rimless, bottle-necked brass case, 2.27in long. Complete round length 3.14in

Ball Lead alloy core. Pink band around case mouth.
Armor-piercing Chrome steel core in brass envelope. Black band.
Tracer Lead alloy nose, cupro-nickel envelope. Green band.
Grenade launcher Solid wood unpainted bullet.

Semi-rimmed, bottle-necked, brass case 2.26in long. Complete round length 3.137in

Ball Lead alloy core, streamlined bullet. Pink band.
Armor-piercing Steel core, brass envelope. Black cap annulus, red or violet bullet tip, black band.
Incendiary Filled white phosphorus. Red or violet bullet tip, pink band.
Observing Filled flash powder. Thin black band.
Tracer Flat base bullet. Green band.

Rimmed, bottle-necked, brass case 2.21in long. Complete round length 3.02in
Resembles British .303 ammunition
Base is headstamped I-III 7.7

Ball Lead core. Black cap annulus.
Armor-piercing Steel core. White cap annulus.
Incendiary White phosphorus filling. Green cap annulus.
Tracer Pink annulus.
Explosive RDX/PETN nose filling. Purple annulus.

APPENDICES

Data tables

For ease of comparison, the basic data for each weapon is tabulated here. The order is that in which the weapons appear in the body of the book.

Pistols

Name	Caliber	Magazine capacity	Barrel length inches	Weight lbs	Muzzle velocity feet/second	Remarks	Page
Webley, Mk 4	.38	6	5.0	1lb 11oz	600	Revolver	18
Enfield, No. 2	.38	6	5.0	1lb 11½oz	600	Revolver	18
Smith & Wesson, No. 2	.38	6	6.0	1lb 8oz	600	Revolver	19
Browning, Model 35	9mm	13	4.65	2lb 3oz	1100	Automatic	19
Colt, M1911A1	.45	7	5.0	2lb 7½oz	860	Automatic	20
Nagant, Model 1895	7.62mm	7	4.3	1lb 12oz	1000	Revolver	20
Tokarev, Model TT33	7.62mm	8	4.57	1lb 13oz	1375	Automatic	21
Pistole '08	9mm	8	4.0	1lb 14oz	1150	Automatic (Luger)	22
Pistole '38	9mm	8	5.0	1lb 13½oz	1150	Automatic (Walther)	22
Mauser 1932	7.63mm	10, 20	5.5	2lb 14½oz	1425	850 rpm full automatic	23
Steyr 1912	9mm	8	5.1	2lb 3oz	1100	Automatic	24
Radom P/35	9mm	8	4.53	2lb 5oz	1150	Automatic	24
Bodeo M1889	10.35mm	6	4.375	2lb 1oz	825	Revolver	25
Glisenti M1910	9mm	7	3.5	1lb 14½oz	1050	Automatic	25
Beretta M1934	9mm	7	3.75	1lb 7½oz	825	Automatic	26
Meiji 26	9mm	6	4.7	2lb 4oz	750	Revolver	27
Taisho 04	8mm	8	4.7	1lb 15¾oz	1100	Automatic	27
Taisho 14	8mm	8	4.75	1lb 15¾oz	1100	Automatic	28
Type 94	8mm	6	3.125	1lb 12oz	1000	Automatic	28
Modèle d'ordonnance M1892	8mm	6	4.5	1lb 10½oz	750	Revolver	29
MAS M1935A	7.65mm	8	4.3	1lb 10oz	1000	Automatic	31

Rifles

Name	Caliber	Magazine capacity	Action	Barrel length inches	Weight lbs	Muzzle velocity feet/second	Remarks	Page
Lee-Enfield No. 4	.303	10	Bolt	25.19	9lb 1oz	2400		34
Lee-Enfield No. 5	.303	10	Bolt	20.0	8lb	2300	'Jungle carbine'	34
US rifle M1903A3	.30	5	Bolt	24.0	8lb 11oz	2800	'Springfield'	34
US rifle M1917	.30	5	Bolt	26.0	9lb 10oz	2800	'Enfield'	37
US rifle M1	.30	8	Gas	24.0	9lb 8oz	2800	'Garand'	37
US carbine cal .30 M1	.30	15	Gas	18.0	5lb	1950		39
Browning M1918A2	.30	20	Gas	24.0	22lb	2800		40
Johnson M1941	.30	10	Recoil	22.0	9lb 8oz	2650		40
Mosin-Nagant M1930G	7.62mm	5	Bolt	28.7	8lb 11oz	2660		41
Carbine 1938G	7.62mm	5	Bolt	20.45	7lb 10oz	2500		41
Carbine 1944G	7.62mm	5	Bolt	20.45	8lb 14oz	2500		41
Tokarev 1940	7.62mm	10	Gas	24.6	8lb 8oz	2725		41
Karabiner 98K	7.92mm	5	Bolt	23.6	8lb 9oz	2450	'Mauser'	42
Gewehr 41 (W)	7.92mm	10	Gas	21.5	11lb	2550		43
Gewehr 43	7.92mm	10	Gas	22.0	9lb 9oz	2450	Also known as Kar 43	43
MP43 or StuG44	7.92mm	30	Gas	16.5	11lb 5oz	2125	Used short cartridge	44
Fallschirmgewehr 42	7.92mm	20	Gas	19.75	9lb 15oz	2500		45
Mannlicher 1891	6.5mm	6	Bolt	30.71	8lb 6oz	2400		46
Carbine 1891/24	6.5mm	6	Bolt	17.7	6lb 14oz	2300		46
Rifle M1938	7.35mm	6	Bolt	20.9	7lb 8oz	2475		46
Meiji 38	6.5mm	5	Bolt	31.45	9lb 8oz	2400	'Arisaka'	47

Sub-machine guns

Name	Caliber	Magazine capacity	Rate of fire cyclic rpm	Barrel length inches	Weight lbs	Muzzle velocity feet/second	Remarks	Page
Sten Mark 1	9mm	32	550	7.75	7lb 3oz	1250		52
Sten Mark 2	9mm	32	550	7.75	6lb 10oz	1250		52
Sten Mark 3	9mm	32	550	7.75	7lb	1250		52
Sten Mark 5	9mm	32	600	7.75	8lb 9oz	1250		52
Sten Mark 2S	9mm	32	450	3.50	7lb 12oz	1000	Silenced model	52
Owen	9mm	33	700	9.75	9lb 5oz	1250		54
Austen	9mm	28	500	7.75	8lb 12oz	1250		54
Thompson M1928A1	.45	20	800	10.5	10lb 2oz	900		55
Thompson M1	.45	20	700	10.5	10lb 9oz	900		55
US M3	.45	30	450	8.0	8lb 15oz	900	Convertible to 9mm	56
Reising, Model 50	.45	12, 20	550	11.0	6lb 12oz	920	Model 55 similar	56
PPD 1940G	7.62mm	71	800	10.5	8lb 2oz	1650		58
PPSh 1941G	7.62mm	35, 71	900	10.5	8lb 0oz	1650		58

Name	Caliber	Magazine capacity	Rate of fire cyclic rpm	Barrel length inches	Weight lbs	Muzzle velocity feet/second	Remarks	Page
PPS 1942G	7.62mm	35	700	10.0	7lb 6oz	1600		59
PPS 1943G	7.62mm	35	700	10.0	7lb 6oz	1600		59
MP 28	9mm	32	500	7.75	8lb 12oz	1250		60
MP 34 (o)	9mm	32	500	7.75	8lb 8oz	1250	Solothurn S1-100	62
MP 34	9mm	32	650	7.75	8lb 15oz	1250	Bergmann	62
Erma MP	9mm	25, 32	500	10.0	9lb 2oz	1250		63
MP 38	9mm	32	500	9.75	9lb 0oz	1250		63
MP 40	9mm	32	500	9.75	8lb 12oz	1250		63
ZK 383	9mm	30	500 or 700	12.75	10lb 8oz	1250		64
Model 39M	9mm	40	750	19.65	8lb 3oz	1500		65
Model 43M	9mm	40	750	19.65	8lb 3oz	1475		65
OVP	9mm	25	900	11.0	8lb 1oz	1250		66
Beretta 1918	9mm	25	900	12.0	7lb 3oz	1250		66
Beretta 1938A	9mm	10, 20, 30 or 40	600	12.5	9lb 4oz	1350		67
Beretta 38/42	9mm	40	550	8.5	7lb 3oz	1250		67
FNAB-43	9mm	20 or 40	400	7.8	8lb 12oz	1250		68
TZ-45	9mm	40	550	9.0	7lb 3oz	1250		68
Type 100/40	8mm	30	450	9.0	8lb 8oz	1100	100/44, 800rpm	69
Suomi 1931	9mm	20, 50 or 40, 71	900	12.5	10lb 5oz	1300		69

Machine guns

Name	Caliber	Magazine capacity	Rate of fire cyclic rpm	Barrel length inches	Weight lbs	Muzzle velocity feet/second	Remarks	Page
Bren, Mk 1	.303	30	500	25.0	22lb 5oz	2400		72
Vickers-Berthier, Mk 3	.303	30	600	23.5	22lb 0oz	2400		74
Vickers, Mk 1	.303	250 round belt	450	28.5	40lb 0oz	2450	Watercooled	74
Johnson M1941	.30	20	300-900	22.0	14lb 5oz	2800	M1944 similar	75
Browning, M1917A1	.30	250 round belt	500	23.9	32lb 10oz	2800	Watercooled	79
Browning, M1919A4	.30	250 round belt	500	24.0	30lb 12oz	2800		79
Browning, M1919A6	.30	250 round belt	500	24.0	32lb 8oz	2800		79
DP 1928	7.62mm	47	550	23.8	20lb 8oz	2750		83
DPM 1944	7.62mm	47	570	23.8	26lb 13oz	2750		83
Maxim 1910	7.62mm	250 round belt	550	28.4	52lb 8oz	2800	Watercooled	83
DShK 1938	12.7mm	50 round belt	550	42.0	78lb 8oz	2900		84
SG 1943	7.62mm	Belt	600	28.3	30lb 4oz	2800		84
MG 15	7.92mm	75	850	23.5	28lb 0oz	2475		85
MG 34	7.92mm	75 round belt	850	24.75	26lb 11oz	2475		85
MG 42	7.92mm	Belt	1200	21.0	25lb 8oz	2475		88
VZ 37	7.92mm	Belt	500-700	26.7	41lb 0oz	2550		89
Knorr-Bremse 35/36	7.92mm	20	500	27.25	22lb 0oz	2600		90
Schwarzlose 07/12	7.92mm or 8mm	Belt	400	20.75	44lb 0oz	2400	Watercooled	90
Madsen	7.92mm	25, 30 or 40	450	23.0	20lb 0oz	2475	And in other calibers	91
Fiat-Revelli 1914	6.5mm	50	400	25.75	37lb 8oz	2100	Watercooled	92
Breda M1930	6.5mm	20	475	20.5	22lb 8oz	2000		93
Fiat-Revelli 1935	8mm	Belt	500	25.75	40lb 0oz	2600		94
Breda M1937	8mm	20	450	26.75	43lb 0oz	2600		95
Taisho 11	6.5mm	30	500	19.0	22lb 8oz	2300		96
Type 92	7.7mm	30	450	29.5	61lb 0oz	2400		98
Type 96	6.5mm	30	550	21.7	20lb 0oz	2400		99
Type 99	7.7mm	30	800	21.65	20lb 0oz	2400		100
Lahti M1926	7.62mm	20 or 75	500	22.3	19lb 0oz	2600		101
Chatellerault 1929	7.5mm	25	500	19.7	20lb 4oz	2700		101

Mortars

Name	Caliber	Barrel length inches	Weight in action lbs	Projectile weight lbs	Maximum range yards	Rate of fire rpm	Remarks	Page
2in	2.0in	21	19	2.25	500	8		104
3in	3.0in	51	112	10	2800 (Mk2)	10		104
60mm M2	60mm	28.6	42	2.94	1985	18		107
81mm M1	81mm	49.5	136	6.87	3290	18		108
5cm M1940	50mm	21	21.3	1.5	875	30		109
82mm M41/43	82mm	48	99.2	7.4	3390	15-20		110
GrW 36	50mm	19.3	30.9	2	550	40		110

Data tables

Name — Mortars	Caliber	Barrel length inches	Weight in action lbs	Projectile weight lbs	Maximum range yards	Rate of fire rpm	Remarks	Page
GrW 34	81.4mm	45	125	7.5	2625	15		111
GrW 42	120mm	73.5	628	34.83	6615	15		112
Brixia 35	45mm	10.2	34	1.0	585	25		113
81mm M1935	81.1mm	45.3	129	7.2	4430	18		113
Gren Disch Type 89	50mm	10	10lb 1oz	1.75	700	25		113
Model 98	50mm	25.6	48	14.1	400	5		114
Model 99	81mm	25.25	52	6.93	2200	15		115
Type 94	90mm	47.8	340	11.5	4050	15		115

Infantry guns

Name	Caliber	Barrel length inches	Weight in action lbs	Projectile weight lbs	Maximum range yards	Muzzle velocity feet/sec.	Penetration (anti-tank guns) depth	range	striking angle	Page
6-pounder 7cwt, Mk 2	2.244in	100.95	2521	6.25	5500	2675	74mm	1000yd	30°	118
95mm Howitzer	3.7in	74.05	2105	25	8000	1083				118
37mm Gun M3A1	37mm	82.5	990	1.92	12,850	2900	2in (54mm)	1000yd	0°	119
57mm RCL M18	57mm	61.6	44.5	2.75	4340	1200	3in (75mm)	all ranges		123
75mm RCL M20	75mm	82	165.5	14.4	6955	990	4in (100mm)	all ranges		123
57mm Gun M1	57mm	117	2810	6.25	10,260	2800	2.7in (68mm)	1000yd	20°	124
105mm Howitzer M3	105mm	66	2500	33	7250	1020				125
45mm Model 42	45mm	117.5	1257	4.72	5460	2690	54mm	500m	30° (APCR)	125
57mm Model 43	57mm	155.53	2535	8.27	9200	2295	100mm	500m	30° (APCR)	128
2.8cm SPzB41	28/20mm	67.51	260	0.31	875	4593	52mm	500m	30° (APCNR)	128
3.7cm PAK 36	37mm	65.5	952	1.5	4400	2500	40mm	500m	30° (APCR)	129
4.2cm PJK 41	40/30mm	92.52	1414	11¾oz	1100	4150	72mm	500m	30° (APCNR)	130
5cm PAK 38	50mm	125.5	2174	4.95	2890	2700	61mm	500m	30° (AP)	130
75mm le IG 18	75mm	35.43	880	13.2	3780	690				130
7.5cm IG 37	75mm	70.75	1124	13.2	5625	918				132
7.5cm IG 42 nA	75mm	70.75	1300	13.2	5030	918				132
7.5cm IK 290(r)	76.2mm	49.5	1720	13.75	9350	1270				133
7.5cm LG 40 (RCL)	75mm	45.27	321	12.85	7435	1150				134
7.5cm PAK 40	75mm	145.75	3139	12.8	8400	2600	115mm	500m	30° (APCR)	134
7.5cm PAK 41	75/55mm	170	2988	5.71	Unknown	3700	171mm	500m	30° (APCNR)	135
8cm PAW 600	81.4mm	116.2	1322	9.59	6780	1375	140mm	all ranges	0°	135
8.8cm PAK 43 & 43/41	88mm	260.25	8150	20.3	19,100	3710	192mm	1000m	30° (APCR)	136
10.5cm LG 42 (RCL)	105mm	72.28	1191	32.6	8695	1099				137
15cm SIG 33	150mm	68.8	3722	83.6	5140	790				138
37mm A/Tk, model 94	37mm	72	815	1.54	5450	2300	32mm	500m	30° (AP)	138
47mm A/Tk, model 01	47mm	99.48	1660	3.37	8400	2700	70mm	500m	0° (AP)	139
70mm inf howitzer, M92	70mm	28.5	468	8.3	3050	650				140
75mm regtl gun, M41	75mm	86	2158	12.5	11,990	1672				140

Anti-tank rifles

Name	Caliber	Barrel length inches	Weight lbs	Action	Muzzle velocity feet/second	Penetration depth	range	striking angle	Page
Boys, Mk 1	.55in	36.0	36.0	Bolt	3250	20mm	500m	0°	144
PTRS 1941	14.5mm	48.0	46.0	Gas	3320	25mm	500m	0°	144
PTRD 1941	14.5mm	48.3	38	Bolt	3300	25mm	500m	0°	145
PzB 38	7.92mm	43.0	35	Recoil	3975	25mm	300m	30°	145
PzB 39	7.92mm	42.75	27.25	Hand	3975	25mm	300m	30°	146
S 18-1000	20mm	57.0	120	Recoil	3000	35mm	300m	0°	146
Type 97	20mm	41.875	115	Gas	2640	12mm	200m	0°	147
WZ/35	7.92mm	47.25	19.5	Bolt	4200	20mm	300m	0°	147

Anti-tank launchers

Name	Caliber	Barrel length inches	Weight lbs	Projectile weight lbs	Range yards	Penetration	Page
PIAT	—	—	32	3.0	100	75mm	148
2.36in rocket launcher	2.36	54	13.25	3.4	400	80mm	150
Panzerfaust 30	5.9 (bomb)	31.5	11.5	7.0	32	200mm	152
Panzerfaust 60	5.9	31.5	15.0	7.0	65	200mm	152
Panzerfaust 100	5.95	31.5	15.0	7.0	110	200mm	152
Panzerfaust 150	4.13	31.5	14.75	7.0	165	200mm	152
8.8cm R PzB 54	88.9mm	62.5	20.25	7.25	165	100mm	155
8.8cm RW43	88mm	63.0	315	7.25	825	100mm	156

Glossary

AP	Armor piercing.
APC	Armor piercing, capped. A steel projectile with a cap over the tip which assists penetration.
APCBC	Armor piercing, capped, ballistic capped. An APC projectile with an additional thin windshield to give better ballistic shape to the nose.
APCR	Armor piercing, composite, rigid. A piercing projectile using a tungsten core and built up to full caliber with light steel and alloy components. It gives a high muzzle velocity but has poor carrying power.
APCNR	Armor piercing, composite, non-rigid. A tungsten cored projectile which is used with a taper-bore weapon and thus reduces in size as it passes up the gun barrel.
APDS	Armor piercing, discarding sabot. A tungsten cored projectile consisting of a core and sheath made up to full caliber by light alloy elements forming a 'sabot'. On leaving the muzzle the sabot elements are discarded, leaving the 'sub-projectile' of core and sheath to go to the target.
All-ways	A fuse which is so designed as to function irrespective of the angle at which it impacts the target. Usually used with grenades, but can be found on mortar bombs.
Annulus	The recessed portion surrounding the percussion cap of a small arms cartridge. Often colored for identification.
Blowback	System of operation of a weapon in which the breech unit is opened by the pressure within the chamber forcing the empty cartridge case backwards.
Cannelure	A groove machined around the body of a bullet, usually for attachment of the cartridge case.
Compensator	A gas deflector on the muzzle of a weapon designed to eject a portion of the muzzle blast upwards and thus force the muzzle down to compensate the tendency for it to rise during automatic fire. Usually found on sub-machine guns.
Cyclic	The rate of fire to be attained if it were possible to fire the weapon continuously, i.e. without having to stop and change magazines. Not quoted for belt-fed weapons since these can be so fired, and thus their quoted rate of fire is, in fact, cyclic.
Fixed round	A round of ammunition in which the projectile is rigidly attached to the cartridge case and thus is loaded in one piece. The propelling charge is sealed off and cannot be adjusted.
HE	High Explosive.
HEAT	High explosive, anti-tank. An abbreviation used for Hollow Charge ammunition.
Headstamp	The stampings on the base of a cartridge case which indicate the type of round, maker, date, etc.
Hollow charge	A method of using high explosive to penetrate armor by forming the face in contact or close to the target with a conical or hemispherical hollow, lined with metal. It works most efficiently when the face of the explosive is 'stood-off' from the target by a small distance.
Hydropneumatic	Type of recoil mechanism used on guns in which the recoil of the weapon is damped by a hydraulic brake and, at the same time, air or gas is placed under pressure so that at the end of the recoil stroke it will return the gun to its firing position.
Hydrospring	A type of recoil system in which the recoil is damped by a hydraulic buffer, and at the same time a spring is loaded up so that it can later return the gun to the firing position.
Muzzle brake	A muzzle attachment for a weapon which deflects some of the emerging gas to the side or slightly to the rear in order to reduce the recoil by forcing the muzzle forward. The more rearward the gas is deflected, the more efficient is the brake.

Bibliography

Military Small Arms of the 20th Century Hogg & Weeks, London 1977

Small Arms of the World (6th edition) Smith & Smith, Harrisburg 1972

Infantry Weapons Weeks, London 1972

German Pistols & Revolvers Hogg, London 1972

The Book of Rifles (4th edition) Smith & Smith, Harrisburg 1972

Assault Rifles of the World Nelson & Lockhoven, Cologne 1968

Pictorial History of the Sub-Machine Gun Hobart, London 1973

The World's Sub-Machine Guns Nelson & Lockhoven, Cologne 1964

Pictorial History of Machine Guns Hobart, London 1972

The Guns 1939–45 Hogg, London 1971

Ammunition Johnson & Haven, New York 1943

Cartridges of the World Barnes, Chicago 1965

German Small Arms Plants Picatinny Arsenal Report PB312, 1945

Development of Weapons by Rheinmettal-Borsig Picatinny Arsenal Report PB17609

German Small Arms Developments Picatinny Arsenal Report PB16695

Development of the 7mm Short Small Arms Cartridge von Lossnitzer Unterluss Interrogation Report No. 281, 1947

The Sturmgewehr *sub-machine gun* von Lossnitzer, UIR No. 297, 1947

Die Fallschirmgewehr FG42 Schultz, UIR No. 352, 1948

Tables of German Armament Equipment Bühler & Jöhnk, UIR No. 295, 1948

Recoilless Gun Development at Rheinmetall-Borsig Combined Intelligence Objectives Subcommittee Report XXVII–27

Armament Design & Development at the Skoda Works, Pilsen, Czechoslovakia Combined Intelligence Objectives Subcommittee Report XXIX–46

Notes on Enemy Ammunition Ord Directorate 21 Army Group, 1945

Acknowledgements

In the course of assembling data for this book innumerable sources have been consulted and every effort has been made to ensure that the facts and figures quoted are from an authoritative source. Wherever possible the weapon has been examined by the author; where this has not been possible, the relevant documents—handbook, drill book, training manual, maintenance manual—have been consulted. Much information on German weapons has come from examination of the vast collection of documents amassed by the Combined Intelligence Objectives Sub-Committee, a body of technical experts and weapon specialists who, after the war, interrogated weapon designers and manufacturers throughout Germany. These documents have only recently been de-restricted, and much of this information has never been published before.

For the opportunity to examine weapons I am indebted to the Committee of the Pattern Room at the Royal Small Arms Factory, Enfield Lock, and particularly to Mr. Herb Woodend who looks after the unrivalled collection there; to Major Myatt of the Infantry Museum, The School of Infantry, Warminster; to the late, Major Frank Hobart and Mr. Arthur Rumbold of the Small Arms Department at the Royal Military College of Science at Shrivenham and WOI (Armament Artificer) George Passant of the Guns and Carriages Branch of the same establishment; to John Weeks who unearthed a number of items in the United States and reported thereon; and to John Walter, Dolf Goldsmith, Don Thomas and others who have produced odd pieces of information at various times.

Picture credits

The author, who has supplied all the photographs in this book from his personal collection except for the following, would like to thank those who have provided illustrative material for this book:
Imperial War Museum: 20 (top right), 52 (top) and 55 (top)
Courtesy of John Weeks: 37 (both), 43 (both), 60 (bottom), 62 (bottom), 72 (bottom), 75 (bottom), 85 (bottom), 91 (bottom), 135 (bottom), 137 (top) and 148 (top)
Bison Picture Library: 2–3, 7, 8, 9, 10, 11, 12, 13, 14–15, 16, 42 (center), 86–87 and 175
Courtesy of Masami Tokoi: 29 (bottom left), 47 (middle), 49 (middle), 97 (top) and 99 (above)
Robert Hunt Library: 57, 61 (bottom), 73, 76–77, 78, 81, 82, 105, 106, 114 (bottom), 120–121, 126–127, 151, 153 (bottom), 155 (bottom) and 167
National Archive: 39 (middle)
Novosti: 4–5 and 61 (top)
Mainichi Newspaper Company: 96–97

The author would also like to thank Helen Downton for providing four technical illustrations which appear on the jacket of this book. He would also like to thank David Eldred, who designed *The Encyclopedia of Infantry Weapons of World War II*.